Unaccompanied Traveler

Irish Studies
Kathleen Costello-Sullivan, *Series Editor*

Select Titles in Irish Studies

For a full list of titles in this series,
visit https://press.syr.edu/supressbook-series/irish-studies/.

Unaccompanied Traveler

The Writings of
Kathleen M. Murphy

Edited and with
an Introduction by
Patrick Bixby

Syracuse University Press

For a listing of books published and distributed by Syracuse University Press,
visit https://press.syr.edu.

ISBN: 978-0-8156-3747-9 (hardcover)
      978-0-8156-3733-2 (paperback)
      978-0-8156-5534-3 (e-book)

Library of Congress Cataloging-in-Publication Data

Names: Murphy, Kathleen M., 1879–1963. | Bixby, Patrick, editor.
Title: Unaccompanied traveler : the writings of Kathleen M. Murphy /
    edited and with an introduction by Patrick Bixby.
Description: First edition. | Syracuse, New York : Syracuse University Press, 2022. |
    Series: Irish studies | Includes bibliographical references and index. | Summary:
    "The editor has selected twelve articles by Kathleen M. Murphy, a little-known
    and understudied Irish writer who regaled readers with stories of her travels to
    Iraq, Russia, Peru, Italy, Vietnam, the Balkans, and other locales near and far.
    In addition to the articles, Bixby provides a scholarly introduction with a thorough
    biographical overview of Murphy, detailed footnotes on the text, and a timeline
    that covers major events in Ireland and the world, as well as significant dates in
    Murphy's life and career"— Provided by publisher.
Identifiers: LCCN 2021006237 (print) | LCCN 2021006238 (ebook) |
    ISBN 9780815637479 (hardcover) | ISBN 9780815637332 (paperback) |
    ISBN 9780815655343 (ebook)
Subjects: LCSH: Murphy, Kathleen M., 1879–1963—Travel. | Women travelers—
    Ireland. | Travel writers—Ireland.
Classification: LCC G269.52.M88 A3 2021 (print) | LCC G269.52.M88 (ebook) |
    DDC 910.4092—dc23
LC record available at https://lccn.loc.gov/2021006237
LC ebook record available at https://lccn.loc.gov/2021006238

In memoriam Sue Wilson and her many adventures.

Contents

Acknowledgments

The editorial process that resulted in this book was something of a winding journey itself and I owe debts of gratitude to the many friends and colleagues who helped me find my way. First, I would like to thank Deborah Manion, acquisitions editor at Syracuse University Press, for seeing the value in a collection of travelogues by a long-forgotten (though, as I argue, ever-fascinating) Irish writer and helping to make this volume a reality. I am also immensely grateful to Brian Kirby, provincial archivist at the Irish Capuchin Archives, who helped me to identify the documents on which this book is based and to secure the rights for their republication here. His attentiveness and generosity have been truly remarkable. Closer to home, I would like to thank Dennis Isbell, subject librarian at the Fletcher Library, Arizona State University, who is always ready with a bright idea to overcome the most insurmountable research obstacles. My gratitude also goes to Louis Mendoza, director of the School of Humanities, Arts, and Cultural Studies for his support, moral and material, of this and other projects. I am very fortunate to have a group of wonderful colleagues in the school, but here I would like to single just a few out for their encouragement of the present undertaking: Annika Mann, Christopher Hanlon, and especially Michael Stancliff, who patiently and skillfully read drafts of the editorial materials contained in these pages. I am also fortunate to have generous colleagues across the field of Irish studies, including Maureen O'Connor, Tadhg Foley, Caoilfhionn Ní Bheacháin, Angus Mitchell, and Feargal Whelan, who all cheered (and, at times, helped to guide) this project along the way. Caoil and Angus, along with Mark Quigley, Anne Ní Choirbín, Deaglán Ó Donghaile,

Méabh Ní Fhuartháin, and Tim Keane have been my dear colleagues away from home at the University Studies Abroad Consortium Summer School, National University Ireland Galway, where I have been reminded of the rewards of travel over and over thanks to the enthusiasm of our students. But, of course, my biggest debt of gratitude is to my family, including my brother, Brian, who designed the maps (modelled on Aer Lingus advertisements from the 1950s) that head each chapter of this book, my wife Nicole, and our children, Claire and Owen, intrepid travelers all.

I would be remiss if I did not acknowledge another (perhaps, the original) inspiration behind this volume. It was an astonishing piece of good luck that I happened to grow up across the street from the home of Sue Wilson, professor of English at California State University, Long Beach—though she was often away on her long-distance sailing voyages. In 1974, a few years before we became neighbors, Sue and a companion sailed a thirty-foot sloop from California to New Zealand, only later discovering that they were the first women-only crew to cross the Pacific. Many other improbable voyages would follow, as would our rather improbable friendship, with nearly two generations separating us. Like Kathleen M. Murphy, Sue was a person of letters *and* a person of adventure, as well as an unfailingly generous soul, always ready to share a story, a book, or a hard-earned bit of wisdom—and it is undoubtedly due to her example that I immediately recognized something familiar in the Irish travel writer. This book is dedicated to her memory.

Note on the Text

The text of this volume derives from a series of travelogues published by Kathleen M. Murphy in *The Capuchin Annual* between 1948 and 1963. The intention in republishing them is to make them accessible to a new generation of readers while maintaining as fully as possible Murphy's singular style. In mechanical terms, this has meant adapting her sometimes idiosyncratic punctuation to contemporary norms (though her distinctive use of ellipses has largely been maintained), closing many hyphenated words, and updating the spelling of a number of place names (but *not* updating place names themselves, if they have been changed since the original publication of the travelogues). Misspelled foreign names and other words have been silently corrected and diacritical marks (unavailable to the typesetters of *The Capuchin Annual*) have been added where needed, though the volume retains Murphy's British English spelling throughout. Last, the effort to appropriately modernize the text has meant removing the honorific capitalization of certain terms and titles while retaining Murphy's uppercase rendering of many religious terms, in keeping with her devout Roman Catholic faith.

Unaccompanied Traveler

Miss Kathleen M. Murphy, ca. 1951. Photograph. Reproduced with permission from *The Capuchin Annual*. Courtesy of the Irish Capuchin Archives.

Introduction

Kathleen M. Murphy, "Ireland's Super-Tramp"

In an obituary published in 1963, Thomas MacGreevy writes that, "insofar as she let herself be known to the public at all," Kathleen M. Murphy, "was known as probably the most widely and most knowledgeably travelled Irish woman of her time."[1] Once a notable writer of short verse, often on Catholic themes, Murphy spent much of the 1920s and 1930s pursuing an abiding fascination with the religious sites and archeological treasures of cultures around the world, only ceasing her idiosyncratic pilgrimages when the Second World War made international travel all but impossible. After the war, she resumed her voyaging and began publishing a series of vivid, humorous, and often harrowing accounts of her travels in *The Capuchin Annual*, a Dublin-based magazine that reached a sizeable audience of mostly conservative, middle-class readers in Ireland and the United States. Murphy wrote for these readers in a manner that, at times, reaffirmed their traditional social values and yet, at others, surely disquieted their sense of Catholic piety and feminine modesty. She may have been devoutly religious but Murphy was not to be constrained by these values, especially the reigning expectation that her place as a woman was in the home. MacGreevy, himself a devout Catholic, notable poet, and regular contributor to *The Capuchin Annual*, remarks with admiration that, when she was back in Ireland, Murphy "came to Dublin

---

1. Thomas MacGreevy, "The Lady of Birr," *The Capuchin Annual* (1963): 384.

1

for every major musical and theatrical event," where "audiences must sometimes have wondered about the tall lady wearing the choice black mantilla (but with no high combs) who, usually unaccompanied, found her way—in good time—to a solitary reserved seat." But unlike the famous writers MacGreevy numbered among his friends, including James Joyce and Samuel Beckett, "very few knew who she was. Miss Murphy went, as she came, unobtrusively."[2] Regrettably, much the same could be said of her career as a travel writer, despite the fact that she published some of the most remarkable travelogues in the history of Irish writing, remarkable precisely because they are poised between religious devotion and searching curiosity, gender decorum and bold adventuring, parochial affiliations and cosmopolitan openness.

This complex, often changeable, positioning is evident in a rather coy autobiographical note that, despite her aversion to public attention, Murphy consented to write for *The Capuchin Annual* in 1952: "there is nothing whatever interesting about me," she begins her communication to the longtime editor of the journal, Father Senan, OFM Cap., "except the fact that I have travelled more than anyone I ever met—indeed I believe I might just claim to be Ireland's super-tramp!" Her proof of this assertion is worth quoting at length:

> Intensely interested in ancient civilizations, I have visited nearly all the famous ruins of the world, including even those of the Khmers and the Incas. Not only have I climbed the Great Pyramid of Egypt and the Great Wall of China but—a far rarer achievement—I have stood on the pillar of St. Simon Stylites in Syria. I have seen pageants of all kinds, ranging from the wonderful carnival of Rio to the weird, colourful cremation ceremony of Bali; have been in a Lap camp and an opium den; dined with a sheikh in Morocco, and accompanied a muezzin at sunset to the summit of a minaret when he chanted across the Sahara the impressive call of evening prayer. I succeeded in penetrating into the palace of the Shah of Persia to see the marvellous Peacock Throne; then, in a Peruvian port, had

---

2. MacGreevy, "Lady of Birr," 384.

to submit to the humiliating experience of being treated as a mere piece of merchandise when I was hoisted by a crane on board a boat just like the cargo. Having lived alone in the stark simplicity in a jungle shack and in the tense atmosphere of a desert hut in Iraq while tribes waged war against the Government, it seemed to me most luxurious to rest in peace when my sleeping apartment happened to be one of the rock tombs of Petra. Among memorable incidents I may mention finding myself locked inside the mausoleum of a Shogun in Japan; a narrow escape from being shot by sentry in the fortress of Belgrade; and being nearly buried alive in Babylon . . . I hope you will be able to select eighty words from the above.[3]

Fortunately, Father Senan saw fit to publish the note in full. Although it can be difficult to gauge the degree of irony in her declarations, it is clear that Murphy is rather self-consciously negotiating the various social and discursive restraints placed on Irish women in particular and women travel writers in general at the middle of the twentieth century.

The term "super-tramp," at once self-aggrandizing and self-deprecating, had been coined by the Welsh writer W. H. Davies at the beginning of the century in *The Autobiography of a Super-Tramp* (1908, with an introduction by George Bernard Shaw), which recounts his impetuous travels from Britain to Canada and the United States. The book, in many ways, exemplifies the traditional masculine narrative of heroic escape from the confines of a staid and stifling home to the more expansive prospects of new frontiers. It is his life on the highways and byways, not where he came from, that makes Davies the man he is. Adopting and adapting the title for herself, Murphy challenges this masculine cultural logic, if only implicitly, by identifying herself as someone who has strayed far from home and, in the process, gained access to these remote domains of self-definition—not just visiting ruins and witnessing pageants, but "penetrating" forbidden sanctums, living in inhospitable surroundings, and escaping a variety

3. "Kathleen M. Murphy," *The Capuchin Annual* (1952): 553.

of dangers, even if these feats come with certain risks to her dignity. As she exhibits over and over in her writings, during a period when the expectations for womanhood in Irish society still dictated introversion, innocence, and domestic servitude, Murphy managed quite successfully to translate herself into the alternative, feminine cultural logic of what Sidonie Smith calls "the individualizing journey."[4]

At the same time, Murphy maintains the sly claim (a piece of strategic false modesty, no doubt) in her autobiographical note that there was nothing of much interest to see here. She ends her letter to Father Senan by asking him to excuse her for not sending a photo: "Very rarely in my life have I been photographed, and the only fair modern one I possess represents me mounted on what I believe was the tallest camel in Africa. I am sure you would consider this far too unconventional to be published in the 'The Capuchin Annual.'"[5] This rhetorical stance could be called "decorous indecorum." Murphy's summary account of her many adventures and misadventures, often undertaken as an unaccompanied traveler, strains at the conventions of Irish womanhood, even as her modesty (however false it might ring) ensures that these conventions are not transgressed in an overtly defiant or threatening way. Her refusal to provide a picture reaffirms this modesty and keeps her hidden, at least temporarily, from the gaze of her readers, even as the description of her one "modern" photograph reasserts her undeniable status as an adventurer.

In the 1920s and 1930s, as Murphy undertook her first journeys, many Irish women were barred from working in the public sector and many Irish politicians openly espoused the notion that the only natural function for women was to raise their children and care for their households. By the 1950s, when she was writing her travelogues for *The Capuchin Annual*, not much had changed.

4. Sidonie Smith, *Moving Lives: Twentieth Century Women's Travel Writing* (Minneapolis: Univ. of Minnesota Press, 2001), xi.

5. "Kathleen M. Murphy," 553.

This is not to suggest that Murphy is entirely alone in the history of Irish letters. Rather, it is to say that although she has remained in near anonymity (albeit an anonymity that she may have at least partially desired), Murphy merits an important place in the (still largely uncelebrated) canon of Irish woman travel writers. Those who came before her include Katherine Wilmot (ca. 1773–1824), Lady Morgan (née Sydney Owenson) (ca. 1781–1859), and Julia Kavanagh (1824–77), whose books—*An Irish Peer on the Continent, 1801–1803* (1920), *Italy* (1821), and *A Summer and Winter in the Two Sicilies* (1858), respectively—contribute an unconventional outlook, in terms of gender and nationality (and, especially in the case of Kavanagh, a devout Catholic, also religion), to the literature of the European Grand Tour; Maria Henrietta de la Cherois Crommelin, known as May Crommelin (1850–1928), whose travels in the West Indies, North Africa, and elsewhere inform the forty-two novels she wrote over a long career, though her reputation as a travel writer rests mostly on her *Over the Andes: From the Argentin to Chile and Peru* (1896); Daisy May Bates (1863–1951), whose efforts to preserve the language and customs of Australian aboriginals, along with her interests in birdwatching and ecology, resulted in a series of articles for the *Australasian* and a landmark book, *The Passing of the Aborigines* (1938); and Beatrice Grimshaw (1870–1953), a record-breaking cyclist, explorer, and novelist, whose extensive travels in the South Pacific were recorded in brief travelogues for *Wide World Magazine* and *The National Geographic Magazine*, as well as in travel books such as *From Fiji to the Cannibal Islands* (1907) and *Isles of Adventure* (1930).

Unfortunately, scholars have long ignored these women travel writers and their journeys beyond Ireland in favor of a focus on travel and tourism within the island nation. A few notable exceptions to this tendency have emerged in recent years along with a mounting interest in Irish travel during the "long nineteenth century," from the Constitution of 1782 to the outbreak of the First World War. Christina Morin and Marguérite Corporaal's wide-ranging essay collection, *Travelling Irishness*, chronicles the rise of Irish tourism abroad and its accompanying literature, especially among an ascending Catholic middle class in the years after Emancipation;[6] drawing out the distinctive features of this writing, Raphaël Ingelbien's groundbreaking *Irish Cultures of Travel* documents the increased global mobility of the Irish men and women during the period, not just in terms of emigration, but of their participation in the democratization of foreign travel.[7] His focus is primarily "on texts that contributed to the public discursive construction of the Irish tourist abroad," including travel books that address an Irish readership, even if they were published by British or American writers.[8] This subgenre encompasses writings that worked to create an image of the Irish woman traveling on the Continent, emphasizing the maintenance of nationalist ideals and social propriety in foreign tourism, as well as the assertion of female independence and political radicalism in various forms of leisure travel. By the end of the century, according to Ingelbien, Irish culture had managed to reimagine the Irish woman traveler as a kind of "national icon," representing Ireland and Irishness abroad.[9] Morin and Corporaal's volume offers several case studies of women's journeys to the Continent, including Anne O'Connor's analysis of Julia Kavanagh's Italian narrative, which demonstrates how the travel writer inflects her experience through both nationalist aspirations and Catholic values.[10] Peter Gray's account of Mabel Sharman Crawford's *Life in Tuscany*, on the other hand, highlights how her activism in the Irish land reform

---

6. Christina Morin and Marguérite Corporaal, eds., *Traveling Irishness in the Long Nineteenth Century* (New York: Spring, 2014).

7. Raphaël Ingelbien, *Irish Cultures of Travel: Writing on the Continent, 1829–1914* (London: Palgrave, 2016).

8. Ingelbien, *Irish Cultures of Travel*, 11.

9. Inbelbien, 181.

10. Anne O'Connor, "Travel Literature and Traveling Irishness: An Italian Case Study," in *Traveling Irishness in the Long Nineteenth Century*, ed. Christina Morin and Marguérite Corporaal (New York: Spring, 2014), 15–34.

and women's suffrage movements informs her depiction of the social conditions she encounters in the region.[11]

Many of these writers, whether traveling as explorers or adventurers, professional journalists or amateur ethnographers, managed to escape the constraints of sanctioned gender roles at home in Ireland and to access alternative ways of life and forms of identity abroad. For much of the nineteenth century, two-way travel for single women from Ireland and elsewhere was generally restricted to where the destination was considered "acceptable" or when the journey was made under the "proper" circumstances, often as a governess, companion, or helpmate. Only with the advent of escorted group travel in the final decades of the century did these restrictions begin to loosen. But, as these recent studies have demonstrated, to focus strictly on what makes these travel writers exceptional women, capable of overcoming the constraints imposed on them and rising to the level of some perceived masculine standard, is to marginalize their achievements; it is, moreover, to overlook their complex interactions with Irish social norms and political exigencies as they wrote about mobile, elusive, and sometimes fiercely independent forms of selfhood. But it is also to neglect their equally complex interactions with the societies they visited in their travels and represented in their writings, which frequently evince an uncommon openness to new experiences and different cultures, even if they too often betray common prejudices regarding race and religion in other parts of the world.

Although Murphy's writing is part of this larger tradition of Irish travel literature, her deployment of various rhetorical strategies provides a particularly remarkable example of these negotiations with other cultures. Often, she addresses her audience in an authoritative manner informed by meticulous historical, geographical, and anthropological researches and punctuated by frequent allusions to the western canon: classical myth, biblical stories, and Romantic verse in particular. At

11. Peter Gray, "Mabel Sharman Crawford's *Life in Tuscany*: Ulster Radicalism in a Hot Climate," in Morin and Corporaal, *Traveling Irishness*, 35–50.

times, her travelogues read like the passages from a guidebook for would-be visitors to these destinations, including descriptions of their principal attractions and warnings for the uninitiated traveler; at other times, she provides a glimpse of her personal motivations for traveling and her impassioned responses to what she encounters along the way. Murphy offers detailed and colorful, sometimes exceptionally ornate, descriptions of these scenes, as well as extended examples of ekphrasis, rendering the finer features of ancient architecture and religious painting. In several instances, she prefaces her travelogues with accounts of why she undertook the journey and what she expected to find in a manner that recalls *Heart of Darkness* as much as the *Arabian Nights* or *The Canterbury Tales*. Perhaps her most remarkable article in formal or stylistic terms is one of the very first she published: "Memorable Masses in Many Lands" (1948) takes the form of a verbal montage comprised of brief scenes that demonstrate her efforts to uphold the Catholic ritual in faraway places. The fragmented tableaus, presented without transitions, demonstrate the immense reach of Catholicism, which she finds practiced among the minarets of Albania, a thousand miles from the mouth of the Amazon, and in a subterranean chapel somewhere in Damascus.

These tableaus also emphasize that, no matter how far away Murphy went, she was always willing to go farther still in order to maintain her religious observance. This persistent emphasis grounds her writings, no matter their ostensible subject, in an oblique form of autobiography, with each of her travelogues framed as a kind of private pilgrimage and rendered in terms derived from her Irish Catholic education and upbringing. Despite this, however, the details of her life story have long remained obscure.

Education and Early Writings

Kathleen Mary Murphy was born on December 15, 1879, in the village of Tulla, County Clare, to Sarah Agnes Murphy (née Egan) and Timothy "Thady" Murphy, and she spent much of her childhood in the family home at the National Bank House. Situated on high ground, Tulla (from the Irish, *An Tulach*, meaning "hill") was and remains the commercial center of its eponymous parish, which is mostly comprised of scenic rolling hills, interspersed with stretches of bogland and dotted with the ruins of ancient castles and towerhouses. Thady Murphy spent nearly forty years as the clerk and officer for the Board of Guardians of the Tulla Union, a position that provided him with a substantial income and later a generous pension. Sarah, who was fourteen years younger than Thady, brought two sons to the marriage when they wed in 1878; the brothers went on to become prominent leaders in the Catholic Church: the Very Rev. J. Maloney, PP, Lorrha, later raised to canon and chancellor of the Diocese of Killaloe, and the Very Rev. A. Maloney, PP, Dunkerrin, also in the Diocese of Killaloe. A younger sister, Agnes Maud Murphy, was born in 1881 and grew up to become a prominent medical doctor, though she predeceased Kathleen by many years. Both girls were educated at Laurel Hill Convent, Limerick, the exclusive boarding school that— with its attention to Catholic rituals, as well as Continental languages and cultural traditions—later served as the (renamed) setting of Kate O'Brien's autobiographical novel, *The Land of Spices* (1941).

Rather remarkably, both sisters went on to enroll at University College, Dublin, of the Royal University of Ireland (founded as the Catholic University in 1853 and later to become University College, Dublin, of the National University of Ireland) at a time when the institution, under the conservative leadership of Fr. William Delany, SJ, admitted very few women. Kathleen matriculated in 1898, entering the university the same autumn as James Joyce and studying alongside Oliver St. John Gogarty, Thomas Kettle, Arthur Clery, and Padraic Pearse, as well as Hannah Sheehy (later Hannah Sheehy Skeffington) and Margaret Gillespie (later Margaret Cousins), among students who would later become notable figures in Irish cultural and political life. Although the Royal University, then based at St. Stephen's Green in central Dublin, had fewer than a thousand students at the turn of the century, this roll call serves as a strong reminder that it was a fertile breeding ground for the great minds of Murphy's generation. Nonetheless, her considerable talents as a student of both English and

French, along with her exceptional height and proud bearing, would have made her stand out among her fellow students, especially at a time when scarcely more than a hundred women were awarded diplomas by the university each year.

Like Joyce and Pearse, the future author of *Ulysses* and the future leader of the Easter Rising, Murphy pursued a degree in Modern Languages. And, like them, she was exposed to Catholic thinkers such as Ignatius Loyola, Thomas Aquinas, and the founder of the university, Cardinal (John Henry) Newman, though by the 1890s the emphasis of the curriculum was firmly on secular subjects. At the time, Ireland was still very much preoccupied with the so-called University Question, regarding how Catholic young men and, increasingly, young women should be educated in a system under the control of the British parliament, which actively restricted course offerings focused on either Catholicism or Ireland. Students of English, of course, read Shakespeare, Milton, and Dryden, but they also became familiar with the work of modern British writers such as Thomas Carlyle, Thomas Babington Macaulay, and John Ruskin. Shortly after taking her degree, Murphy was back in Tulla with her family, but she returned to Dublin within a few years and boarded on Harcourt Street, just around the corner from the university buildings, where she took up "private study" for a time. In 1917, drawing on this further learning—especially her reading in the genre of Christian autobiography, but also her familiarity with the philosophy of G. W. F. Hegel and the painting of Henri Matisse—she published a probing and rather lyrical essay in the *Catholic Review* titled, "The Newman of the *Apologia*," which was republished almost three decades later as her first contribution to *The Capuchin Annual*.

In the years after her graduation, despite a later aversion to public attention, Murphy began to seek (and attain) some modicum of recognition for her writing as she dabbled in a variety of genres and contributed to a range of periodicals. The first record of these efforts is to be found in the April 26, 1907, issue of *T. P.'s Weekly*—a popular miscellany founded a few years earlier by the Liverpool-based Irish nationalist politician, Thomas Power O'Connor—which presented her with a third prize for "the best comments, not to exceed 200 words, on any point or topic in the March 29 issue".[12] A decade later, in the April and October 1917 issues of *The Bookman*, then under the brief editorship of G. G. Wyant, she received a "special commendation" for lyrics entered in the journal's monthly prize competitions.[13] During this period, Murphy was again in Tulla helping to care for her aging father, who eventually passed away on February 25, 1918. Shortly thereafter, from March 1918 to June 1919, she published a series of short verses—"Noumena," "To the Moon," "Sonnet for Lady Day, 1918," and "To Time"—in the prominent Jesuit quarterly, *Studies*, which began to gain her some attention in Ireland as a poet. These poems, all of them sonnets, address both classical and Catholic subjects, invoking Apollo, Proserpine, and Lethe, as well as the Feast of the Annunciation in a poignant lament to the Virgin Mary. Murphy's verse could soon be found in other, far less orthodox, venues, including the February 13, 1920, issue of *The New Witness*, which published her poem "The Hunchback," and the April 1920 issue of *Vision: A Magazine & Review of Mysticism and Spiritual Reconstruction*, which published her poem "On Reading the Apocalypse" and awarded it the prize of half a guinea for "the best mystical poem."[14] During these turbulent years in Irish history, Murphy and her elderly mother stayed on in Tulla before moving in the midtwenties to Stada Cona, a charming Georgian house on the outskirts of Birr, County Offaly. There, for several years, they lived in close proximity to the parishes of her stepbrothers in Lorrha and Dunkerrin until Sarah Agnes died at the age of 81 on September 24, 1928. A few years later, Kathleen experienced her greatest literary success with the publication of *Poems* (1932), which won First Prize in the *Aonach Táilteann* literary competition of 1932 and soon led her to receive the papal decoration *Pro Ecclesia et Pontice*.

12. "T. P.'s Competitions," *T. P.'s Weekly* 9 (April 27, 1907): 524.
13. "Special Commendations," *The Bookman* (April 1917): 12; "Special Commendations," *The Bookman* (October 1917): 15.
14. "*Vision* Competitions," *Vision: A Magazine & Review of Mysticism and Spiritual Reconstruction* 2, no. 4 (April 1920): vi.

Despite these accolades, *Poems* is perhaps most noteworthy for the record it provides of Murphy's early experiences as a world traveler. The volume gathers the verses she published in periodicals more than a decade earlier, along with dozens of other lyrics on a range of conventional poetic themes: plaints lamenting unrequited love, meditations on solitude and human frailty, and odes to the natural world, especially the enigmatic seasonal cycles of decline, death, and rebirth. Generally speaking, the poems read like accomplished, if rather derivative, exercises in Romantic versification, here recalling the Wordsworth of *The Prelude* or Coleridge of "The Aeolian Harp," there echoing the Shelley of "Ode to the West Wind" or Keats of "La Belle Dame sans Merci." What distinguishes Murphy from these forerunners is a more orthodox sense of the natural world providing direct access to God along with an insistence on overtly Catholic themes, often in poems with Latin titles such as "*Quia Multum Amavit*," "*Te Deum*," or "*In Aeternum*." But these verses are interspersed with others that reflect on her travels to Norway ("Spitzenbergen—An Impression"), the United States ("New York—An Impression," "To Niagara"), Italy ("In the Dolomites," "The Sculptor of the Vatican Eros," "Venice—An Impression"), and Egypt ("The Temple of Karnac—An Impression," "To Egypt," "To the Sphinx").

Although these poems provide an itinerary of her first forays beyond Ireland, they are hardly travelogues. Much like her Romantic predecessors, Murphy seizes on these various locales not so much for their own sake as for the stimulus they provide to her imagination, which moves beyond the world of everyday experience into wild flights of fancy. Her New York is populated by Titans who seek to restrain her soul, like a Minotaur, in the city's concrete and steel labyrinth; her Venice is the home of Cerberus and Charon, though it leaves her feeling like "a sin-stained Peri outside Heaven's gate,"[15] unworthy to enter its loveliness; her Egypt beguiles visitors "with

15. K. M. Murphy, "Venice—An Impression," in *Poems* (Dublin: Talbot, 1932), 124.

wondrous charms,"[16] and yet the timeless Sphinx evokes a dread of "Death," until she is reassured by her Christian faith. From time to time, her early travels brought Murphy in contact with other religious traditions, such as when she visits the Temple of Karnac, closely associated with Theban deities, and imagines that "not men but gods have made thee; nothing mars / With mortal touch thine awful majesty."[17]

World Traveler, Domestic Traveler

Although Murphy would publish very little poetry after the success of *Poems*, the passing of her mother—and the inheritance that it brought—meant she was freed to pursue her career as a world traveler more intently. For much of her life, dating back to her study of French at Laurel Hill Convent, she had demonstrated the traits of a Francophile and in the 1920s she became a Member of La Société d'histoire ecclésiastique de la France. In 1931, she visited the massive Paris Colonial Exhibition, where she encountered displays presenting the various cultures of the French overseas empire, including native arts, crafts, and architecture from Indochina, Algeria, and elsewhere. During the early 1930s, among her many other sojourns, she traveled widely in Spain, where she befriended several prominent families. In September 1935, as announced in a brief article from the *Offaly Independent* headlined "Young Noble in Birr," Murphy received a visit from a member of one of these families, Don Carlos de Coyeneche y Silvela, a seventeen-year-old whose ancestors included Charlemagne and Theodore the Great.[18]

A little more than a year later, after the outbreak of the Spanish Civil War, Murphy used the pages of the *Irish Independent* to question recent claims made by a Revered Precentor Lewis-Crosby at the Protestant Synod regarding the brutality of the Nationalist forces.

16. K. M. Murphy, "To Egypt," in *Poems* (Dublin: Talbot, 1932), 108.

17. K. M. Murphy, "The Temple of Karnac—An Impression," in *Poems* (Dublin: Talbot, 1932), 68.

18. "Young Noble in Birr," *Offaly Independent*, September 21, 1935, 5.

Convinced that the Reverend had exaggerated the crimes committed against Protestant pastors in Spain, Murphy demanded documentation of the atrocities but promised to forward the information, if it was produced, "at once to Spanish friends, who, being related to King Alfonso, have much influence in the country, and who will place it in the hands of Franco himself."[19] She appears to have been incensed by competing reports that Spanish Communists, opposed to Franco and his Nationalist allies, had begun murdering Catholic priests, while sparing their Protestant counterparts. The brutal conflict in Spain would give rise to some of the most important travel writing of the 1930s, including Kate O'Brien's *Farewell Spain* (1937), W. H. Auden's *Spain* (1937), and George Orwell's *Homage to Catalonia* (1938), though it prevented Murphy from resuming her sojourns there.

Nevertheless, she continued to travel widely, visiting Syria, Iraq, Persia, and Haiti in 1936; French Indo-China in 1937; and Bolivia and Peru in 1939; among many dozens of other destinations around the world, before the start of the broader global conflict all but put an end to her wanderings. "In the Spring of 1939," as she reflected later, "I visited a Peruvian farm in the foothills of the Andes, and saw there a condor in a cage. Overwhelmed with pity at the sight of this gigantic bird gazing through iron bars at his home among the majestic mountain peaks, I had no presentiment that a few months later I too should be doomed to a similar fate."[20]

Despite her dismay at ceasing to travel for a time, Murphy was quite happy at home in Ireland and became an integral part of the local community in her midlands town. A founding member of the Birr Gramophone Society and the Birr Historical and Arts Group, she helped to promote cultural activities in the municipality, which was home to just one small purpose-built theater, Oxman Hall, dating back to the end of the nineteenth century. When Murphy did slip away from town on one of her long journeys, she did so quietly,

19. "Protestant Synod Speech," *Irish Independent*, November 20, 1936, 6.
20. "Kathleen M. Murphy," *The Capuchin Annual* (1950–51): 523.

without ceremony, "only to pop up some later at some attractive film-show, art exhibition or other local attraction in town." Although she was known to go to Dublin for major musical and theatrical events, she became admired for sharing, with great wit and merriment, her extensive knowledge of the arts with her friends and acquaintances in Birr. During the periods she spent at Stada Cona, she also gained a reputation for offering "kindness to so many poor and needy," and "never turn[ing] a deaf ear to anyone in trouble."[21] She gave generously to Irish charities such as the Achill Relief Fund, established after ten young men from the island died tragically in a fire on a farm in Kirkintiloch, Scotland, where they had been working as itinerate potato pickers.

Perhaps it is no surprise, then, that when Murphy began to write for *The Capuchin Annual* after the war, her first travelogue was not about some far-flung destination but about the village of Keel on Achill Island. To be sure, the literature considered "Irish travel writing" is typically dominated by accounts of travel to or within Ireland, though "Slippin' into Keel" offers a remarkable contrast to "Memorable Masses in Many Lands," published in the same 1948 issue of the journal. While the latter travelogue recounts her escapades in dozens of countries all over the globe, offering glimpses of the foreign cultures and exotic customs that nonetheless accommodate the familiar ritual of the Catholic Mass, the former describes her journey to a single destination just off the west coast of Ireland, where she seeks something like an "authentic" Irishness untouched by the rest of the world. In this sense, like the Irish Revivalists who came to the region before her, Murphy endorses a variety of native primitivism, which addresses the western regions of the nation as the site of an enduring peasant culture somehow beyond the reach of capitalist modernity.[22] In this sense, moreover, her domestic travel, despite its proximity to

21. "Obituary: Miss Kathleen M. Murphy," *Offaly Chronicle*, April 4, 1962, 1.

22. See Gregory Castle, *Modernism and the Celtic Revival* (Cambridge: Cambridge Univ. Press, 2001), 98–133; and Sinéad Garrigan Mattar, *Primitivism, Science, and the Irish Revival* (Oxford: Oxford Univ. Press, 2004), 130–84.

home, forms a crucial prelude to her journeys far from the familiar coordinates of her native culture and national traditions.

Murphy emphasizes the primitivism of Achill by attempting to transcribe the island dialect, which has long been of interest to linguists due to the influence from Ulster Irish. The use of dialect, which recalls similar efforts more than thirty years previous by Douglas Hyde and J. M. Synge, lends the piece an air of ethnographic expertise insofar as it works to capture what is essential in the local culture, the peasant life, for an audience of readers elsewhere in Ireland and the United States. Of course, coming from Murphy and other university-educated outsiders of comparable experience and social position, such efforts also risk sounding like a form of class and regional condescension (even if the accent Murphy heard may have been rather exaggerated, staging a version of "authenticity" for her, the outsider). But for Murphy, as for Synge in his early writings on the nearby Aran Islands, the attempt to reproduce western intonations is just as much a matter of a novice travel writer finding a voice, generating a form of discursive authority.[23]

Throughout the article, Murphy repeatedly associates what she saw years ago on Achill with what she has seen since in her travels abroad: relating what she encounters on the island to nomads in the desert, to beards worn in China, to winding trails in Peru, and so on. In this way, she enacts a curious reversal of a standard travel writing trope, the "traveler's simile": that is, the comparison of what is foreign and unfamiliar to the reader with what is native and familiar in order to render the strange knowable or at least less strange. But Murphy's reversal—the comparison of the familiar with the foreign precisely to render it less familiar—is vital for the neophyte travel writer's voice, precisely because it displays her credentials as a traveler. She repeatedly gives the impression of one who has wandered the distant reaches of the globe and encountered all manner of unexpected and

23. See Giulia Bruna, *J. M. Synge and Travel Writing of the Irish Revival* (Syracuse: Syracuse Univ. Press, 2017), 17–64.

extraordinary things; who has become, moreover, worldly enough to appreciate what is strange, but also valuable, in her own culture. In this way, then, Achill is subtly established as a touchstone for the evaluation of other cultures, even as, in article after article over the next fifteen years, those other cultures also become an implicit measure of Ireland and Irishness for Murphy and her audience.

Ireland and *The Capuchin Annual*

As Murphy published her travelogues in *The Capuchin Annual*, Ireland was slowly emerging from the isolation of its neutrality during the war, though it remained home to a relatively closed society through the 1950s. In the popular imagination, the decade is still generally defined by insularity and poverty, brought on by the failure of protectionist economic policies that served an increasingly outmoded vision of Ireland as a steadfastly idyllic and preindustrial society. Financial necessity, especially for those employed in agriculture and other semi-skilled labor, led more than four hundred thousand men, women, and children to emigrate during the decade. Meanwhile, under the leadership of Éamon de Valera—who served as *Taoiseach* (Prime Minister) from 1937 to 1948, from 1951 to 1954, and again from 1957 to 1959—economic conservativism was matched by social conservativism, as official rhetoric continued to promote a vision of an essentially Catholic and pastoral nation. If many Irish women and men were compelled to leave the island for economic reasons, others departed in search of social freedoms available elsewhere, even as members of the Catholic middle class began to enjoy new opportunities emerging after the war to travel for pleasure and recreation.

Since the beginning of the nineteenth century, tourism in much of Europe and North America had been closely linked with the idea of modernity and the increasingly commercial and consumerist societies that industrialization had brought into existence. *Travelling Irishness* and *Irish Culture of Travel* have demonstrated the slow but steady rise of new forms of leisure travel along with the emergence of a new middle class in Ireland after Catholic Emancipation. But in the middle of the twentieth century, Ireland still seemed to lag behind the rest of Western Europe in these developments, even though it played a significant role in pioneering of international air travel—especially after Shannon Airport, just sixty miles (one hundred kilometers) from Birr, opened to commercial airlines with its first transatlantic proving flight in 1945. Aer Lingus, which had been formed by the Irish Free State government in 1936, expanded rapidly after the war, soon introducing new routes to London, Liverpool, and Glasgow, as well as to Brussels, Amsterdam, Rome, and other Continental destinations. Nonetheless, as Ingelbien has noted, to speak of "Irish travel" as outbound leisure trips taken by Irish citizens, rather than inbound tourism, is "largely to go against the grain," since travel from Ireland remained "fairly uncommon" into the 1960s.[24]

It was in these circumstances, with Ireland standing between tradition and modernity, insularity and openness, that Murphy began to write her travelogues for *The Capuchin Annual*. Just ten pages ahead of her very first article, the 1948 issue contains a full-page advertisement for Aer Lingus touting the national airline as "linking Ireland with the world": "whenever, wherever you want to travel—go by air. Aer Lingus services cover many of the European capitals and link up with the other major airlines of the world. Travel in luxuriant comfort—via Aer Lingus."[25] The articles and advertising in the journal repeatedly emphasize this vision of tourist travel and the tourist industry, which are dependent on the basic binary relationship between home and away, between the ordinary and the extraordinary. Murphy's travelogues address an audience that may have been unlikely to follow in her footsteps but that was nevertheless encouraged to see something of the world and to believe in the promise of travel. Her articles help to construct a set of expectations for her readers about what might be encountered beyond their everyday routines at home in Ireland; her travelogues play on a desire for experiences that required

24. Ingelbien, *Irish Cultures of Travel*, 3.
25. Aer Lingus advertisement, *The Capuchin Annual* (1948): 42.

different modes of perception than were typically exercised in their quotidian lives. But her writings also address an audience that, by and large, continued to believe in the sort of traditional gender roles and conservative social values that were institutionalized by the Roman Catholic Church and deeply engrained in the legal principles of the Irish republic.

The Capuchin Annual was skillfully edited not only to uphold these social and political norms but to actively promote them in the modes of a Catholic universalism and an emergent consumerism in Ireland. Published almost every year for nearly a half-century, from 1930 to 1977, the *Annual* became, according to Malcolm Ballin, "the journal of choice in many Catholic middle-class households with nationalist politics," with a print run of 25,000 issues per year in 1940, which expanded through the decade and into the 1950s as Murphy published her travelogues. Individual issues extend to as many as seven hundred pages, containing articles on a variety of Catholic and nationalist topics, as well as poetry, photo essays, and cartoons, including numerous caricatures of Capuchin friars engaged in all manner of modest and benevolent activities: hanging pictures, sewing robes, playing the piano, frolicking with children. Each issue of the journal also includes page after page of advertisements for Catholic-owned, mostly Dublin-based, business concerns selling consumer goods ranging from wine and poultry, jams and jellies, to musical instruments, umbrellas, fine china, gramophones, automobiles, and so on. Many advertisements in each issue appeal to Irish "homemakers" with items that might ease their domestic duties, while others promote Irish holidays for readers in the United States and the United Kingdom. These advertisements were accompanied by lengthy photospreads and articles highlighting the landscapes and other attractions of Ireland for a readership of potential tourists who might return to their family roots or simply come to see the charming sights of the island.

The journal was thus quite capacious in its scope and rather eclectic—one might even say, catholic—in its taste, despite its general objective to publicize the activities of the Roman Catholic Church in Ireland and abroad. From 1934 until the end of its run, the sturdy cardboard covers of every volume featured the name and date of the journal in large gothic script above a block print of a rather sullen-looking St. Francis kneeling in a grassy clearing to scratch the chin of what appears to be an Irish Wolfhound pup, who receives his attentions gladly. Below the image, the motto of the journal is written in Irish: "*Do ċum Glóire Dé agus Onóra na hÉireann*" ("For the Glory of God and the Honor of Ireland"). Notwithstanding this patriotic sentiment, the international breadth of the journal—which included titles such as "Parish Priest of the Pacific," "Jerusalem," "A Black Boy's Soul," "Dublin to Rome," "Portuguese Journey," "Lebanon to Me," "The Legion of Mary—a Work of God for our Day"—also evokes the global reach of the Catholic Church and its history of missionary activity. In this regard, *The Capuchin Annual* also was one of the principal venues for the publication of Irish travel writing at mid-century, though many of the articles concern Irish priests and nuns attending to the sick and impoverished in other parts of the world. But unlike much of the Irish travel writing published in the nineteenth and early twentieth centuries, these articles were not directed at an English audience so much as a readership in Ireland and across the Irish diaspora. While many of the contributors were Irish Catholic clergymen, they also included government ministers, academics, artists, and notable Irish Catholic writers such as Thomas MacGreevy and Francis Stuart. As a woman, Murphy was certainly part of a small minority in each table of contents, but she was not entirely alone, as the journal also numbered the likes of the singer Delia Murphy Kiernan and the sculptor Julester Shrady Post among its contributors.

In some of her early writings, following shortly after "Slippin' into Keel," Murphy offers her readers something akin to the travel advisories now published in lifestyle magazines, which highlight the attractions to visit in a particular destination and provide tips for navigating the local customs, culinary offerings, and transportation options. They clearly promote what John Urry has called "the tourist gaze," which scans destinations for a set of predetermined signs that have been identified as authentic or essential by various discourses on travel and tourism. Murphy's articles might even be called didactic pieces intended to educate the readers of the *Annual* in the appropriate ways of traveling abroad. "A Treasure Island," for instance, guides the reader through the splendors of Venice, Fiume (now Rijeka), Zagreb, and other locales around the perimeter of the Adriatic Sea, albeit with a wit and range of reference seldom matched in commercial travel writing. Similarly, "Benedictine Byways," escorts the reader through a series of churches, abbeys, and other religious sites across Europe, recounts key events in their histories, and describes the artistic treasures they contain. In these articles, then, Murphy offers her audience access to a kind of knowledge and sophistication that would prepare them to be cosmopolitan consumers of these Continental tourist destinations, should they have the opportunity to visit them.

Varieties of Cosmopolitanism

Despite their elements of touristic appeal, Murphy's foreign travels more often took the form of rather unorthodox pilgrimages to destinations of spiritual significance for her own faith—the biblical sites of Jerusalem, the great cathedrals of Western Europe, the fresco-lined churches and monasteries of the Balkans—but for many other faiths as well. She sought out sites sanctified by the divinities and holy men of various world religions, as well as ruins associated with the grand achievements of numerous lost civilizations, both eastern and western—though, as we have seen, Murphy also brought a desire to observe her Catholic faith wherever she found herself, whatever way she could. Often that desire worked to sustain a distance between her and the local peoples she encountered, who are identified as fundamentally different due to their religious beliefs; but just as often, it brought her into communion with marginalized groups of Catholics or with other wanderers—priests, friars, and observant laypersons—who shared a boat bound up the Amazon, a dimly lit basement in Morocco, or the restaurant car of a train bound for Peking (Beijing).

   Her shifting responses to these experiences are as remarkable as the vast extent of her travels. At times, Murphy evinces rather parochial ways of addressing ethnic and religious difference, especially in her allusions to a variety of a Catholic universalism which views the Catholic faith as a fundamental category that supplants all other social, cultural, or political distinctions. For example, observing the congregation gathered at a Mass in the Amazon, she remarks: "I had never seen so many diverse shades together; they obviously belonged to a medley of numerous races; and the sight produced in me a quickened sense of the essential unity of the Church, a comforting sensation of companionship in the knowledge that we all professed the same doctrines, recited the same prayers, were nourished by the same Bread of Life; in short, were all brethren in the Faith."[26] What determines her attitude toward others in this instance is not their difference but their similarity, their common embrace of Catholicism, so that her sympathy is premised on a shared set of religious beliefs. This sympathy, then, comes at the cost of a basic, structural intolerance to alterity, which must be obscured or ignored before a sense of fellow feeling can arise. In this way, her Catholic universalism asserts a standard that allows the admittance of other ethnicities, cultures, or voices only in the form of sameness and self-confirmation, so that differences are devalued and ultimately excluded from her consideration.

At other times, however, Murphy evinces a species of what Ulrich Beck calls "religious cosmopolitanism," which does not devalue cultural and religious differences but, instead, accepts or indeed positively affirms their merits in relation to her own affiliations.[27] For instance, witnessing "a diminutive Franciscan who wore above his brown habit the tarboosh of Mohammed," she is gladdened to see "this friendly union of the Crescent and the Cross."[28] Beck identifies another an example of this kind of cosmopolitanism in the resolutions of the Second Vatican Council (1962–65), which he sees as replacing the missionary zeal of the Church with an emphasis on the tolerance for

26. K. M. Murphy, "Memorable Masses in Many Lands," *The Capuchin Annual* (1948): 299.

27. Ulrich Beck, *A God of One's Own: Religion's Capacity for Peace and Potential for Violence* (Cambridge: Polity, 2010), 69.

28. Murphy, "Memorable Masses," 299.

other faiths and the expansion of global civil society. In the years leading up to these resolutions, Murphy periodically provides her readers glimpses of the transition to a religious cosmopolitanism when
she opens herself to other orthodoxies—moments when she recog-
nizes and values religious otherness as much as religious sameness—in
encounters with Muslim clerics, Buddhist monks, and representatives
of other faiths.

The tensions between universalism and cosmopolitanism can
already be perceived in the opening paragraph of "Memorable Masses
in Many Lands." These initial statements begin to frame the perspective that would define Murphy's writing in *The Capuchin Annual*
for the next one and one-half decades, as she went on to present her
middle-class Irish Catholic audience with exemplary scenes, belief systems, and cultural traditions from distant parts of the world: "The
prophetic words of Scripture, 'In every place there is sacrifice and
there is offered to my name a clean oblation' have been transmuted,
by my world wanderings, into vital sparks that set my imagination on
fire; and have become for me an 'Open Sesame' to a treasure-house
of precious memories. Whenever I read or hear this text, I realize I
have been privileged to witness its truth, and my thoughts take flight
to the various places all over the globe where I have assisted in the
offering of that 'clean oblation.'"[29] Her fondness for these lines from
the Old Testament, which predict the conversion of the Gentiles and
the emergence of a spiritual priesthood in the time of the Gospels,
suggests that Murphy shares in the missionary zeal of the Roman
Catholic Church rather than in a cosmopolitan embrace of other religious traditions and cultural perspectives. But there is at least a minor
disruption of this perspective in the claim that these words serve as an
"Open Sesame," invoking the famous phrase from "Ali Baba and the
Forty Thieves" in the *Arabian Nights* to explain how the biblical lines
influence her recollections. For a moment, that is, there is a tenuous
equivalence between western and eastern cultures, which unsettles the

29. Murphy, 295.

hierarchical outlook assumed by Catholic universalism by suggesting that, in some sense, the other tradition is equally valid and equally valuable. Something similar happens a few pages later when Murphy describes her experience with "a most self-sacrificing Mahomedan" who drives her around and around the streets of Constantinople in search of a Catholic Mass and then waits patiently outside the cathedral for the duration of the service.[30] Her faith remains foremost, but her appreciation of those who practice other faiths, their generosity and their tenacity, is not compromised by this priority.

The religious cosmopolitanism Murphy displays in these instances can be understood as a variety of what Kwame Anthony Appiah has called, more generally, "rooted cosmopolitanism."[31] Like her self-applied title, "Ireland's super-tramp," the notion of a rooted cosmopolitanism is potentially oxymoronic: to be rooted is to be inserted in a particular nation, people, or history; to be cosmopolitan is to claim affiliation with a broader transnational community. But commentators in a number of fields have begun to question the simple opposition between "national" and "global" experiences and to assert a more nuanced awareness of the relationship between a familiar homeland and the broader world, between cultural specificities and general sympathies. In books such as *Ethics of Identity* (2005) and *Cosmopolitanism: Ethics in a World of Strangers* (2006), Appiah has elaborated on "the possibility of a cosmopolitan community in which individuals from varying locations (physical, economic, etc.) enter relationships of mutual respect despite their differing beliefs (religious, political, etc.)."[32] If cosmopolitanism has traditionally entailed an obligation to others that transcends the local bonds of family and community, along with recognition of the value of alterity or otherness, rooted cosmopolitanism suggests these commitments begin with an attachment

30. Murphy, 297.

31. Kwame Anthony Appiah, *Ethics of Identity* (Princeton: Princeton Univ. Press, 2005), 213–72.

32. Kwame Anthony Appiah, "Cosmopolitan Patriots," *Critical Inquiry* 23, no. 3 (1997): 617.

to an ethically and affectively significant community. Critics have countered that "Appiah's 'rooted' cosmopolitanism finds a way to accommodate prejudice without really challenging us to uproot ourselves and forge a new world community with an enlarged sphere of concern."[33] It is an appealing notion, that is, because it seeks to moderate some of the demands of a radical cosmopolitanism that would have us abandon our duties to friends, family, and fellow citizens, but it does so precisely by diminishing the most consequential implications of cosmopolitanism, especially that we owe profound obligations to strangers from other cultures from other parts of the world distant from our own.

It should be apparent already that Murphy's writing is demonstrative of the very contradictions raised by Appiah and his critics. Her curiosity drives her to seek out otherness, which is often valued in and of itself, and her sympathy goes so far as to hint at the integration of other cultural and religious perspectives with her own. And yet her point of view remains firmly tethered to her Irish Catholicism, as evinced in the final paragraph of "Memorable Masses in Many Lands":

Meandering up and down the highways and byways of the world, my thoughts, like homing birds, return at last to Ireland, and there forge two final links to close this golden chain of memories, which encircles the globe. First, that unforgettable Eucharistic Congress Mass in the vast natural cathedral of the Phoenix Park, when, above the bowed heads of many thousands, "breathless with adoration," the clear, crystal notes of our famous tenor rang out in the ecstatic prayer of "Panis Angelicus." The second took place at midnight, on a moonlit Christmas Eve, in a village a few miles from my own home. One lone star, the brightest in the northern hemisphere, guided my feet over the frost-paved road, through the

33. Ethan J. Leib, "Rooted Cosmopolitanism," Review of Kwame Anthony Appiah, *Cosmopolitanism: Ethics in a World of Strangers* in *Policy Review* (June 2006): n.p., accessed July 1, 2020, https://www.hoover.org/research/rooted -cosmopolitans.

silent night, to where I found a simple crib, surrounded by earnest worshippers.[34]

Her obligations to the people most familiar to her remain foremost, so that her exposure to otherness during her travels—and the estrangement from the familiar that it brings—is overcome by her return to Ireland and the abandonment of difference. This is the case whether she is communing with more than a million Irish Catholics at one of the largest eucharistic congresses of the twentieth century as they listen to the renowned John McCormack sing at an outdoor Mass or with a small congregation of fellow believers as they gather around a humble nativity scene on a cold winter night in the Irish midlands.

Openness *and* Ambivalence

There are times, in her subsequent articles on more distant destinations, when Murphy is concerned to stress the hazards associated with her unrestrained inquisitiveness, which occasionally looks more like comic naïveté. For example, wandering the thronged streets of Saigon, in search of "the exotic colour needed to banish [her] depression," Murphy's "curiosity [is] aroused by seeing dejected-looking, slouching figures entering what appeared to be a shoddy cinema": "penetrating" the interior of the dilapidated building she finds, to her considerable surprise, an opium den, where she nonetheless lingers "sufficiently long to witness the whole process."[35] In another instance, when she applies to the authorities in Tehran for an exit visa, she discovers that she has "broken the law by bringing into the country a sum of money which [she] had failed to declare at the frontier," and "for two miserable days" thereafter she fears that her trip will end in a Persian jail.[36] But these scenes, played out in a pose of comparative ignorance, are not just cautionary tales for would-be travelers. Instead,

34. Murphy, "Memorable Masses," 307.
35. K. M. Murphy, "I in Indo-China," *The Capuchin Annual* (1952): 266.
36. K. M. Murphy, "Patches of Persia," *The Capuchin Annual* (1960): 151.

they provide a kind of vicarious thrill for those who will never follow in her footsteps, because the scenes cast her in the role of a sympathetic everyman—or, better, everywoman—figure with whom they might identify.

Murphy's rhetorical positioning is rendered even more complex precisely by the issue of gender and her need, as an Irish woman at midcentury, to produce discursive authority by other means. Take, for instance, "I, in Indo-China," which begins with her account of the 1931 Paris International Colonial Exhibition and a model of the five towers of Angkor Wat "discovered" by French naturalist Henri Mohout in 1861. Seeing the model sparks a "fervor" in Murphy to see the magnificent ruins for herself, but a French friend tells her, "in a tone suggestive of soothing a wayward child," that a such visit would be "impossible."[37] In this context, her account of Mohout comes to look like an effort to position herself as a more knowing, more capable, more intrepid character than her male predecessor as Murphy mocks his cynicism and his naïveté as well as the simplicity or backwardness of his local guides. The article goes on to detail her triumph over the prejudice expressed by her friend: in her disappointment that the trek to the "marvelous Khmer temple" was not more arduous, her awe at finally exploring the Brahman and Buddhist temples, her anthropological reflections on modern Cambodians, her interest at seeing a monk bathing nude in a river on a hot afternoon, and, finally, her delight at discovering a "tiny wooden Catholic church" near a Buddhist monastery.[38] Murphy pushes back against the social conventions that would keep her at home and yet, in the process, she also adopts a number of assumptions that had guided European colonial rule abroad and French expansionism in particular.[39] It is as if adopting

37. Murphy, "I in Indo-China," 265.

38. Murphy, 269.

39. The scholarly effort to place women travel writers within the colonial context rather than focusing on their struggles against social conventions began with Sara Mills, *Discourses of Difference: An Analysis of Women's Travel Writing and Colonialism* (1991). It remains a key text for understanding these dynamics.

these assumptions is the only way to highlight her own adventurous spirit, her mastery of other cultures, her expertise as a woman traveling through foreign lands.

All this suggests that the "rooted cosmopolitanism" on display in Murphy's articles does not entirely escape the patriarchal, colonial legacy of the travel writing genre. Like many travelogues, that is, her articles depend on the *production* of difference as much as the *appreciation* of difference, so that the places described can be rendered sufficiently foreign, sufficiently exotic. In many of her articles, not just in "I in Indo-China," Murphy claims to offer her readers a behind-the-scenes view of distant cultures as she adopts the stance of a masculine adventurer directing a "masculine gaze" capable both of piercing the obscurities of those cultures and revealing the essence of their allure for her readers. On another occasion in Iraq, she pauses briefly at a signpost pointing toward a Catholic church: "I soon gazed incredulously at my surroundings, where, with bewildering abruptness, I was swept back to the age of the *Arabian Nights*, as Baghdad, like a beautiful Mohammedan maiden, dropped her veil, and revealed to me an indescribable charm, which has never been effaced from my memory."[40] Here Murphy casually reproduces an orientalist perspective, which fixes the East in images that date back to its representation in folk literature centuries earlier, even as it implicitly reaffirms cultural and political hierarchies in the present. Given the long history of the English denigrating the Irish, we might expect her background to temper the use of racial stereotypes and disparaging representations of poor or disadvantaged peoples, and yet Murphy occasionally lapses into the familiar tropes of colonial discourse as she portrays these distant regions.

In this way, her writing works to reassure her readers of their superior position insofar as she assumes the moral authority of the Catholic faith, which remains consistent with the intertwining missionary and colonial activities of the Church in previous eras. This

40. K. M. Murphy, "An Eyeful of Iraq," *The Capuchin Annual* (1959): 217.

reassurance tends to bolster certain ethnic and cultural stereotypes: much of this—especially her use of dismissive, racialized terms such as "Chinaman," "negro," "savage," or her insistence on calling her driver in Baghdad "Anonymous"—sounds entirely dissonant more than a half-century later, even though in many cases she uses the terms to announce perspectives that are far less doctrinaire and intolerant than those that predominated in earlier examples of travel writing. She manages to maintain a genuine openness to alterity, which makes these encounters with other cultures qualitatively different from those so often recorded in colonial discourse. Her openness, that is, operates in a dialectic of authority and admiration so that cultural difference is examined as something to be revered for its foreign beauty and charm as often as it is to be fixed in familiar discursive forms.

This dialectic generates highly ambivalent representations of the various "others" Murphy encounters, depictions that often work to make them sympathetic to her audience and transvalue longstanding ethic and cultural stereotypes even as the depictions repeat common tropes regarding different races and societies. In the remarkable opening paragraph of "Chasing Chunchos," for instance, she describes a fondness, dating back to her childhood in Tulla, for "the humble blossoms of the field and hedgerow" over the "haughty blooms of garden or greenhouse":

> And, so what I may call the wild flowers of humanity—the Bedouins of the desert, the Lapps within the Arctic Circle, the Caboclos of the Amazon, the Kabyles of the Atlas Mountains, the Mois of Indo-China, the Igorots of the Philippine Islands, and the Indians of the Andes—all these true children of Nature, who dwell along the remote byways of the world, their "clouds of glory" undimmed by "shades of the prison-house," aroused in me, during my wanderings, a far deeper interest than did their sophisticated brethren who tread the crowded highways of civilisation.[41]

41. K. M. Murphy, "Chasing the Chunchos," *The Capuchin Annual* (1955): 209.

The analogy is a troubling one: its breezy generalities not only wipe away the specificity of each culture she names but risk too-easy application of ideologically loaded binary distinctions between civilization and its opposite. As I have been suggesting, however, her rooted cosmopolitanism generates a complex, sometimes tangled, system of differentiation that alternates between, on the one hand, a colonial paradigm of cultural and racial superiority and, on the other, a more pluralistic and sympathetic approach to difference: later in "Chasing Chunchos," when her driver objects to giving a ride to two members of the tribe "on the ground they were too dirty," Murphy overcomes his opposition by assuring him that since she left Lima she "had only had a pint of washing water each day."[42]

If travel writing is often prone to emphasize the difference between home and away, between the community of the writer and those "who dwell along the remote byways of the world," there is frequently an element of atavism, or at least nostalgia, in the insistence on encountering societies still inhabited by the "true children of Nature" (along with a sense that these societies are quickly disappearing). In many of her travelogues—recording her journeys to Indo-China, the Andes, Jerusalem, and elsewhere—Murphy presents her destinations as romantic sites of adventure and spiritual experience that have since been lost to tourism in the age of commercial travel and transcontinental flight. She gives the impression that a Golden Age of Travel has come to an end, not just because the tourist industry is on the rise around the globe, but because the war has intervened to spoil many of these destinations with its almost inconceivable violence and destruction.

In this way, Murphy brings her audience a world not beyond their geographical reach, with the proliferation of package tours and airline routes, so much as beyond their temporal reach, at a time when "real" travel, "real" adventure, seems less and less possible. This is a sense of loss that, by the 1950s, Murphy herself feels deeply: "Since the

---

42. Murphy, "Chasing the Chunchos," 215.

end of the war I have taken an occasional flutter as far as my clipped wings would allow me, but only along familiar paths, condemned to follow 'the dusty road of commonsense.' Gone forever is the glamour of the Unknown. Jungles and deserts, sheiks and dervishes, bandits and gauchos have all vanished from my life; and only in dreams can I hear again the muezzin's call to prayer, or the magic music of camel bells."[43] Beginning with her very first travelogue about Achill Island, many of her articles are written from this position of wistful retrospect, not just for her own loss of mobility but for the disappearance of "authentic" cultures, of the unfamiliar places and peoples, of the foreign customs and conventions she sought to experience on her journeys. Such was the allure of other cultures, however, that Murphy began to travel again as she neared her ninth decade of life: visiting Benedictine sites in France, Germany, and Switzerland; peeking behind the Iron Curtain in Poland, Czechoslovakia, and the USSR; and, on her final adventure, tracking down the magnificent frescoes to be discovered in secluded monasteries throughout Yugoslavia.

Final Years and Legacy

During her final years, in addition to writing travelogues for *The Capuchin Annual*, Murphy actively composed letters to the editor for both local and national newspapers—letters that combined her devout Catholic faith with a historical, geographical, and anthropological knowledge derived from her researches and her many wanderings. In 1957, for instance, she published a letter in *The Catholic Herald* about *mestizos* in Peru, referencing both her extensive travel in that country and her in-depth study of the Incas.[44] Two years later, in the same periodical, she published another letter defending "the

---

43. Biographical note, *Capuchin Annual* (1950–51): 523.

44. K. M. Murphy, letter to the editors, *The Catholic Herald*, January 25, 1957, 2.

followers Zoroaster" against the slander that they were mere "fireworshippers," and, in the process, recalling her visit many years before to two Zoroastrian altars in Persia.[45] Her brand of cosmopolitanism does not entirely escape the predominant discourses of the Catholic tradition insofar as it continues to rely on its terminologies of discrimination, but her use of these terms is far more muted than the articles she responds to in such publications. With her more strident claims, Murphy argues that readers of *The Catholic Herald*, like the readers of *The Capuchin Annual*, do not have to appreciate other cultures and traditions despite evident differences from their own, but they can learn to value the differences in and of themselves.

In this sense, Murphy's variety of cosmopolitanism regards other religions, other traditions, not as a threat to her own religious affiliations but, rather, as what Beck's formulation identifies "as an enrichment in a quite personal sense, and ultimately even as part of the normal state of affairs."[46] Take a final example from a passage in "Balkan Byways," the posthumously published account of an arduous journey Murphy undertook well after her eightieth birthday:

> In Dalmatia, Bosnia, Herzegovina and Serbia, I travelled in the ordinary local buses, thus establishing an intimate contact with many places in which, at that time, so universally worn were the picturesque and colorful, national costumes, that the weekly markets resembled fancy dress balls. In some districts the majority of the inhabitants were followers of Mohammed, in others the Cross was triumphant over the Crescent; and once, as I approached a distant village, I saw a mosque, a Catholic and an Orthodox church, all three, silhouetted clearly against the horizon. Everywhere one witnessed a fascinating blend of East and West, found nowhere else in Europe; and no traveller could ever complain of monotony where the scenery was as varied and interesting as the people.[47]

45. K. M. Murphy, letter to the editors, *The Catholic Herald*, April 24, 1959, 2.
46. Beck, *A God of One's Own*, 71.
47. K. M. Murphy, "Balkan Byways," *The Capuchin Annual* (1963): 111.

The travelogue frequently emphasizes, sometimes comically exaggerates, the hardships that Murphy endures as she travels along the backroads of the Balkans, but these sufferings are relieved by her stirring encounters with local splendors, not just art and architecture but the varieties of native social and cultural life.

To be sure, throughout her account she draws on a discourse that Maria Todorova has labeled "Balkanism": that is, a tradition of writing that constructs the Balkans as "a region geographically inextricable from Europe" and yet culturally other.[48] Like orientalism, Balkanism offers exoticizing, patronizing, and sometimes denigrating representations (often of Islamic peoples), representations that serve as a foundation on which a self-congratulatory image of European culture has been built. Murphy describes Sarajevo, "with its dim-lit bazaars, veiled women, and countless minarets; and picturesque Jajce where [she] heard the muezzin's cry resounding through its majestic gorge and at sunset watched groups of gaily clad men performing the ceremony of washing themselves at a fountain before evening prayer."[49] Just as often, however, she seeks out difference not to make hierarchical distinctions but precisely (as in the closing lines of this passage) to celebrate the diversity of cultural influences coalescing in the Balkans. Other faith traditions are not rendered as inferior or divisive or menacing. Rather, they offer Murphy the possibility of integrating alternative imageries and customs and viewpoints into her own religious experience.

Despite the persistent ambivalence of her writing, it is difficult to deny the insistence of Murphy's curiosity—her sheer drive to come into contact with other cultures, to encounter new places, new peoples, new experiences—regardless of the many physical and emotional hardships of travel. In part, of course, this is also a rhetorical stance on her part taken up to distinguish her from everyday travelers and mere tourists at a time when international travel was becoming more and

48. Maria Todorova, *Imaging the Balkans* (Oxford: Oxford Univ. Press, 2009), 188; see also 3–20.

49. Murphy, "Balkan Byways": 111.

more accessible, less and less demanding. For Murphy, moving beyond
the relative security and luxury of the expanding tourist industry was
essential to the pilgrimages she undertook, even when she traveled
with groups of other sightseers toward the end of her life. In the opening paragraph of "Balkan Byways," she reflects on these themes: "The
hardships and misadventures inseparable from travel in remote areas
of the world may be likened, in my opinion, to the nucleus needed
by the oyster for the formation of a precious gem." In this way, the
journey she goes on to describe, like many of the journeys that came
before it, is framed as an authentic test or trial: not a trivial or hedo-
nistic getaway but an opportunity to take away a treasured experience
that cannot be garnered any other way. This too is a common feature,
perhaps even a necessity, of much travel writing, which justifies itself
as a genre precisely by deriving a valuable lesson, if only in retrospect,
from the activity of moving through the world with all its discomforts
and distractions: "The remembrance of these unpleasant experiences
would inevitably tarnish some of my most splendid moments, were it
not that in course of time they became encrusted with a layer of something magical that develops into a thing of beauty completely concealing the ugliness of the inner core."[50] By the end of the journey, she
can claim—in one final rhetorical flourish—that she "had discovered a
chapter of absorbing interest hitherto missing from my history of art,
another 'magic casement' had been opened on far horizons, and my
lengthening string of travel memories was enriched by the addition of
another priceless pearl."[51]

By the time she died, on March 22, 1962, Kathleen M. Murphy
had collected many such priceless pearls. In one sense, this claim is
nearly literal: the few obituaries dedicated to her, along with the auc-
tion notifications at the time of her death, report a treasure trove
of "artistic mementoes of visits to all parts of the globe," including
Persian rugs, Italian oil paintings, antique furniture, bric-a-brac, and

50. Murphy, 110.
51. Murphy, 124.

a small collection of unique jewelry.[52] It is fitting that just before she passed away at the age of eighty-two Murphy was in the midst of planning another journey, this one to visit Constantinople and the Middle East; the tributes written for her recall both an immense curiosity and an unstinting generosity, especially to the poor and downtrodden of Birr; others mention her bequests to parish priests in Birr, Dunkerrin, Westmeath, and elsewhere, as well as to the Capuchin Fathers, Church Street, Dublin. There can be no doubt, however, that Murphy's greatest legacy is to readers of travel writing as well as to the travel writers who followed her, though for too long that legacy has gone largely unacknowledged and unclaimed. It is not too much to say that Kathleen M. Murphy is the most significant predecessor of that other Murphy, Dervla (no relation), who is widely recognized as one of the most important travel writers of the late twentieth century. It is also fitting that, in 1963, as Kathleen published her last travelogue in *The Capuchin Annual*, Dervla was setting off on the journey that became the basis for her first, and still most celebrated, travel book—*Full Tilt: Ireland to India With a Bicycle* (1965). Like her predecessor, she highlights the many dangers and hardships that befall the traveler, especially the woman traveler, in search of distant cultures and alternative ways of living. And like her predecessor, Dervla relates these adventures and misadventures in a way that is both self-deprecating and yet implicitly self-aggrandizing, detailing the life of an intrepid individual willing to step away from the comforts of home in order to gather experiences that will one day become the pearls of memory. But Kathleen M. Murphy remains singular in her mode of rooted, Catholic cosmopolitanism, which filters these experiences through both her devout faith and her openness to other cultures, her sympathy for other peoples, in a way that once revealed—and now can continue to reveal—more expansive vistas to her readership in Ireland and elsewhere.

52. "Obituary: Miss Kathleen M. Murphy," 1.

The Travelogues

2. Map for "Slippin' into Keel," Brian Bixby, 2020.

1

"Slippin' into Keel"

Long before it became the popular summer resort it now is, I set out to explore the island of Achill with so limited a knowledge of its geography that I assumed the village of Keel, where I had secured accommodation, to be only a short walk from the railway terminus. So vague too were my ideas of the length of the journey that when I lunched at a town en route, I imagined myself enjoying an early supper in the cosy corner promised me on the edge of the Atlantic. Meandering at a leisurely pace for the greater part of a day, and shedding its passengers until I alone remained, the train at last limped into "The Sound" station shortly before sunset on an August evening. Grown accustomed to many hours of solitude, and to the thinly populated country through which I had travelled, I expected to see the individual sent to meet

Published in the *The Capuchin Annual* for 1948, Murphy's first travelogue recounts her journey many years earlier to the village of Keel on Achill Island off the northwest coast of Ireland—a part of the country the writer confesses to barely knowing before her arrival. She nonetheless brings with her a rather romantic vision of the hardy inhabitants of the small island and their "unceasing warfare against elemental forces," including the "primeval simplicity and rugged strength" of the landscape. In this regard, Murphy's account draws on the example of the Irish Literary Revival, from domestic travelogues such as J. M. Synge's *The Aran Islands* (1907) to folkloric compilations such as W. B. Yeats's *The Celtic Twilight* (1893) and Lady Augusta Gregory's *Visions and Beliefs in the West of Ireland* (1920), although it also incorporates ample reference to her many travels abroad. Perhaps most importantly, then, her first travelogue begins to establish Murphy's credentials as a savvy world traveler, even as it depicts her "at home" in Ireland. Reproduced with permission from *The Capuchin Annual*.

me standing isolated on the platform, like a palm tree in the middle of the Sahara. When a battalion of warriors sprang from the dragon's teeth Jason[1] could hardly have been more bewildered than I was when a living mosaic of faces slid past the window of my compartment, and I stepped out into the midst of a multitude, swaying and heaving like a windswept cornfield. Suddenly, all this commotion was petrified as if by the wave of a wand; hats were doffed as if by a single hand; and, to the accompaniment of a soft, murmuring chorus of prayer, a coffin was removed from the van. The famous picture by El Greco of *The Burial of Count Orgaz*[2] came to my mind, with the thought that this scene too was a subject worthy of the brush of a great painter. Here were no human weeds such as so often spring from city pavements; no glazed expressions fixed by constant staring at mere man-made monuments; but men of all ages with powerful limbs developed by centuries of unceasing warfare against elemental forces, and eyes filled with a yearning for the infinite, generated by lifelong gazing on starry spaces and limitless horizons. "Ah, there ye are, asthore, and I blind from lookin' out for ye," said a warmly affectionate, but reproachful, voice at my elbow. Thinking it a case of mistaken identity, I turned and saw, beaming at me, a middle-aged giant, who instantly seemed an old friend of childhood, so striking was his resemblance to the figure supporting the globe on the cover of my school atlas. "I'm Sonny Magee that's come to dhrive ye," and he cracked his whip with a vehemence implying a capacity to drive a herd of buffaloes. Believing I had only a very short distance to go, I had intended to walk; but, in the circumstances, I urged him to fetch my luggage at once, and to start on our way as soon as possible. "Is it goin' without payin'

---

1. In Greek mythology, Jason encounters a dragon with magical teeth on his quest for the Golden Fleece.

2. El Greco, byname of Doménikos Theotokópoulos (1541–1614), was a Spanish painter and sculptor. Generally regarded as his masterpiece, *The Burial of Count de Orgaz* (1586–88) depicts a local legend concerning the death of a charitable Toledo nobleman, who is surrounded at his funeral by an array of prominent men including the Spanish King Philip II and Pope Sixtus V.

yer respects to the poor corpse ye'd be?" he exclaimed with horror, as if I had pronounced a blasphemy. I squirmed beneath his gorgon glance, and, muttering something inarticulately apologetic, followed him meekly to find my transport. The horse was abnormally tall and slender, with a tail so sparsely haired that it reminded me of a Chinaman's beard. He furnished a most interesting object lesson in natural history; the legs, neck, and diminutive head proclaiming giraffe ancestry, the huge floppy ears of obvious elephantine extraction, and the backbone betraying direct descent from a brontosaurus. He appeared to have been assembled in sections, carelessly and precariously riveted even after the lapse of countless millenniums. The car, on the contrary, was what house agents describe as a solid structure. "Jaunting" was an insultingly flippant epithet to apply to a vehicle apparently constructed to occupy a position stationary as Boadicea's chariot on the Thames Embankment.[3] That this was a true estimate of its character was proved when the horse seemed to have nearly as much difficulty in obeying the signal to move as if he had been harnessed to the Rock of Cashel.[4] With the innate courtesy of people in close communion with nature, I was assigned a place of honour among the chief mourners; and, then discovering the absence of a hearse, I realised, with dismay, that the rate of our progress must be measured by the footsteps of the coffin bearers. Even at such a solemn moment, so potent is the domination of matter over mind, that a troop of mocking demons, masquerading in the guise of delectable dishes, paraded before my inner vision with exasperating persistence. Making a desperate attempt to adjust the balance of my mental faculties, and finally succeeding in

3. Thomas Thornycroft's sculpture *Boadicea and Her Daughters* (1856–85) depicts the Celtic queen leading a revolt against Roman rule in ancient Britain. In 1902, it was placed on the western end of Westminster Bridge, where it has faced Big Ben and the Palace of Westminster ever since.

4. The Rock of Cashel, also known as St. Patrick's Rock, is a spectacular limestone outcropping in the otherwise flat landscape of County Tipperary, Ireland. According to legend, the rock was set in place when St. Patrick banished Satan from a mountain cave some twenty miles (thirty kilometers) away.

doing so, my aesthetic sense was thrilled by the sight of the procession crawling like a colossal caterpillar through scenery, of which the inhabitants were the living embodiment. There was in this melancholy land no touch of softness or tenderness, but a primeval simplicity and rugged strength, a wild grandeur and brooding mysticism, which, against a sky of livid grey flushed with vermilion, was reminiscent of a landscape by Salvatore Rosa.[5] Lines of horsemen wearing undyed homespun jackets added a most impressive and picturesque note, to which the crimson petticoats and short plaid shawls of the women lent a delightful glow of colour, intensified by the browns and blues of bogs and mountains. Again, I deemed it a fitting subject for the canvas of an Old Master, and again, in spite of my efforts, the baser side of my nature gradually became ascendant, and I looked for a crossroads as eagerly as a thirsty nomad for a well in the desert. Round twists and turns, over hills and hollows, we wound wearily on . . . and on. The motion had become quite automatic; there was no evidence of volition; we seemed a mere machine worked by unseen hands. Our route was rough and plentifully strewn with stones; and I felt like a puppet with strings so clumsily manipulated that my movements became a series of spasmodic jerks, exactly as if I were afflicted with St. Vitus's dance.[6] I thought of Christian's pilgrimage through the Slough of Despond;[7] I thought of Dante's ascent of the Mount of Purgatory;[8] I thought of the unfortunate Jew condemned to wander till the Day of Judgment; and, for the first time in my life, I understood why

5. Salvator Rosa (1615–73) was an Italian artist of the Neapolitan school best remembered for his haunting paintings of rugged and romantic landscape scenes.

6. An antiquated name for Syndenham's chorea, a neurological disorder distinguished by involuntary and erratic movements of various muscle groups that follow a streptococcal infection.

7. The "swamp of despair" in John Bunyan's Christian allegory, *The Pilgrim's Progress* (1678).

8. The second part of Dante Aligheri's *Divina Commedia* (*Divine Comedy*) (1320), *Purgatorio* (*Purgatory*), is an allegorical account of the poet's climb through seven levels of suffering and spiritual growth on Mount Purgatory toward the Earthly Paradise at its summit.

the *summum bonum*[9] of human desire is eternal rest. Stealthily, the shadow of twilight crept around us; a single star shyly announced the approach of night; and, at last, the funeral turned off from the main road, and we were left alone. Much to my surprise, I was the only one who noticed any change in our environment, the other two being quite unconscious of having parted from the cortège; our pace remained unaltered. At the foot of a steep hill Sonny awoke from his trance, and suggested that "to stretch my legs and aise the little horse I ought to walk up the shlope." I did this with alacrity, believing my reward would be a glimpse of the Promised Land where food and shelter awaited me. Reaching the top, I was paralysed by the sight of a boundless expanse, populated by cottages widely separated as raisins in a wartime cake. Heroically suppressing a keen pang of disappointment, and strangling the least tremor of emotion in my voice, I asked how far we had yet to go. Grinning like a gargoyle, Sonny screwed up his eyes and peered towards where a few shreds of scarlet and gold still lingered in the sky. "Ye see that mountain with a mouthful out o' her side," he replied, nodding at a nebulous formation dimly visible in the west. "Well, with the help o' God," and he braced himself as if for a herculean task, "when we're after skirtin' round the waisht o' *that*, we'll never feel shlippin' into Keel."

Feeling as if a pound of flesh had been cut from my own side, I had not sufficient vitality to dispute the point when he declared that the road was "as shlippy as the shkin of an eel" after a heavy rainfall, and that "'twould be safer not to be over-hashty goin' down the incline." Informing me that "Dainty" had only recently been shod, he said "'twould be daft to make bould with new shoes, anyway"; and while admiring his exquisite irony in naming his steed, I assured him of my full confidence in his ability to avoid anything rash or reckless. When we reached a surface level as a billiard table, our pace at last accelerated into a trot; and the car lurched from side to side, like a ship on a stormy sea. Years later, in my desert wanderings, I felt a strange

9. [Latin] "the highest good."

familiarity with my mode of locomotion, and, recalling that night in Achill, I realised that when enumerating the various ingredients in my horse's pedigree, I had omitted a strong dash of dromedary blood. At regular intervals afterwards he trotted to the tune of the constantly reiterated "Aisy, Dainty, *aisy*" of the driver; but, evidently, the funeral had the effect on him of intensive training, and, in a few minutes, he always stopped abruptly, as if apologising for his irrever- ence, and relapsed into the majestic rhythm of the *Dead March* in *Saul*.[10] So regular, too, was the peremptory command to climb every excrescence for the good of my health, that mounting and dismount- ing from the high-stepped car became an exhausting form of exercise, admirably adapted to develop in my anatomy the sinews and muscles of a frog. Like the discoverer of the Pacific, from the summit of every hill I gazed with eagle eyes at the horizon, but, for any evidence of the proximity of the sea, we might as well be in the middle of Siberia. I had learned that time and space are merely forms of thought due to the limitations of the finite human intellect. My experience on that drive forced me to conclude that, through a rapid phase of evolution, produced by inhaling some element in the island's atmosphere, I had reached a superhuman plane of knowledge in which space was elimi- nated, our movement being but a method of measuring time, as sand in an hourglass. We had been moving constantly ever since we left the railway station, but it seemed to be on a revolving platform, like the chariot race in the film of *Ben-Hur*,[11] photographed in slow motion. Unlike the latter, however, our gyrations were accomplished in a lone- liness awful as that of the sole survivors from the destruction of the world by an atomic bomb. Moments became like the years described by Yeats as great black oxen treading the world and crushing mankind

10. The funeral march in Georg Friedrich Händel's oratio *Saul* (1739), which is often used to accompany important state occasions, such as the burial of a king or queen.

11. *Ben-Hur* (1925) is a silent historical drama starring Ramon Navarro and directed by Fred Niblo.

beneath their hooves;[12] but these cruel beasts had relinquished the extended sphere of influence allowed them by the poet to concentrate all their energy on me. My companion seemed to share the ecstasy of Ponchielli when he composed the *Dance of the Hours*,[13] depicting them as ethereal nymphs whose twinkling feet scarcely ruffled the petals of a daisy. Radiant as his name, time was a word of no importance in Sonny's vocabulary. "All for the best in the best of all possible worlds" was manifestly his philosophy of life; and my restlessness and periodic surges of rebellious emotion broke like waves against the granite cliff of his angelic serenity. Striving to convey a purely speculative interest in the latitude of the country, I inquired once more how much farther we had to go. "Do ye see yon heathery hill?" he asked, pointing a vague finger towards infinity. I strained my eyes, but quickly realised that the heather must be a daylight memory, the visibility being then poor enough to tarnish the purple of ancient Tyre.[14] "Well," and he drew a deep breath, like a whale about to submerge, "when we're afther climbin' a taste and roundin' the chest o' that"— and his bust measure increased perceptibly—"*then*," making a most eloquent pause, "we'll never feel shlippin' into Keel."

A waning moon, thickly curtained by clouds, shed a spectral pallor on what seemed a lunar rather than an earthly landscape. Indeed I could have well believed myself a second Jonah, disgorged by some aerial monster on the surface of our satellite, were it not for my acute consciousness of the laws of gravitation. The absence of trees from the land and stars from the sky added to the forlorn aspect of the scene. A small lake, set amid the shadows, reflected the ghastly light, and glared at me with cyclopean malignity. Desperately, as a drowning

---

12. W. B. Yeats, *The Countess Cathleen* (1892), scene 5: "The years like great black oxen tread the world, / And God the herdsman goads them on behind, / And I am broken by their passing feet."

13. "Dance of the Hours" is a brief ballet that forms the act III finale of Amilcare Ponchielli's best-known opera, *La Gioconda* (1876).

14. Tyrian purple, also known as royal purple or imperial dye, is a natural dye traditionally used to color fabrics worn by people of royal or imperial rank.

man a straw, I had grasped some frail links with humanity forged by the red glow of lamps in occasional windows, but these had long disappeared, leaving me chilled with a sense of utter homelessness and desolation. I seemed to be surrounded by a "blasted heath,"[15] where all the weird tales I had ever read could find their ideal setting. Every tussock became a werewolf crouching to seize its prey; solitary squat bushes were transformed into grimacing goblins: the raucous cry of a seabird was the cackling laughter of a witch riding her broomstick. A vampire bat seemed to be draining the blood from my brain, until I became a veritable robot incapable of thought. Predominant in my mind was so intense a longing to terminate my *status quo*, that I would have accepted eagerly a seat in the Headless Coach,[16] or even on the back of the flame-breathing Pooka himself,[17] to hasten the advent of my journey's end. No inquiries about my welfare having come from Sonny for a considerable time, I concluded he had gone to sleep. That Dainty had not followed his example was scarcely proved by the monotonous, metallic clang, eerie as the hammering of a leprechaun, with which the hooves accentuated, rather than dispelled, the oppressive stillness that lay on everything like a pall . . . Suddenly, the silence was lacerated by a shrill, grating noise a series of shrieks and growls suggestive of the jungle; and, simultaneously, I felt myself jerked upwards like a Jack-in-the-Box, while the other side of the vehicle seemed to sink into an abyss. Standing on the only remnant of *terra firma*[18] left to me, I literally took a leap in the dark, and made a safe landing, just in time to see a wheel whirling down the road with the joyous elation of a spirit freed from the bondage of the body. Despite his great bulk, Sonny too landed on his feet, demonstrating himself endowed with no mean acrobatic skill. He gazed wistfully after the rapidly departing

15. William Shakespeare, *Macbeth* (1606), act I, scene 3.

16. According to Irish legend, the passing of the Death Coach (Irish: *Cóiste Bodhar*), driven by a headless horseman, is a harbinger of imminent death.

17. In Irish folklore, the pooka (Irish: *púca*) is a shape-shifter able to take on a range of forms, both terrifying and benevolent.

18. [Latin] "solid earth" or "dry land."

wheel. "Musha, bad 'cess to yerself and yer capers, an' we getting' on so fine," he muttered angrily, as the object of his scorn, with a grace worthy of the Russian ballet, fluttered languidly and lay prone on the roadside. "But, sure, the walk will do ye a power o' good," he added, addressing me with his unfailing solicitude. "'Twill limber ye out afther sittin' so long, and ye'll be able for a toppin' gran' breakfast. Glory be to God, 'twas lucky we were yoked to such a quiet craythur. Any other baste, hearin' that hullaballo, would lep like a hare, and lave oursels and the poor car in smithereens. Things do be mighty conthrairy sometimes," and his tone switched to a minor key. "If only that little inconvaynance had happened a few miles farther ahead—a goat's bleat nearer that black-browed hill," and he pointed to a rain-sodden cloud above the horizon, "*then*"—with an emphasis like an anvil-beat, "we'd never feel shlippin' into Keel."

I "dragged my slow length along"[19] in true Alexandrine style, and eventually reached a village, where groups of whitewashed cottages resembled tombs in the pallid light of dawn. The sea was wailing, poignantly as a woman keening over her dead, and my eyes clung like limpets to the fishermen's upturned boats on the beach as to the only symbol of life. Knowing I had arrived at my destination when I came to a two-storied house which, with aristocratic aloofness, looked down on its neighbours, I knocked loud and long. In the sepulchral silence the sound seemed to reverberate across the ocean, each echo fraught with the dramatic significance of the knocking at the gate in *Macbeth*.[20] Screeching and snorting in prolonged protest, the door opened reluctantly, and before me stood a figure in a flowing white nightgown, startlingly like Lady Macbeth in the sleep-walking scene.[21]

---

19. Alexander Pope, *An Essay on Criticism* (1711), part II, lines 355–56: "A needless Alexandrine ends the song, / That, like a wounded snake, drags its slow length along."

20. The knocking brings a close to act II, scene 2, and initiates act II, scene 3. It is the subject of Thomas De Quincey's most famous piece of literary criticism, "On the Knocking at the Gate in *Macbeth*" (1823).

21. *Macbeth*, act V, scene 1.

Fortunately for me the likeness was merely physical. Whether from custom or courtesy she made no reference whatever to the unconventional hour of my arrival, but melted my frozen heart with the fire of a real Irish *céad míle fáilte*;[22] and, with a speed a chef might envy, served a gargantuan repast of bacon and eggs, home-made bread, and tea. I have since travelled all over the world, tasting many exotic dishes, treading many winding trails from China to Peru, but never again have I recaptured the gastronomic delight of that simple meal, nor the exhilarating sense of achievement I felt, when, on that morning long ago, I had at last accomplished the feat of—"shlippin' into Keel."

22. [Irish] "a hundred thousand welcomes."

3. Map for Memorable Masses in Many Lands, Brian Bixby, 2020.

2

Memorable Masses in Many Lands

One of the most striking results of a visit to the Holy Land is the fact that the Gospel narrative, which hitherto has been a photographic record of Our Lord's life on earth, is transfigured for ever afterwards into a picture painted in glowing colours, complete in every detail of light and shade, of form and perspective. Jerusalem and Jericho, Cana and Caphemaum,[1] Bethlehem and Nazareth, are no longer seen "as in a glass darkly,"[2] but have become living realities; and when we meditate on the sacred events associated with them, our mind's eye is fixed on scenes no longer nebulous or distorted, but clear and vivid as those surrounding our own everyday existence. Similarly, the prophetic words of Scripture, "In every place there is sacrifice and there is

This kaleidoscopic account of Murphy's extensive travels shows her always in search of opportunities to practice the Catholic ritual—and, in the process, it alludes to more than sixty destinations around the globe. Appearing in the same 1948 issue of *The Capuchin Annual* as "Slippin' into Keel," "Masses in Many Lands" introduces readers to Murphy's "nomad spirit," which took her far beyond Ireland and into all variety of other cultures; at the same time, the travelogue manages to remind her readers of just how successful Roman Catholic missionary activity had been in spreading the faith. Murphy carries with her a number of assumptions about the people she encounters along the way, sometimes viewing them as a threat to her safety, at other moments romanticizing their beauty and innocence. Nevertheless, as the travelogue makes clear in its closing passages, Ireland remains for Murphy the center of the Catholic world, no matter how far she strays. Reproduced with permission from *The Capuchin Annual*.

1. More commonly spelled "Capernaum."

2. 1 Corinthians 13:12.

51

offered to my name a clean oblation"[3] have been transmuted, by my world wanderings, into vital sparks that set my imagination on fire; and have become for me an "Open Sesame"[4] to a treasure-house of precious memories. Whenever I read or hear this text, I realise I have been privileged to witness its truth, and my thoughts take flight to the various places all over the globe where I have assisted at the offering of that "clean oblation."

The great cathedrals of Europe pass before my mental vision in stately procession; from Seville and Toledo to Cologne; from the gargoyles of Notre Dame to the white marble sculptures of Milan; the hoary grey of St. Gudule's in Brussels; the war-scarred walls of St. Stephen's in Vienna; the classic asceticism of the Duomo in Florence; and the pile of St. Vitus's crowning Prague's historic hill.

I kneel again in Granada, close to the mausoleum of that wonderful woman, Isabel of Castile;[5] and I am distracted, not so much by thoughts of her, as of Alonso Cano,[6] who, when a canon of this cathedral, chose, for his studio, an alcove perched high above the pavement, and there, in presence of the Blessed Sacrament, created his immortal masterpieces.

In brilliant sunshine I had often watched the towers of Burgos look down on the ancient city; but it was on a dark winter's morning, when I walked through the silent streets to hear Mass in one of its dimly lit chapels, I clearly recognised, in the shadow of the Cid's[7] tomb, that the mighty cathedral is the embodiment of the very spirit of Spain.

I have been present at many ceremonies amidst the splendour of the great Venetian basilica, but the name of St. Mark's will ever recall

3. Malachi 1:11.

4. A magical phrase, used to open a cave containing an immense treasure, in the Middle Eastern folktale "Ali Baba and the Forty Thieves" from the *Arabian Nights*.

5. Isabella I (1451–1504) reigned as Queen of Castile from 1474 until her death.

6. Alonso Cano (1601–67), known for his elegant religious paintings, was appointed canon in the Cathedral of Granada by Philip IV in 1652.

7. El Cid, byname of Rodrigo Díaz de Vivar (ca. 1043–99), was a Castilian warlord and national hero.

for me a Mass at which I knelt near a side altar, in an unusual position in front of the priest. I scarcely uttered a single articulate prayer, and yet I felt that I had never prayed so well. My eyes were fixed on the celebrant's face, wherein I read, as in a missal, the whole sacred service; the luke-warmness of my devotion flushed beneath his fervour, his faith kindled mine into a white flame, and I understood, as never before, how intimate can be the union between man and his Maker.

Straying among the Umbrian hills, my thoughts nestle in Assisi, where, surrounded by the frescoes of Giotto,[8] I seemed to inhale, in that beautiful church, a subtle fragrance from the soul of the seraphic St. Francis.

Retracing my steps, I come to the Madeleine in Paris, where I once had a curious experience. The elaborately draped black curtains at the entrance proclaimed that the Mass would be a requiem; and, absent-mindedly, I allowed an usher to escort me to a special seat, where, too late to protest, I realised I had been mistaken for one of the mourners. This fact was most embarrassingly emphasised later on, when, according to a local custom, an acolyte, bowing low, handed me an asperges; and, with all the dignity I could muster, acutely conscious of the many eyes focused on me, I marched round the coffin, performing a ceremony which I had ever regarded as the sole prerogative of the priesthood. During those solemn moments I recited a "De Profundis"[9] for the deceased, though ignorant of whether it was for "him" or for "her" I ought to beg eternal rest.

Again I linger in that strange corner of France known as the Camargue, and look down from a low gallery on a colourful tapestry of reverent figures in the eleventh century shrine of Saintes Maries-de-la-Mer, which stands, defiantly as a fortress, on the edge of the sea, and is the scene of an annual pilgrimage attended by gypsies from all over Europe. Like them, my nomad spirit wanders far afield to the village

---

8. Giotto, in full Giotto di Bondone (ca. 1267–1337), was a late medieval Italian painter and architect, whose works predict the innovations of the Renaissance style.

9. [Latin] "from the depths." The phrase refers to Psalm 130.

churches in the mountains of the Tyrol, in Balkan byways, or on the plains of Hungary, where I felt so drab and commonplace among the picturesque natives in their distinctive costumes.

I once travelled by bus to the Bosnian town of Banjaluka, my companions being, on one side, a veiled woman, and, on the other, a moustached friar. To western eyes, this hirsute adornment, combined with the Franciscan habit, produced an unusual effect; but, soon learning that it was a clerical characteristic of this country, I was not surprised, at the following Sunday's Mass, to see the celebrant's upper lip unshaved. It was startling, however, to find that a beard could hardly have made myself more conspicuous than the fact that I was the only woman present who wore a skirt. All the others were resplendent in national dress, of which the most striking feature was that intricately cut garment, the Turkish trousers.

A Mass in Belgrade was memorable because it was there, and not in his own cathedral of Zagreb, I first saw the handsome, spiritual face of Archbishop Stepinac;[10] and I always remember a Mass in Constantinople because of its association with a most self-sacrificing Mahommedan. Late one Saturday night I arrived at the Bosphorus on board a boat from Beyrout.[11] An excursion, which I was anxious to join, had been arranged to start at eight the next morning. I interviewed a taxi driver and explained to him that I wanted a Mass at 6:30, or, at the very latest, seven o'clock. He promised to do all in his power to gratify my wish, and swore to be on the quay at 6 a.m. After a wakeful night, I arose too early, and when I stepped out on the deserted deck, before the sun had risen over the Golden Horn,[12] I saw the faithful fellow standing beneath in the grey light, gazing up at me. He drove

10. Aloysius Viktor Stepinac (1898–1960) served as Archbishop of Zagreb from 1937 until his death. In a highly controversial trial, shortly after the end of the Second World War, the communist Yugoslav government convicted him of high treason for collaboration with the fascist Ustaše regime.

11. Alternative spelling of Beirut.

12. The Golden Horn is a horn-shaped fjord and the principal inlet of the Bosphorus in Istanbul.

to several churches, and insisted on making all the inquiries himself, while I sat comfortably in the car. In each he was told there was no service before eight, but at last he found one where Mass would be at seven. Accompanying me into the empty church, he led me to a seat near the altar, and then waited patiently outside for one and one-half hours. At the end of that time he flew like a lightning-flash back to the boat, and was almost as pleased as I, when we found there were ten minutes left for my breakfast. A few weeks before, my car, driven by a Persian with whom I could not exchange a word, broke down on a dark night in the desert of Iraq, one hundred and fifty miles from my destination. In answer to my frenzied prayers, an English-speaking Turk, who seemed an angel from Heaven, appeared on the scene, and rescued me from a prolonged sojourn in the wilderness. After these two experiences it is not surprising to find in my heart a very soft spot for Turkey.

Like migrant birds, attracted by the far-flung beams of a light-house, my vagrant thoughts are lulled to rest in the radiance of the Eternal City; and, of the many ceremonies I witnessed there, the most outstanding was Pontifical Mass in St. Peter's. After a long wait among the tensely expectant throng, it was indeed a thrilling moment when a sudden fanfare of trumpets announced the arrival of the Pope, wearing the triple crown, borne on the Sedia Gestatoria,[13] preceded and followed by members of the papal court. "Rich not gaudy" was the keynote of this wonderful pageant, in which colours were blended with consummate artistry to produce a perfect mosaic, harmonious as a piece of music. No procession of mere men it seemed, but rather as if a gallery of superb portraits by Old Masters, here the sombre tones of a Rembrandt,[14] there the dazzling brilliance of a Titian,[15] had come to

13. [Italian] "chair for carrying." The throne used to transport popes to and from ceremonies in St. Peter's Basilica.

14. Rembrandt van Rijn, in full Rembrandt Harmenszoon van Rijn (1606–69), was a Dutch painter and printmaker.

15. Titian, in full Tiziano Vecellio or Tiziano Vecelli (ca. 1488–1576), was a Renaissance painter of the Venetian school.

life at the wave of a magic wand, and stepped majestically from their frames. The enthusiastic applause which greeted the Pontiff surged through the vast building, and ebbed into a hush which almost stilled one's breath; and, in the midst of this intense silence, commenced the solemn service, culminating at the sacred moment when the silver trumpets rang out, in what is surely the most ethereal sound on earth.

In striking contrast was the simple, but beautiful ceremony which took place in the Church of St. Agnes on the feast-day of that youthful martyr. Accompanied by the chanting of the choir, a basket decked with red ribbons and containing two tiny snow-white lambs was carried to the nave and placed on the altar, where it remained during High Mass. After the blessing, the little animals, looking the very embodiment of innocence, were brought to a neighbouring convent to be reared by the nuns until their wool was fit to be woven into the pallium of an archbishop.

In the Church of Ara Coeli, on the Feast of the Holy Innocents, I had a touching experience of the truth that "out of the mouths of babes comes wisdom,"[16] when, according to a time-honoured and charming custom, I listened to short sermons preached by children to adult congregations. But the Roman ceremony which wrung the most profound emotion from the chords of my soul was a Mass on a sunny May morning under the blue sky in the Colosseum. Thousands of worshippers took their places among the tiered stone seats of the huge amphitheatre, exactly as did the spectators of the ancient games; the altar was erected on the very spot sanctified by the blood of martyrs; and when the softly tinkling bell heralded the Elevation of the Host, I seemed to hear Christian voices hailing their God with the poignant cry of the pagans of old—*morituri te salutamus.*[17]

Another year I lingered in Rome, day after day postponing my departure. I had visited all my favourite haunts in a last farewell,

16. Psalms 8:2.

17. From the Latin, *"Ave, Imperator, morituri te salutant"* ("Hail Emperor, those who are about to die salute"). The phrase is quoted in *De Vita Ceasarum* (*The Twelve Ceasars*) (121) by Roman historian Gaius Suetonius Tranquillus.

and had even thrown a coin into the Fountain of Trevi to ensure my return; and yet I was loath to go. It was early in February, the month in which was celebrated the anniversary of the Pope's coronation, and I could not suppress an ardent desire to be present at that ceremony; but, considering it was to be held in the very limited space of the Sistine Chapel, my obsession seemed a mere longing for the moon. My only hope centred in a French friend, through whom I had enjoyed the privilege of a private audience with Pius XI,[18] and whom I had accompanied, a short time before on a visit to Cardinal Van Rossum.[19] She had gone back to Paris, but I wrote begging her assistance; and eagerly looked out for an answer until the very eve of the celebration, when at last I despaired. I was in my room, dejectedly about to pack, when a page knocked and presented me with a card, a glance at which filled me with excitement. I hastened downstairs to find a secretary who brought the Cardinal's apologies for being unable to obtain for me the coveted invitation, because the application had been too late, but he sent me a ticket of admittance to an adjoining antechamber, where I could see the exit of the procession and receive the Papal blessing. Next morning I occupied a position which was a perfect illustration of the truth of the saying "So near, and yet so far." All my companions seemed quite content with their lot, but the sight of that closed door filled me with the desperation of Tantalus,[20] and I felt as miserable as a peri outside the gate of Paradise[21] . . . Suddenly, like a gust of wind across a meadow, a tremor of agitation swept

18. Pope Pius XI, born Ambrogio Damiano Achille Ratti (1857–1939), succeeded Benedict XV as head of the Roman Catholic Church in 1922.

19. Willem Marinus van Rossum (1854–1932) was a Dutch priest who was elevated to the cardinalate in 1911.

20. In Greek mythology, Tantalus was subjected to eternal punishment, never able to eat or drink, though he was poised between a fruit tree and a pool of water.

21. In Persian mythology, a peri is a fairy-like being that suffers from being shut out of paradise. The Irish poet, Thomas Moore, wrote a verse tale titled, "The Story of Paradise and the Peri" (1817), which is later referred to in *Ulysses* (1922) by James Joyce.

through my fellow outcasts, and looking round, I saw, to my amazement, the Pope and his suite only a few dozen yards away. In a flash of inspiration I began to writhe, gently but doggedly, through the crowd, until, at the very moment the massive portal was flung open, I stood close beside the Sedia. Abandoning all further effort, and becoming passive as a cork in a strong current, I was whirled into the chapel in the wake of the procession; and, on recovering my equilibrium, found myself anchored in the midst of the Diplomatic Corps. There, under the marvellous ceiling of Michelangelo, I witnessed a spectacle which would have gladdened the eyes of the great master, who had himself designed some of the picturesque costumes of the Court, which blended in admirably with the scarlet robes of the cardinals, the purple cassocks of the bishops, the gold-laced uniforms of the diplomats, and the glittering vestments, to produce a symphony of gorgeous colour, which was transmuted into sound by the angelic voices of the world-famous choir.

Music of a different kind lured me a few days later to climb one of the Seven Hills to the Benedictine church, where I was eloquently convinced that Plain Chant is the most worthy accompaniment of the Mass. The rich volume of harmony rising from the cloister, gradually swelling as the line of monks slowly advanced, and breaking in waves along the nave, overwhelmed me with awe, and paralysed the cold voice of criticism, leaving only the warm, childlike emotion of wonder. Since my eyes were dazzled by the glory of Chartres, I can see but dimly the beauty of all other stained glass; since that morning on the Aventine, Gregorian chant has become for me a shell, within which I for ever hear the faint and distant echoes of San Anselmo's.[22]

On my first day in Albania I was strolling early through the streets of Scutari, a stranger in a strange land; but entering an open door in the shadow of the minarets, I found a multitude assisting at a Mass

---

22. Sant'Anselmo all'Aventino is a Roman Catholic church located on Cavalieri di Malta Square on the Aventine Hill in Rome, well-known for the performance of Gregorian chant during Sunday mass.

which had just begun. Dropping on my knees, I felt no longer an alien, but home among my own people, enfolded in the tender arms of our common Mother, the Church. This too was my predominant feeling during a Mass in Manáos, a thousand miles from the mouth of the Amazon. I arrived there on a boat belonging to a company which held the exclusive monopoly of the Brazil nut trade; and I lived on board during her stay in the jungle city. The fierce rays of the sun being intolerable to workers, the loading of the cargo, which was a tedious process, took place during the hours of darkness. All night the rattling of chains, the groaning of the crane, the shrieks of the windlass, the creaking and straining of heavily laden barges, and the shouts of the men, rang through a cabin sweltering like a furnace; while my whole body became a feeding-ground for ravenous hordes of innumerable species of insects, which the Amazonian forest produces with prodigal fertility. On Sunday morning I rose before dawn, but, with the startling suddenness of the tropical sunrise, I soon saw the cathedral towers clearly framed in the porthole, and heard a bell which, after the nocturnal pandemonium, seemed to drop on my ears soothing notes of the sweetest melody. During the Mass I looked round at the congregation, at serried ranks of faces ranging through every gradation of colour, from those white as my own to some black as ebony. I had never seen so many diverse shades together; they obviously belonged to a medley of numerous races; and the sight produced in me a quickened sense of the essential unity of the Church, a comforting sensation of companionship in the knowledge that we all professed the same doctrines, recited the same prayers, were nourished by the same Bread of Life;[23] in short, were all brethren in the Faith . . . It was, too, as if I stumbled against the threshold of my own house while believing myself lost in a fog, when, after a nerve-racking journey of five hundred and fifty miles across the desert, I wandered through a labyrinth of narrow streets, haunted by the ghost of the famous caliph himself, and arrived at the door of the Franciscan Church in Baghdad. High

23. John 6:22–59.

Mass there on some special festival was celebrated in a most colourful setting. The splendid vestments of the bishop and priests were accentuated by the white-coiffed Sisters of Charity in charge of troops of gaily dressed children; and the women were clad in the lovely garment known as the "izaar,"[24] which transformed them into the semblance of a garden of flowers.

High Mass on Palm Sunday in the Haitian Cathedral of Port-au-Prince, at which the seminarists sang so well, and many of the people prayed with extended arms, served to exorcise the eerie feeling which possessed me the moment I set foot on that mysterious land, where the nights are vibrant with the muffled, but incessant beating of voodoo drums.

In the neighbourhood of many Hindu temples, a Mass in Singapore on St. Patrick's Day tempered the inevitable nostalgia of an exile; but all symptoms of homesickness evaporated completely during lunch at my hotel, when the orchestra played only Irish music; and, in the oppressive heat of a tropic night, I lay awake listening to the heroic dancing of jigs and reels, at what I afterwards learned was a ball held by the Irish colony to celebrate their national festival.

A Maronite Mass[25] on Whit Sunday in Aleppo was impressive, and another in Tehran, where the Chaldean rite[26] and the ceaseless wailing of the acolyte produced a weird, exotic note . . . While travelling in southern India, a priest, who was a fellow passenger, said Mass under the shade of a tree beside a railway station; and, on the long journey from Shanghai to Pekin, I was equally fortunate in hearing Mass in the restaurant compartment of the train, which had been converted by the attendants into an oratory.

24. An izaar, also spelled "izar," is a cotton garment worn by Muslim women, which typically covers the whole body.

25. The Maronite Church is an eastern Catholic church with communities in Cyprus, Israel, Lebanon, and Syria.

26. The Chaldean Catholic Church is an eastern Catholic church prevalent in Lebanon, Iran, and Iraq, and united with the Roman Catholic Church since 1830.

I spent some weeks in Morocco during the fast of Ramadan, and frequently, while exploring the tortuous streets of the old city of Fez, I saw a diminutive Franciscan who wore above his brown habit the tarboosh of Muhammad. This friendly union of the Crescent and the Cross amused me; and I was always glad to see the little figure darting here and there, with the rapidity of a rabbit, through the densely thronged bazaars. Knowing that he did not serve the fine church in the modern French quarter, I shadowed him one day through curiosity, and when only a short distance in front of me, I happened to turn my eyes for a moment in another direction, he disappeared, as if into a burrow. I hurried excitedly to the spot, and found a steep flight of stone steps leading to a deep basement. Descending these, I discovered, to my astonishment and joy, a small dark chapel lighted only by a sanctuary lamp. Next morning, with some French and native soldiers, I received the ashes from the little friar, who looked strangely unfamiliar without his red cap. In another subterranean chapel, near the Street called Straight in Damascus, I heard Mass in the House of Ananias, the disciple charged by Our Lord with the baptism of St. Paul.

In faraway Rio de Janeiro I had the interesting experience of spending another Ash Wednesday. No transformation scene in a pantomime was ever so bewildering as the effect produced on that city by the coming of Lent. For three days of carnival the entire population of one and one-half million surrender themselves whole-heartedly to the absolute rule of the "king of the revels." Every man, woman, and child, with effervescent *joie de vivre*[27] dons fancy dress of the most varied and artistic kind; ordinary clothes promptly proclaim one a foreigner. The magnificent procession—the highlight of the whole fiesta—is timed to finish at the stroke of midnight on Shrove Tuesday. In similar circumstances, Cinderella, in her haste, betrayed herself by dropping her glass slipper; but the spirit of the Rio carnival vanishes suddenly without leaving behind a single footprint. The following

27. [French] "joy of living."

morning I received the ashes among a crowded congregation, the members of which seemed to bear, not merely on their foreheads, but in their hearts, the *"Memento, homo, quia pulvis es"*[28]; and I walked through streets ruthlessly stripped of all decoration. There was no trace whatever of the tons of confetti and miles of multicoloured streamers; and the solemn faces and sombre garb of the citizens transmuted the brilliant scenes of gaiety I had witnessed into a wonderful dream from which I had but just awakened.

During a journey in North America I left Detroit one Saturday night for Buffalo, but finding I could not arrive until the afternoon, I decided to hear Mass at a Canadian town where the train stopped about 5 a.m. Unaccustomed to the extraordinary sleeping compartments of the American railways, it was with sheer terror I awoke, in the obscurity of my bunk, to see the rolling eyes and gleaming teeth of a negro bending over me. Luckily, before I screamed, I realised that he had no intent to commit a felony, but was merely the attendant obeying my instructions to call me half an hour before reaching Hamilton. Awaiting me there was the unpleasant surprise of being obliged to pay a substantial supplement on my ticket, my abnormal detours and zigzags having far exceeded the mileage. This unexpected outlay devoured all the dollars in my possession, leaving me only sufficient to buy a scanty breakfast at a workmen's cafe, and compelling me to walk many sun-scorched miles for lack of a cent to pay the bus fare. In this state of utter destitution I was tempted to stand at the church door, begging for alms.

I once spent the last days of Holy Week in the Javanese town of Djocja.[29] Arriving in the early afternoon of Good Friday, I called at the seminary to inquire the way to the church, and a student accompanied me, clad in his picturesque sarong, his bare feet demonstrating the fact that, in some eastern countries, men always go unshod even

---

28. From the Latin, *"Memento homo, quia pulvis es, et in pulverem reverteris"* ("Remember, man that thou art dust and unto dust shalt thou return").

29. Also spelled Jogja or Yogyakarta.

when otherwise most elaborately dressed. I found a service conducted by a Dutch priest, who also officiated at the Mass I attended on Easter Sunday. In Japan I had already grown accustomed to churches where the seating accommodation was the floor, always scrupulously clean owing to the universal custom there of shedding one's shoes at the entrance to every house. In this Javanese church the European colony occupied ordinary pews on one side of the nave, while, on the other, the natives sat on cocoanut matting in characteristic eastern fashion. Except when standing at the Gospel, they remained seated the whole time, wrapt in prayer, until the moment the bell rang at the Consecration, and then, all together in perfect unison, they raised their arms on high and flung themselves prostrate in the most impressive gesture of adoration I have ever seen.

A couple of weeks later I crossed to the neighbouring island of Bali, the inhabitants of which I had been told were all pagans—a fact which seemed obvious from the innumerable pagodas scattered over the country. On a Saturday evening, I drove out from the small town of Denpasar to a clearing in the forest, where myriads of monkeys were so tame that they slid down from the trees and boldly ate from one's hand. Engrossed in feeding and watching the antics of these comical little beasts, I suddenly felt I was not alone; and looking up, I saw, within a few yards of me, what seemed an apparition—the white soutane of a priest. And there in the jungle, introduced by the monkeys, I first met the Dutch missionary Father Buis.[30] At that time he had a flock of newly baptised converts, to whom he was both pastor and physician; and this, in a few years, developed into a flourishing mission. He was then residing temporarily in the town, awaiting the completion of his own house; and early next morning I accompanied him to the scene of his labours a few miles distant. We walked across the emerald green rice fields, and soon, at regular intervals, began

---

30. Father Simon Buis (1892–1960) was a Dutch missionary and ethnographic filmmaker who was instrumental in establishing the Roman Catholic Church in Bali after his arrival in 1936.

to meet children bearing offerings of flowers, so that by the time we reached the church, the good Father was carrying what resembled a bridal bouquet. The Balinese are born wood-carvers, and it was evident that the elaborately carved altar was literally a labour of love. Kneeling there, in what I felt was the atmosphere of the primitive Church, I assisted at a Mass which is forever etched on my memory. As an antidote to all distracting thoughts, I had merely to look at my fellow worshippers' passionate absorption in the ceremony to realise its awful sanctity; and when I reluctantly sailed away from that lovely land, the missioner's words echoed in my ears, and I saw again the tenderness in his eyes, as he said softly, "These people have beautiful souls."

I have heard Mass on board ship in nearly all the Seven Seas, and three of these occupy special niches in my mind. One took place on Easter Sunday among the Isles of Greece; another on a South American liner, where I was impressed by the fervent devotion of the "Swallows," as Portuguese labourers are called, who migrate to Brazil for the harvest, as our Achill islanders to Scotland. The third was celebrated on the deck of a Messageries Maritimes[31] vessel in the Dardanelles by the "immortal" historian of France, Monsignor (afterwards Cardinal) Baudrillart.[32] It was a requiem for his compatriots who had fallen so tragically there during the First World War; and the words of his sermon, as they floated over the silent waters, acquired a sublimity and eloquence which even that noted preacher of Notre Dame had probably never before achieved. A few weeks later, as the sun was rising over the Dead Sea, I knelt on the sand beside the Jordan at a Mass by the same celebrant on the traditional site of Our Lord's baptism. And then followed a series of Masses in all the places sanctified by the footprints of the Saviour. High Mass on Holy Saturday in the Church of the Holy Sepulchre was preceded by an imposing

31. A state-owned French merchant shipping company established in 1851.
32. Alfred-Henri-Marie Baudrillart (1859–1942) was a French historian and Roman Catholic prelate who became a cardinal in 1935.

procession in which an acolyte carried a colossal Paschal candle.[33] The officiating clergy and a choir of boys blended in the perfect harmony of superb singing; and the congregation, with its curious conglomeration of types, was possible only in Jerusalem. Their expressions transfigured from sorrow to joy, I saw again my fellow penitents of the Via Dolorosa on Good Friday. Black Ethiopian priests rubbed shoulders with smart naval officers; Bedouin women and babies crouched beside members of the Diplomatic Corps; an old man with the long hair of an anchorite, incongruously clad in a grey Norfolk suit, jostled the dignified figure and flowing burnous of a White Father[34] from the desert. After the conclusion of the Latin service I reached the door in time to witness the formal entry of the Greeks. The indescribable richness of their vestments; the gold-covered, gem-studded missals and pectoral crosses; the gorgeously attired Patriarch, with his jewelled crown, holding a priceless ikon; even the charming national costume worn by an official of the embassy; all combined to produce a pageant, overpowering in its magnificence. In both Latin and Greek processions the beadles wore Turkish dress, and carried enormous staffs, the rhythmic beating of which against the ground reverberated throughout the whole edifice.

At the Mass I heard in the crypt of the Church of the Nativity the people were so packed within the narrow space that I was unable even to kneel, and so my fervour was damped by sheer physical discomfort. But one evening, during my last visit there, I was fortunate enough to find myself alone. For several minutes I knelt in prayer, and then, in the deep silence, I heard footsteps resounding along the pavement of the great church above, and down the staircase came a woman, dressed in the Biblical costume of the country, carrying an infant in her arms. She too knelt for some time, and then, bending low, kissed

33. The Easter candle, made of beeswax shaped around a wooden core, with a candleholder proportionate to its size.

34. The White Fathers, also known as the Society of the Missionaries of Africa, are a Roman Catholic society of apostolic life, founded in 1868 by the Archbishop of Algiers, Cardinal Charles Lavigerie.

the ground and laid her child on the spot, marked by a star, bearing the awe-inspiring inscription *"Hic de Maria Virgine natus est Jesus Christus."*[35] The sight of that tiny babe lying in that sacred place, with its little arms outstretched towards me, will ever remain my outstanding memory of Bethlehem.

On a journey across Algeria, between Algiers and Tunis, I arrived one evening in November at Boghar, which, owing to its elevated position, has always been; since Roman days, the site of a military post. When I had explored my immediate surroundings I returned to the lounge of the hotel, where the principal piece of furniture was a monumental delph stove, ghastly as a tombstone, from which not the faintest glimmer betrayed the presence of a fire. Seated there, pressed against its portly form, but obviously failing to extract therefrom any warmth or comfort, was a melancholy Englishman, who also had been a passenger in the car. In a moment of forgetfulness of everything but the fact that I was at last in close proximity to the Sahara, I exclaimed enthusiastically, "Isn't this thrilling?" He "gorgonised me from head to foot with a stony British stare,"[36] and completed the process of my petrifaction by the glacial irony with which he answered, "You think so?" I saw no sign of human habitation in the adjoining country, except a cluster of houses and large barrack clinging, like the hotel, to the lofty mountain side. The next day being Sunday, I asked mine host if there was any Catholic church in the neighbourhood, a question which seemed superfluous, judging from the surrounding desolation. To my surprise and delight, he said that a small French mission was tucked away in a valley a few kilometres distant. He offered to send a messenger to the priest to inquire the hour of Mass, and I asked him to provide a guide to escort me in the morning. The night was intensely cold and still, the only sound the occasional howl of a jackal,

---

35. The Latin is usually rendered, *"Hic de Virgine Maria Jesus Christus natus est"* ("Here of the Virgin Mary Jesus Christ was born").

36. Alfred Tennyson, "Maud" (1855), section XIII, stanza 2, lines 8–9.

and before dawn I stepped from my bed on to a tiled floor, which seemed a sheet of ice. Finding an Arab boy awaiting me outside, we tramped along a steep and rugged path in the glory of the rising sun; until we reached a village, where I assisted at a Missa Cantata[37] sung by children, and impressive by its very simplicity.

A kind of charabanc, with several seats, brought me on the next lap of my journey, and landed me on Saturday evening on a route so perilous that even specially trained drivers were forbidden by law to travel there at night. A breakdown had kept us stranded on the way for most of the afternoon, making it impossible to complete the trip by daylight, but the chauffeur insisted on continuing in the dark. Soon we began to climb, gradually higher and higher; the weary passengers slept peacefully; but, sitting in front, I remained abnormally wakeful, realising, as I did, that we were on an extremely narrow, unfenced road, with a precipice on the right, and a sheer rocky mountain towering above me on the left. Soon, too, I realised that something was wrong. Instead of hugging the security of the inner side, the car seemed to be trying to balance itself on the outer edge, like a tight-rope dancer . . . Suddenly, something stabbed me with terror, and I shrieked "Arretez, arretez."[38] The brakes groaned loudly, everybody jumped out; and we "looked at each other with a wild surmise" when we saw . . . one wheel over the abyss! The nearest village was some miles away, but we walked there joyfully, thankful for the safety of our feet. The unexpected arrival of so many travellers overtaxed the capacity of the local inn, obliging me to share a room with another woman. Again I rose early to attend a Mass, memorable because offered in thanksgiving for a narrow escape from a terrible fate; and with, perhaps, a subconscious presentiment of approaching danger. That very day, while ascending another precipitous pass, we collided with a lorry when rounding a hairpin bend, but fortunately suffered no serious injury. As a result of the accident, the car had to undergo extensive repairs, and many legal

37. [Latin] "sung Mass."
38. [French] "stop, stop."

formalities had to be observed. Soldiers were fetched from a distant outpost to arrest the driver, and an official from somewhere else to conduct an investigation. The whole proceedings were so prolonged that before the other passengers resumed their journey, I had walked over twelve miles through the glorious scenery of the Kabyle country, inhabited by an ancient race of pure Berbers, who belong to a heterodox Moslem sect whose women are unveiled, their virtue so jealously guarded that it was dangerous for a strange man to wander there alone, and death was literally the penalty for dishonour.

Still wending their way to Mass, my thoughts climb to Costa Rica's lofty capital; or scale the dizzy path to Venezuela's lovely Caracas; or tread the long trail over the pampas of Argentina, from Buenos Aires to earthquake stricken Mendoza, where I spent Palm Sunday, on the eve of my first crossing of the Andes. Holy Week then followed in Santiago; another Andean pass to Bolivia was surmounted, and Lake Titicaca, the highest in the world, navigated, before reaching Cuzco, the metropolis of the Inca Empire. Arriving there on Saturday night, I determined to hear Mass next morning in the Temple of the Sun, much of which has been incorporated in the present Dominican Church. Kneeling at the end of a bench, thrilled by the realisation of where I was, and lost in a maze of distractions, I suddenly heard a stern voice from behind ordering me to remove my hat. Thinking I must have the misfortune of possessing a back which had caused me to be mistaken for a man, I quickly looked round, expecting an apology. To my bewilderment, I saw a priest glaring at me, and he repeated the order with even greater sternness. I hastily removed the offending headdress, and carried it with me to the altar rails when receiving Holy Communion, fearing to leave it behind lest somebody might sit on my sole defence against the ancient Peruvians' beneficent god, who to me, at that time, proved a pitiless tyrant. Later I learned that all the Indian women in Peru take off their hats, exactly like men, on entering a church; and those of Spanish descent wear mantillas. In many village churches I visited I was pursued by a mob of urchins, whose shouts to remove my sombrero fell on deaf ears; and once the request was politely made by a sacristan, who was showing me a famous carved pulpit. I looked at him with horror, exclaiming "San Pablo" in a tone implying that my disobedience would cause St. Paul to collapse in what, to a disembodied spirit, is the equivalent of an apoplectic fit. One day in the Cathedral of Cuzco, while admiring some of its numerous works of art, I became conscious of being shadowed by an angry canon. I glided in and out between the columns, slipped under arches, and made my exit, with covered head, before he overtook me. This experience reminded me of my first visit to St. Sophia's in Constantinople. It was then the only mosque I had ever entered, and I did not fully realise the gravity of the crime of not removing my shoes. In a dim, secluded corner of the interior, as I wandered about, I was suddenly aware that an infuriated old imam was bearing down on me; but him too I succeeded in eluding by playing hide and seek among the pillars, and reaching the open air before his rage exploded. One Sunday morning I drove out several miles from Cuzco to hear Mass in the remote little village of Pisac. The church, obviously a relic of colonial days, was situated in a spacious plaza with a background of mountains, crowned by Inca ruins. Hundreds of Indians from surrounding districts were gathered in this large square; some seated on the ground, or on the steps of a gigantic crucifix; others standing in isolated groups; and all dressed in the various costumes of their tribes, producing a perfectly harmonious medley of brilliant colours, worthy of the palette of a great painter. Completing the picturesque scene, sprinkled here and there through the throng, were the haughty llamas, the Indian's constant companion, the ubiquitous beast of burden of the Andes. At the sound of the bell all voices were hushed, and, with an air of the deepest reverence, the people entered the church, and remained on their knees the whole time. A primitive organ accompanied the service, to which was added a unique note when, in the tense silence at the Elevation of the Host, a most impressive salute was blown upon conch shells. This duty was performed by tribal chieftains, bearing staffs elaborately ornamented with silver, who, when the last prayers were said, standing in two rows facing each other, formed a bodyguard in front of the church. When the priest came out, the two men at the end, doffing their hats with the grace of hidalgos, advanced up the middle, kissed his hand, and retired to their places, to be succeeded by the next pair, and so on all up the line. Then the priest walked down the middle, and led the procession along a narrow passage, until it stopped at an entrance in a high whitewashed wall, and, with a fanfare of conch shells, dispersed. Overcome by curiosity to see the parochial residence to which its owner had been escorted with such pomp, I followed in their footsteps. Expecting to find a colonial mansion similar to those characteristic of Cuzco, I peered furtively into a little courtyard, and gasped with astonishment when I saw a mud hut exactly the same as that of the poorest Indian; and, to my embarrassment, standing at the door, was the pastor himself. I was about to stammer an abject apology for my intrusion, when, with a profound bow and graceful wave of his hand, which plainly expressed the Spanish offer of hospitality, "My house is yours," he invited me to enter. I had visited a priest who lived in a state of apostolic simplicity among the snow-capped peaks of the Tyrol; I had met another in the wilds of Haiti in his little wooden shack, half-smothered by the purple blossoms of bougainvillea; I had been in a Japanese presbytery where the European owner sat, ate, and slept on the floor, as did the members of his flock. But all these dwelt amid princely luxury compared to this Peruvian shepherd of souls; the furniture was limited to the barest essentials; and yet this poor cabin reflected, as in a mirror, the refinement and spirituality of its occupant, and I inhaled there the unmistakable aroma of culture, so often lacking in a castle.

Among the mountains once more I assisted at a Missa Cantata in a little thirteenth-century Romanesque church, perched amid the Pyrenees, in the miniature capital of Andorra. The chanting of the men's choir seemed lite rally to raise the roof, and clamour for spacious aisles and soaring transepts; and the dim light was shot by fitful gleams of pale gold from the magnificent reredos of the High Altar. On the morning of my departure I had to catch the 6:30 bus which, in recent years, has prosaically replaced the mule train I had expected. I stole on tiptoe from my room in the ancient hostel, where the tunnelled entrance, furnished with mammoth wine barrels, the stone floors and staircase, the patio and balconies, had transported me back to mediæval Spain. Descending a steep roughly cobbled lane, along which my steps resounded like the giant's seven-leagued boots, I paused for a moment outside the church, to take a deep breath of the delicious atmosphere of peace which emanated from the sleeping houses. Round the corner came the old sacristan, whose heavy bunch of keys jingled in my ears as musically as did the cow bells in the adjacent valley. Greeting me with a smile, he hastily unlocked the door, and we both entered—he, to ring the Angelus,[39] and I, in the words of the Angelic Salutation,[40] to bid farewell to that unique country, where war is unknown, and which has proudly preserved its sovereign independence since the days of Charlemagne.[41]

Meandering up and down the highways and byways of the world, my thoughts, like homing birds, return at last to Ireland, and there forge two final links to close this golden chain of memories, which encircles the globe. First, that unforgettable Eucharistic Congress Mass in the vast natural cathedral of the Phoenix Park,[42] when, above the bowed heads of many thousands, "breathless with adoration," the clear, crystal notes of our famous tenor[43] rang out in the ecstatic prayer of "Panis Angelicus." The second took place at midnight, on a moonlit Christmas Eve, in a village a few miles from my own home. One lone star, the brightest in the northern hemisphere, guided my feet over the frost-paved road, through the silent night, to where I found a simple

39. The Angelus bell is rung as a call to the Angelus prayer, a Catholic devotion commemorating the Incarnation of Christ.

40. Hail Mary (Latin: *Ave Maria*) prayer.

41. Charlemagne or Charles the Great (742–814) was first emperor of the Holy Roman Empire.

42. The 31st International *Eucharistic Congress* was held in Dublin, June 22–26, 1932, and attended by approximately one quarter of the Irish population.

43. John Francis McCormack (1884–1945) was an Irish American tenor, renowned as one of the finest singers of his time. In 1928, he was given the title of papal count by Pope Pius XI.

crib, surrounded by earnest worshippers. School children sang the *Adeste Fideles*,[44] the priest read the sublime words of the Gospel, and all present received Holy Communion. When the congregation had ebbed away in reverent silence, and I stepped out into the little street, where every window shone with a ruby glow, every roof glittered like burnished silver, I felt I had emerged from the very stable of Bethlehem, my soul suffused by an emotion so unutterable that "speech was but broken light upon the depth of the unspoken."[45]

44. The original Latin version of the Christmas carol, "O Come, All Ye Faithful."

45. A slight misquotation of a line from George Eliot's *The Spanish Gypsy: A Poem* (1886), Book I: "Speech is but broken light upon the depth / Of the unspoken."

4. Map for A Treasure Island, Brian Bixby, 2020.

3

A Treasure Island

Always a believer in Browning's dictum that "a man's reach should exceed his grasp,"[1] I doubt if even the poet himself would commend my reaction when I heard, one day in Venice, that a beautiful picture by Rosselli[2] was preserved in a monastery on a remote island. For some time I had been treading reverently the labyrinths of a veritable treasure-house; countless churches and palaces adorned with Old Masters, the Venetian Academy rich in priceless works, numerous and glittering as the gems in Aladdin's cave:[3] and yet an ardent longing to see something far beyond my grasp tarnished the lustre of these jewels that literally lay at my feet. The story of the Sleeping

This travelogue, published in *The Capuchin Annual* for 1951, finds Murphy in the role of the "tourist" more than that of the "adventurer." As she travels around the northern rim of the Adriatic Sea, she visits a number of sightseeing destinations, beginning with Venice and continuing as far south as the island of Rab and city of Spalato (now Split) down the Yugoslavian (now Croatian) coast. Murphy thus takes her readers from a familiar site on the Grand Tour to places well off the beaten track, which lure her audience into Continental travel with images of local color and artistic brilliance. Along the way, she offers lively accounts of her misfortunes and the countless minor hazards that await the unsuspecting tourist. Reproduced with permission from *The Capuchin Annual*.

1. Robert Browning, "Andrea del Sarto" (1855), line 97.

2. Cosimo Rosselli (1439–1507) was a Florentine painter who was a contemporary of Sandro Botticelli and Domenico Ghirlandaio.

3. From the Middle Eastern folktale of "Aladdin" collected in the *Arabian Nights*, the cave is a secret place containing vast treasures including gold, jewels, and the famous magic lamp.

Beauty hidden in the gloom of an almost impenetrable forest, or of Brunhild[4] surrounded by a circle of flame, symbolises a deep-rooted characteristic of human nature; and the fact that it was to be found, not in the midst of a great metropolis, nor even in a secluded countryside, but in the cloistral isolation of a distant island, flung for me around the precious object an irresistible glamour. In answer to my eager inquiries, I was informed that a boat plying between Venice and her ancient rival Ragusa, called at Hvar, the Hy-brasil[5] of my dreams. Excited as a schoolboy in search of adventure, I stepped into a gondola one evening on the Grand Canal and was rowed across the lagoon to where the Dalmatian steamer was anchored. As I climbed the ladder, the whole crew assembled on top to give me an unmistakable welcome, which they did with such an avalanche of unknown words, that I turned helplessly to the captain and appealingly asked him if he spoke English. My heart sank when he answered, with a beaming smile, "Mooch leetell"; and during the following days this apparently contradictory phrase aptly described the conversation he reserved for me, which consisted of such a large quantity of "leetell" that I found it as incomprehensible as his native Slav. With a scarcely perceptible movement, we glided out to the open sea, and I stood on deck gazing wistfully at the lovely city which, under a most unusual and ominously leaden sky, had shed her brilliantly coloured wedding garments and donned diaphanous raiment, in which she looked a spectral bride. Like a deposed king stripped of all his accustomed splendour, the sun sank unseen behind a heavy grey curtain, and an eerie silence ushered in the brief twilight. Darkness soon urged me towards the comfortable saloon, of which I had a complete monopoly.

4. In Icelandic legend, the supreme God Odin punishes the warrior maiden Brunhild (also spelled Brunhilde, Brunhilda, Brrynhildr) by making her fall into an everlasting sleep surrounded by a wall of fire.

5. Hy-Brasil (also spelled Hy-Breasal, Hy-Brazil, Hy-Breasil) is a phantom island that appears in various Irish myths, as well as on many maps from the fourteenth to nineteenth centuries.

The passengers were few, the peace and restfulness so soothing that I quickly became absorbed in the pages of an interesting book . . . Suddenly, the boat, which had been floating like a rose-leaf on a stream, staggered beneath the impact of a titanic blow, and the next moment I seemed to be transported, as if by magic, to the back of a bucking bronco. Dazed by the shock, I gradually realised with horror that we were writhing in the grip of the dreaded *bora*—the ruthless wind that drives all the fishing fleets on the Adriatic to seek safety within the nearest harbour. I crawled to my cabin and flung myself miserably on the bunk, feeling as if my limbs were paralysed by the slimy tentacles of an octopus. Instantly, with a promptness worthy of the Slave of the Lamp,[6] a steward appeared at my side, obviously expecting that his services were urgently needed. Repeatedly I waved my arms in the direction of the door, with what I believed were eloquent gestures of dismissal; but my attendant evidently mistook them for symptoms of epilepsy. Assuming a professional air, he soaked a large towel in the washhand basin, and, while a deluge descended on the blanket, he wrapped the dripping folds round my aching head. Then stifling my moans most effectively by stuffing my mouth with slices of a lemon so bitter that its seeds must have sprung from the waters of Marah,[7] he poured a ceaseless cataract of Slav on my fevered brain. Desperately I waved once more a feeble hand towards the exit, but found that the more I gesticulated the greater to him seemed my need for his assistance, the tighter he squeezed the towel round my temples, and the more copious became the icy drops that trickled down my spine. Fearful of provoking him to search for other instruments of torture, I lay at last so deceptively still that he congratulated himself on leaving me in profound slumber—a blissful state infinitely exceeding my grasp on a night of such external and internal tumult.

6. The genie who frees Aladdin from the magic cave and then does his bidding in the *Arabian Nights*.
    7. Exodus 15:23.

Next morning we arrived at Fiume, the scene of D'Annunzio's daring exploit in the First World War;[8] and there the delightful sensation of standing on solidity proved a powerful tonic which induced a rapid recovery. The next stepping stone was the island of Rab, with its many picturesque ecclesiastical buildings; and the following afternoon we landed at Spalato, which is built within the precincts of the gigantic palace where Diocletian[9] spent the last years of his life, close to his own birthplace. Approaching this royal residence from the sea, the well-preserved façade, seven hundred feet long, makes a most imposing and memorable impression, which is intensified when we wander through the narrow streets with their curious medley of architectural styles, and realise the stupendous scale on which the majestic structure was planned. The site occupies about ten acres, and the emperor's mausoleum has been a cathedral for more than eleven hundred years, his private temple serving as a baptistry. The brooding sphinx, of immemorial age, brought from Egypt to guard the tomb, has been left undisturbed at the entrance of the church, exemplifying that strange union of paganism and Christianity which gives the town its distinctive charm. So enthralled was I by the exotic atmosphere of this unique post that, like Ulysses on Calypso's isle, I almost forgot the inspiration of my voyage, and it was with thoughts that strayed back and lingered in the days of Imperial Rome I first saw the coast line of Hvar. Drawing nearer I could see distinctly the belfry of the monastery which, to my dismay, was a very considerable distance from the landing stage. In all the other ports of call ample time was allowed to explore the locality, but here we were warned that the delay would be short. I started off at a brisk pace, under a broiling sun, and arrived at my destination exactly

8. After the Paris Peace Conference of 1919, Italian poet, playwright, journalist, and fighter pilot Gabriele D'Annunzio led a takeover of Fiume (now Rijeka, Croatia) from the inter-Allied occupying forces. The march on the city by his ultranationalist irregular forces became known as the Impresa di Fiume ("Fiume Endeavour").

9. In May 305, Gaius Aurelius Valerius Diocletianus (245–316) became the first Roman emperor to abdicate his position voluntarily before building his retirement palace in the neighborhood of Salonae (now Split, Croatia).

as if I had emerged from a Turkish bath. This temperature dropped rapidly when I gazed at my surroundings, where I seemed to be the only living thing. Stealthily as a snake, a chill silence crept round me; the whole edifice stared at me with hostility; and I shuddered beneath a cold douche when, on reaching the church, I was confronted by a locked door! Then, with stunning suddenness, the truth struck me that I had the misfortune to arrive during the siesta, when, in hot countries, all business and pleasure are suspended, and Morpheus[10] brooks no rebel against his despotic sway. Maddened by the irony of a fate that snatched the object of my quest almost from my very grasp, I seized a bell rope dangling above my head and gave it a violent tug. A melodious peal rang out across the island, each note falling on my ears with the thud of a sledge hammer. Transfixed with terror, I heard a window in the top storey open with a screech, and looking up saw a monk glaring down at me with all the fury of a gargoyle; while, like the defender of an ancient castle, he drenched the hapless invader with a torrent of words sizzling like molten lead. My first impulse to flee from the wrath so overwhelmingly present was restrained by the thought that it was literally a case of "now or never"; and this alone stimulated me to hold my ground. In tremulous and halting Italian I begged for mercy with the whine of a mendicant, declaring I had come all the way from Ireland to see the great picture, and I hinted gently that only an inhuman monster, an unworthy son of his saintly founder, could turn me away after such an arduous journey.

In the days before Rineanna[11] had found a place on the map of the world I was accustomed, in certain circumstances, to speak of my native land as though she were an offspring of the moon, still attached to the maternal apron-strings; and this habit of mine often proved an "Open Sesame" to many hermetically sealed doors. I once

10. In Greek mythology, the god associated with the realm of dreams and sleep.

11. In 1936, the Government of Ireland chose Rineanna as the site for Shannon Airport, the country's first landing field for transatlantic commercial flights; the first transatlantic flights set down there nearly a decade later.

arrived in Zagreb, the Croatian capital, when its magnificent museum was closed for a season, but the huge building was thrown open and innumerable dust sheets removed from the glass cases, so that I might enjoy, in Olympian aloofness, a leisurely survey of its many treasures. I had a similar experience in the Syrian town of Latakia which I visited for the sake of its collection of antiquities, resulting from local excavations, which have shed much light on the lives and customs of some very ancient races. Unfortunately I arrived there in the early afternoon when the majority of its inhabitants were sleeping peacefully; but my prolonged knocking awoke the curator who, in colourful robes, appeared on his balcony, looking like a caricature of Juliet; and with all the ardour of Romeo I pleaded successfully and secured his consent to the opening of the museum. He aroused the police by telephone, and a stalwart but drowsy sergeant escorted me, mounting guard outside until I was satisfied with my study of its most interesting contents . . . One late afternoon too in a little Javanese town where I was making but a brief stay, I found the church closed, and, not remembering the reason, called at the presbytery to ask where the sacristan lived. My knock was answered by the priest himself, resplendent in vividly striped pyjamas that would have dazzled even a zebra. Waving aside all my apologies he expressed his pleasure in being of service to a native of the "Isle of Saints and Scholars" with such obvious sincerity that he evidently assumed me a member of both categories. Fetching a bunch of keys, he stepped out into the street with no more trace of embarrassment than if he strolled along Piccadilly in an orthodox morning suit; and, compared to his scantily clad parishioners, he was as fully dressed as if fresh from the hands of a Savile Row tailor[12] . . . In an American city where I spent only one day I was driven round for hours in a forty-seater charabanc, although I was the only passenger, because I convinced the driver that it would be little less than a national calamity if I were forced to return to Ireland without seeing

---

12. Savile Row is a street in central London, known since the mid-nineteenth century for its bespoke tailoring.

the sights of his "home town." And now as I stood outside the monastery of Hvar, listening to footsteps descending the stairs, and the ponderous bolts being slowly withdrawn, I knew the talisman had worked once more. With icy courtesy the monk conducted me along a stoneflagged passage, and flung open a massive door. At the end of the apartment, in exactly the same position as Leonardo's, was the "Last Supper" of Rosselli; but, unlike the pallid ghost of the famous Milanese masterpiece,[13] here, after the lapse of centuries, were figures firmly drawn in gorgeous colours, as if newly born from the painter's brush; and the sight wrung from me exclamations of the warmest and most spontaneous enthusiasm . . . I had often found that the key to an Italian's heart is a love and appreciation of beauty, and I was soon conscious that the fervour of my admiration had completely melted my companion's coldness. With perfect understanding he remained silent until an indelible photograph of the fresco was imprinted on the sensitive plate of my memory; and then, leading me to the garden, he gave a final proof of forgiveness for my turbulent intrusion by presenting me with a leaf from the tree beneath which was Rosselli's favourite seat. In this hallowed place I would fain have lingered, forgetful of time, but my reverie was suddenly transformed into a nightmare by the boom of a siren. Bidding an abrupt farewell to my host, I rushed towards the boat, the raucous shrieks punctuating my pace in a most irritating crescendo of urgency. Goaded by the gesticulations of passengers and crew, my body the target of the sun's burning arrows, I flew on winged heels; and at last stumbled across a gangway wrenched from under me, and collapsed into the nearest deck chair, gasping for breath, exhausted . . . but triumphant.

And as we sailed over a calm sea beneath a sunny sky, I dreamed of Florence, the birthplace of Rosselli, in the last quarter of the sixteenth century. Twilight had long succeeded the golden days of the

---

13. Leonard da Vinci's *The Last Supper* (ca. 1498) is a painted mural covering a wall in the Convent of Santa Maria delle Grazie in Milan.

Renaissance, when those streets beside the Arno were thronged with scholars, sculptors, painters and poets, when the very air was redolent of culture; but days too of dark deeds that stained even the sanctity of the Duomo, which resembles the city's emblem, the lily, in the austere purity of its style. Born amid a more peaceful if less brilliant era when the Medici, after many banishments, had securely established their power, Rosselli was employed by the Grand Duke Cosimo II[14] to glorify the achievements of that illustrious family. Little is known of his life and that little not always reliable. The statement made in one history of art that after studying in Rome he returned to his native place which he never afterwards left, is refuted by this picture in Hvar, its size alone being sufficient evidence that the artist spent a considerable time in this sequestered spot, his world bounded by its shores, its inhabitants his only models. Some sturdy fisherman spreading nets on the beach, or basking contentedly on the sun-splashed quayside, had probably posed for the portrait of St. Peter; a humble young novice, with pale spiritual face, may have gazed with wondering eyes at finding himself seated beside the Master, immortalised as the Beloved Disciple. We can imagine Rosselli following the monastic routine, rising before dawn to sing matins with the monks, drinking inspiration from the inexhaustible fountain of the liturgy; and, like Buddha beneath the banyan, or Tasso[15] under his oak, plunged in profound meditation in the cool cloister garden, shaded by the foliage of that fragrant orange tree. That those hours were filled for him with peace and happiness can scarcely be doubted by anyone whose soul is gladdened by the pure, glowing colours of his palette, which surely were never blended in a mood tainted by moroseness or melancholy; and we may well believe that it was with reluctant feet he left at last this sheltered haven to return once more to the storm-swept haunts of men.

14. Cosimo de' Medici (1590–1621) was the fourth grand duke of Tuscany from 1609 until shortly before his death.

15. Torquato Tasso (1544–95) was an Italian poet. He is said to have planted an oak on Janiculum Hill in western Rome, where he sat and wrote some of his greatest works.

Into my thoughts too glided the spirit of another Court painter who shines in the firmament of Art as a star of the first magnitude. If Velázquez,[16] grown weary of portraying the insipid features of Philip IV,[17] had fled to some remote island monastery, where, in serenity and solitude, free from the trammels of royal patronage, he could listen undistracted to the imperative voice of his own genius, might not the world have been enriched by a masterpiece, beside which even *Las Meninas*, with all its consummate mastery of technique, would seem but a candle before the noonday sun?

16. Diego Rodríguez de Silva y Velázquez (1599–1660) served as court painter to the King of Spain during three separate periods totaling nearly thirty years. His masterpiece, *Las Meninas* ("The Maids of Honor"), was painted in 1656, during his final tenure in the court.

17. Philip IV (1605–65) was King of Spain from 1621 until his death.

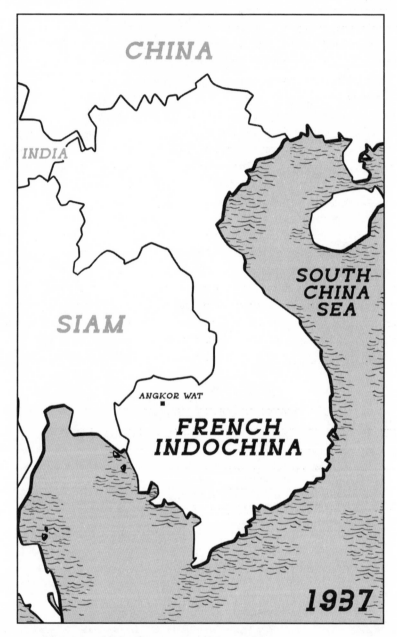

CHINA

INDIA

SIAM

SOUTH CHINA SEA

ANGKOR WAT

FRENCH INDOCHINA

1937

5. Map for I in Indo-China, Brian Bixby, 2020.

4

I in Indo-China

One night in Paris, many years ago, while wandering through the native section of a Colonial Exhibition[1] and thinking that such scenes, when deprived of their natural environment, were even less expressive of reality than words wrenched from their context, I turned from a village of bamboo shacks and was suddenly transfixed by seeing before me, modelled in plaster, the colossal facade of the Temple

Published in the *The Capuchin Annual* for 1952, this travelogue demonstrates Murphy's enthusiasm for exotic destinations as she journeys to the temple complex of Angkor Wat and several other notable sites across Southeast Asia. The term Indo-China, indicating the influence of both Indian and Chinese civilizations in the region, dates back to the early nineteenth century and was used until 1954 to name a group of French colonial territories (including present-day Cambodia, Laos, and Vietnam). Inspired by the investigations of French naturalist Henri Mouhot and determined to overcome the dismissive attitude of her "French friend," Murphy sets off like a latter-day explorer to discover the ancient sanctuary for herself. Again, she brings with her a number of tacit colonialist assumptions, though she also displays a detailed knowledge of the history and geography of the region. Through the course of the journey, she witnesses Hindu and Buddhist traditions, gazes on bathing monks and laboring women, but Murphy is also fascinated (and a bit surprised) to observe the modernity of Saigon and Hanoi, including the shops, theatres, cafes, and other new attractions she finds charming. Reproduced with permission from *The Capuchin Annual*.

1. *L'exposition coloniale international* ("The Paris Colonial Exhibition") was held in the Bois de Vincennes from May 6 to November 15, 1931, and was attended by approximately eight million visitors from around the world. It included large-scale reproductions of native architecture, including huts and temples, from a number of French colonial possessions.

of Angkor. Henri Mouhot,[2] the French naturalist, on an expedition in search of the flora and fauna of Cambodia, had scoffed at the terrified whispers of enchanted cities which scared the scanty population from venturing beyond the fringe of the forest, and wrote in his journal that it was manifest there had never been any civilisation in that region. But soon afterwards, in January, 1861, he was almost as terror-stricken as his simple companions when he saw rising, from the very heart of the jungle, the five mighty towers of Angkor Wat. And so overwhelmingly impressive to me was the mere model of a fraction of the great temple seen by artificial light in most commonplace surroundings that I determined forthwith to share some day Mouhot's thrilling experience. My fervour overflowed into my conversation with a French friend whose uncle had been a diplomat in the Far East, and I spoke of my decision to visit Angkor. "Impossible," he protested, in a tone suggestive of soothing a wayward child. "Impossible. You would have to go there on an elephant." My enthusiasm had been a red glow, his words fanned it into a white flame. And so one morning in 1937 I sailed up the river from Cap St. Jacques to Saigon, the capital of Cochin China. In search of a cobbler to mend my can case, my first experience there was a rickshaw ride, during which I got practical proof of oriental contempt for time, and glimpsed many facets of local life in streets where I was the only European. Saigon is a city of fine buildings—a stately cathedral facing on imposing square; a museum of exceptional interest; a governor's palatial residence; lovely private houses; boulevards and parks; botanical and zoological gardens containing specimens of all the animals and plants of Indo-China; tennis courts lighted by night; good shops, theatres, cafés, swimming pools; in fact, every amenity conducive to the pleasure and comfort of its large foreign colony. A Frenchman there could scarcely suffer much from nostalgia; except for the secluded native quarter, a few pagodas,

2. Henri Mouhot (1826–61) was the first explorer to alert western scholars to the ruins of Angkor, though he succumbed to malarial fever shortly after reporting his findings.

and the ubiquitous rickshaw, he might indeed believe himself to be in *la belle France*.[3] I looked in vain for any trace of the glamour of the east, and then remembered that the French came here only in 1858 and built the city on a marshy site occupied by clusters of palm-thatched cabins scattered through the rice fields. The wonderful transformation wrought in such a short period failed to kindle any emotion within me, and the final frigid touch was laid on my adventurous soul when I learned that Angkor was only three hundred and forty-three miles from Saigon, and that I could motor there in a day. Vanished forever was my dream of seeing the marvellous Khmer temple, for the first time, from the howdah of an elephant; and, in a passionate reaction against the prosaic elements in my surroundings, I set out for Cholon, an important town in the neighbourhood, founded by Chinese in the seventeenth century and which is now the industrial and commercial centre of the country. There I found the exotic colour needed to banish my depression, blended with the peculiarly distinctive sounds of a Chinese city, and saw the strange houseboat life so characteristic of China. Strolling at night through the thronged streets, in the midst of brilliantly lighted scenes of animation, my curiosity was aroused by seeing dejected-looking, slouching figures entering what appeared to be a shoddy cinema. Penetrating in I found myself in an opium den. Both attendants and addicts ignored my presence as completely as though I were a piece of furniture, and so I remained sufficiently long to witness the whole process, and to dissipate forever any vestige of the glamorous atmosphere which De Quincey's poetic prose contrived to fling round the subject of his "Confessions."[4]

Next morning at dawn I started for Angkor. Rice fields with groups of workers wearing large lampshade hats; farmhouses, villages, thatched huts on piles—all went past in rapid succession. The landscape is so flat that a high and quite solitary mountain, rising sheer

3. [French] "Beautiful France," a clichéd patriotic expression.

4. English essayist and critic Thomas De Quincey (1785–1859) is best known for his autobiographical narrative *Confessions of an English Opium Eater* (1822), which set out to be a warning to his readers, but paints a rather seductive image of the drug.

out of the plain, is silhouetted against my memory of this part of the drive. It is the site of an immense pagoda of the Black Goddess,[5] in the shape of an enormous granite block, and a famous place of pilgrimage revered by Annanites, Cambodians, and Chinese. Soon commence on each side of the road the forests which cover almost half the surface of Indo-China. The fact that the country has been the scene of many invasions accounts for the diversity of its people, but its animal is even more diverse than its human population. The dreaded cayman haunts some of its rivers; and its jungles shelter tigers, elephants, rhinoceros, boats, buffaloes, bears, panthers, monkeys, and a gigantic species of wild ox called the "gaur." The previous year, when travelling through an uninhabited wilderness in Haiti, I urged my negro chauffeur to stop the car for a short time, so that he could have some lunch; but he firmly refused, answering gloomily that if a breakdown occurred there "neither of us would ever eat again." This incident now flashed through my mind, and I too, reflected sadly that if the motor rebelled in this lonely spot, fate would undoubtedly spare us the ordeal of death from starvation! I crossed the wide Mekong river, which is 2,625 miles long, in a little steamer with such limited seating accommodation that I was obliged to sit on the floor with my head bent beneath the very low roof of the deck—a trying position in the torrid heat. My suffering was rewarded on reaching the other side by a delightful ride to the Cambodian town of Kampong Cham in a rickshaw drawn by a man on a bicycle—in my opinion, an ideal mode of locomotion. The end of the journey was in darkness, and I could see little of my surroundings when I reached the hotel a few miles from the ruins.

I had dreamed for so long of visiting Angkor that when I awoke next morning I could hardly believe myself to be at last on its threshold. And when the reality rose before me, across the broad causeway, lapped by the waters of the moat; when I climbed the innumerable

---

5. Black Virgin Mountain (Vietnamese: Nui Ba Den) is found in the Tay Ninh Province of Vietnam. It is the site of a pagoda dedicated to Ba Den, a local deity of Khmer origin.

steep steps of a monumental staircase, and saw around me a boundless forest in which the fiercest wild animals roam, I felt myself inside the very Gate of Dreams,[6] and could well understand why the inhabitants believe this miracle in stone to be no mere work of man but the creation of spirits. I had visited the famous Dravidian temples of southern India, but all memories of the impressive gopuras[7] of Madura, the equestrian carvings of Srirangam, and the symmetrical elegance of Tanjore were obliterated by the sight of an inconceivable majesty and sublimity that filled me with awe. The sense of unreality became still more overpowering as I continued to explore the stupendous structure. I lingered within the innermost sanctum where candles and joss sticks burned before a gilt image of Buddha; wandered through sunsplashed galleries; groped through dim-lit cloisters; and finally walked the whole length of nearly a mile round the verandah that surrounds the main building. Its entire space is covered with thousands of sculptures, all tense with life. Brahmanic and Buddhist gods in fraternal intimacy; battlefields with warriors mounted on horses, richly caparisoned elephants, or sumptuous chariots; an inferno rivalling that of Dante in its realism; a heaven where the blessed are the embodiment of joy. And it was my good fortune to be alone among all these marvels; the temple, being remote from populated districts, is almost deserted, except for occasional visitors and a few bonzes who tend the altar of Buddha. At intervals my reverie was broken by what seemed a sudden apparition, so silently along those winding passages glided some bare-footed wayfarer; but, so acute was my sense of having stepped beyond the range of ordinary experience, that, if a tiger from his lair so close to me had come and crouched at my feet, I think I should have felt as little fear or surprise as Eve did in the Garden at the words of the serpent. Everywhere was it stillness so profound that my own heartbeats sounded as irritating as the ticking of a clock

6. In the *Odyssey*, book 19, lines 56–69, Homer divides dreams between those that are true ("passing the Gate of Horn"), and those that are false or unreal ("passing through the Gate of Ivory").

7. The entrance gateway to a Hindu temple in southern India.

punctuating the seconds of a sleepless night; and that silence would cling around those towers until, at sunset, myriads of bats, tumultuous as a rushing wind, would fly out from the dark recesses and, like a pirate's flag, flutter across the rose-flushed sky. After many hours of mental exhilaration, rare in its intensity, I became conscious of my body, and, crossing the causeway, sat down to rest on the roadside wall facing the great shrine. It was then the hottest time of the afternoon, and two Buddhist monks had come to bathe. One had just dressed, the other was still bathing; but, in a in few moments, he scrambled up the parapet to join his companion, quickly his gleaming robes around him. They both stood high above the water on the dark grey stone, the mighty pale-grey temple in the background, a turquoise blue sky, brilliant sunshine, and the flame-coloured figures reflected, as in a mirror, in the lotus-studded moat. It was my last daylight vision of Angkor Wat; and I say "vision" advisedly, because everything there seemed to belong to a visionary world . . . I saw it again under the full moon, when exquisitely graceful dancers might have stepped straight from its sculptured panels, so accurately copied were their costumes and poses; their hands lissome as lily-petals, their lithe limbs weaving the intricate pattern of their ancient dance . . . I next visited Angkor Thom, that amazing capital, with its eight hundred temples and palaces, which was abandoned, either by its builders or its conquerors, to the insatiable hunger of the jungle. Treading the labyrinths of that phantom city, the five striking gate towers, carved in the form of the god Lokeshvara,[8] seemed to follow me stealthily as though the four-visaged deity himself were shadowing my footsteps; and, whenever I raised my eyes from examining the details of a piece of sculpture, I found staring at me a hostile face, stern with resentment at my intrusion on its solitude. That eerie locality, haunted by the ghosts of its former glory, impressed forcibly upon my mind the truth that there is no such thing as dead matter. Everything around

8. One of the most renowned figures in Buddhist legend, Lokeshvara is the *bodhisattva* ("buddha-to-be") of infinite compassion and mercy.

me—every stone and every tree—seemed instinct with a vigilant, furtive, vital principle antagonistic to mine. Sometimes, when crossing a clearing, I met a genuine wild man of the woods, armed with a bow and arrows and, occasionally, heard legions of monkeys screaming, like infuriated demons, above my head. A vivid mirage of an ancient royal procession seemed to rise in the midst of ruins which had witnessed many such splendid spectacles. Trumpets and banners heralded the bejewelled king, grasping the Sacred Sword, and standing erect on his golden-tusked elephant, while throngs of courtiers similarly mounted preceded a female bodyguard equipped with shields and lances. Hundreds of maidens, with flower-wreathed hair and flowing garments, bearing lighted tapers; innumerable gold-handled, red and white umbrellas countless chariots and palanquins; the whole gorgeous pageant of the past vanished amid the shattered porticos and pillars of the present. Scattered for miles through the forest are buildings startling in their size and magnificence. The sculpture of the fifty-one towered Temple of Bayon is hardly less wonderful than that of Angkor Wat; and representing, as it does with meticulous realism, activities and episodes of everyday experience, it has the supreme interest of an open book in which to study the habits and customs of the Khmers. On all sides were melancholy, awe-inspiring scenes where trees, transformed into ravenous beasts, literally devoured the masonry. Some, like vultures, had clawed their victims' flesh with ruthless talons, destroying all clues to identity by leaving only a few mouldering bones. Others, like anacondas, were swallowing shrines, so beautiful that they resembled an Andromeda who had awaited in vain a Perseus to rescue her from the jaws of the monster. Something akin to a python's fascination for its prey lured me within the shade of a wide-spreading banyan to gaze in horror at its repulsive display of gluttonous rapacity. The sinuous tendrils of its roots had crept through the pores of a massive structure, and a bloated buttress of the lofty trunk sprawled on top, like a giant octopus. Deeming those loathsome tentacles capable of creeping even round my own body, I felt myself in the midst, indeed almost in the grip of a preternatural and sinister form of life that mocked my frail humanity and filled me with terror . . . Then, suddenly, as upon a wintry day flashes the first daffodil of spring, along the path came a Buddhist priest who exorcised the powers of darkness with his glowing yellow raiment . . . At an early hour on the mornings I spent near Angkor, I was awakened by the distant beating of a drum mingled with the ringing of what sounded like an Angelus bell. On the eve of my departure I explored the thick plantation from which this reveille had come and found a small Buddhist monastery containing a most uncommon temple, with a number of statues, some of them wearing teal clothes and, among many curious things, the large gong that had enticed me hither. The belfry belonged to a tiny wooden Catholic church, so like a stage property in its fragile construction that, when I shook the door in an attempt to open it, I feared to emulate Samson by pulling down the whole edifice! These two religious centres stand on the outskirts of a little riverside village, nestling in banana groves, and completely hidden by dense foliage though only a short distance from the hotel. So peaceful and remote from the maelstrom of mundane affairs is Siem Reap, as it is called, that on emerging from its welcome shade, I felt I had been favoured by a brief glimpse of another world.

Cambodia is strewn with the remains of spacious cities and imposing temples, but the origin and destiny of the people responsible for this civilisation is a mystery, intensified by the contradictory conclusions reached, in persistent efforts to solve it, by French historians and archaeologists. These savants disagree even about the period in which Angkor Wat was built; one says the seventh, another the twelfth century; but all admit its Hindu inspiration, and all fix the end of the fourteenth century as marking the decline of the Khmer Empire. One historian names, as founder of this dynasty, the son of a king whose capital stood on the site of Delhi; another states no less dogmatically that the country's present occupants are of the same race as the Khmers, who were influenced by Indian culture diffused not by conquerors but by merchants and missionaries. In Egypt, Iran, Greece, in fact all over the globe, we find so many examples of a similar degeneracy that there is no more difficulty in believing modern Cambodians to be direct descendants of the architects of Angkor than that the Peruvian peasant is descended from the builders of Cuzco, or that the ancestors of the Persians today were the consummate artists who created the beauty of Persepolis. The unique naga[9] motif—the monstrous multiheaded cobra—which crawls like a macabre melody through the whole architectural symphony of this land, may well be the exclusive emblem of the original inhabitants, who were snake worshippers long before they adopted Brahmanism. In the small rock-hewn pagodas of Mamallapuram the student of archaeology can find the seeds from which have developed all the vast temples of southern India; but the glories of Khmer architecture sprang in full bloom from the soil of Cambodia, miraculously as Minerva, fully formed, from the brain of Zeus.[10] No wonder its finest flower—the temple of Angkor—is believed by the present dwellers within its precincts, to be a work of magic, conjured from the earth by the supernatural power of jinn.[11]

Taking a different route for my return to Saigon, I left early for the drive of two hundred miles to Phnom Penh, which became the metropolis of the kingdom of Cambodia in 1434. Situated on the Mekong, it is surrounded by a fertile region producing abundance of fruit, rice, cotton, rubber, and maize; and the manufacture of silk is one of its chief industries. A finely laid-out city with tree-lined boulevards, gardens, squares, a large cathedral, and a museum where I reveled in the rich treasures collected from the numerous ruins spread through-out the country. By evening light I climbed the little wooded *phnom* or hill, crowned by a most picturesque pagoda, enshrining the four sacred images of Buddha saved from the flooded river by a woman named Penh, whose heroism is immortalised by her birthplace. But my

9. Naga is a member of a race of mythical serpentine deities in Buddhist, Hindu, and Jainist traditions.

10. Here Murphy conflates the Roman and Greek pantheons. Minerva is the Roman goddess of wisdom, warfare, commerce, and the arts, who is in many ways comparable to the Greek goddess Athena (who sprang, fully grown and clothed in armor, from the head of her father, Zeus).

11. Jinn, also called genies, are supernatural beings in pre-Islamic Arabian and Islamic mythology.

outstanding memory is of my visit to the Royal Palace, when I walked a short distance from a modern hotel straight into an enchanted kingdom of the *Arabian Nights.* Unlike those of Europe, oriental palaces are never single large buildings, but, invariably, large groups of small buildings, so exotic in design and colouring that a mere photograph conveys little of their charm to western eyes. The luxury of this rural residence may be imagined from the fact that its private temple contains a life-sized statue of Buddha in solid gold studded with diamonds, and the whole floor is paved with engraved silver. A famous "Emerald Buddha," a few feet high, was too far above me to examine closely but, realising that gems of that size were unknown even in Aladdin's cave, I decided the image was rare and precious enough if carved in jade. I noticed here, as in the Hindu temples of India, many cheap, tawdry articles mingled with beautiful and priceless works of art. In the pavilion specially dedicated to its preservation is the Sacred Sword, reputed to be a divine gift to a Khmer ancestor of the ruling sovereign, which is guarded night and day by Brahman priests. I saw the king's three crowns—one to wear in a palanquin, a second for use when riding an elephant, and the third reserved for occasions of great ceremony, such as the annual festivals when the Royal Corps de Ballet[12] revive traditional dances amid scenes reminiscent of the ancient civilisation. The Throne Room is no mere apartment, but a detached kiosk, which is an artistic masterpiece; and, when I noted that within a few yards of the throne itself is a sanctuary, furnished with urns filled with the ashes of the royal family, I surely saw a most striking demonstration of the truth of *sic transit gloria mundi.*[13] I was shown an array of glittering robes and dazzling jewels; gorgeous ceremonial parasols, brocades, and embroideries specimens of flawless craftsmanship

12. The Royal Corps de Ballet ("Royal Ballet of Cambodia") performed highly stylized dances, with elaborate costumes, during royal ceremonies and state occasions.

13. [Latin] "Thus passes the glory of the world," a phrase evoking the transitory nature of life and worldly honors, which was used in papal coronation ceremonies from 1409 to 1963.

destined for household and personal adornment; and, finally, dazed and bewildered, I went into the palace grounds, and, like an awakening sleepwalker, tried to regain my grasp of the ordinary, everyday world. But when, as a parting gesture, I was conducted to the royal mews and found that the sacred elephants were *white*, I felt that the last step had been taken in my transport to the realm of Harun-al-Rashid![14]

Once again I started from Saigon for a drive of about two hundred miles to Dalat, the most important of the many hill stations of Indo-China, my chief object being to see some of the oldest race in the country—the tribe, or rather collection of tribes, called the Mois, who inhabit the upland regions. Rubber, kapok, and cacao plantations, fields of sugar cane, rice, and cotton, line the route to Phanthiet, a seaside resort, where I lunched on the balcony of a beautifully situated hotel. After leaving here, the road begins to ascend through tropical forests, and for many miles winds through magnificent scenery. Palms, banyans, ferns, and pines frame foaming cataracts; turbulent rivers rush through wild gorges, to the precipitous sides of which the car clung while, at intervals, sudden vistas reveal the mountain chain beyond, or the immense plain far below. Soon Mois began to appear, getting more numerous as we approached the Langbian Plateau. The first was a young girl who looked at me with the shy, startled eyes of a gazelle; and, as she stepped lithely through the brushwood, this child of nature seemed truly a dryad who had but just emerged from the shade of her native tree. Fine types of humanity, their bronze-coloured bodies formed a gallery of living sculpture, superbly set amid the Doric columns of the forest. Here and there small shacks were perched on stakes so abnormally high that access to these eyries was possible only by using a long ladder; an obvious explanation of which is the fact that the men are always armed with cross-bows to defend themselves from tigers. As evening came I made a detour off the main road to visit a colony of lepers, where I found a Catholic church and

---

14. Harun al-Rashid (763 or 776–809) was the fifth caliph of the Abbasid dynasty, whose court provides the setting for portions of the *Arabian Nights*.

heard that these unfortunate people are under the care of a priest who lives in Djiring—a large village a short distance away. Towards nightfall I crossed a river by ferry boat, the road still running through dense jungle, the darkness lit by the glare of many camp fires. At last I arrived at a big hotel which, next morning, I found was situated on a height overlooking a lake, beyond which a wide tract of country rising to bare hills contrasted strongly with the extensive range of tree-clad mountains traversed the previous day. Dalat has first-class hotels, excellent schools, a modern hospital, a Pasteur institute, cinemas, golf links, tennis courts, lovely villas and gardens; and yet, within a two hours' ride, is a paradise for big game hunters, who congregate there from every corner of the earth. I drove into the bleak tableland adjoining the town to visit the tombs of some chieftains, which resemble little huts completely covered with thatch, surmounted by curiously carved ornaments not unlike deers' antlers. In this neighborhood I found a whole settlement of Moi; and, for the first time, saw women with the lobes of their ears enlarged to look like colossal earrings. That this may have been their intention when undergoing such horrible mutilation is probable from the fact that they have a passion for jewellery, shared by the men, many of whom wear strings of beads and I met a small boy lavishly adorned with necklaces and anklets though he lacked all other clothing. When bearing heavy burdens on their backs, the women rest by sitting on sticks, which are rough replicas of those used, for a similar purpose, by their western sisters at race meetings! Before leaving Dalat I went to the market, which I found very interesting because of the various types gathered there from all the surrounding districts. Squatted on the ground were groups eating bowls of rice with short-handled, dainty porcelain spoons, which I afterwards found for sale in Saigon. On my return journey I lunched at an inn in Djiring, and met there a Frenchman who had spent most of his life in Indo-China. A hunter by profession, he told me many thrilling tales of his adventures and described the formidable appearance of the gaur, which is an animal peculiar to this country. With him was his son, who had seen a tiger prowling round their house a few nights before; and, recently, in the neighbourhood, a man had been badly mauled while sleeping in his bed. In such circumstances it was not surprising to hear that, with a primitive people's instinctive desire to placate evil spirits, the Mois had erected, in certain isolated spots, shrines consecrated to "His Lordship The Tiger"! It was in Djiring I also met a French official who took me to visit a Moi village, the residents of which were well-known to him. There I saw this friendly tribe really at home; the women cooking, pounding big basins of rice with tall poles, and absorbed in the numerous chains of their ordinary domestic work. My companion and I climbed on to a platform facing the entrance to a thatched bamboo dwelling and stooped to enter the low door. The house consisted of one narrow, exceptionally long apartment, with a fire at the remote end, but no chimney and no windows. We also visited the residence of the chief, which was similar, but had two or three rooms, in which I was surprised to see religious pictures. He was a Catholic, and wore national dress, with a black Tonkinese cap or turban. The house was extremely simple, with little furniture except a large collection of pitchers, filled with rice wine, ranged in tiers against the wall. He received me with exquisite courtesy and, for my entertainment, he and a young man played a selection of music on crudely fashioned instruments. In a Moi household the wife is the dominant partner of a husband of her own choice, and some tribes have even matriarchal form of government. On the way back to Saigon we met many of these forest-dwellers, some carrying bows and arrows, others armed with spears; and during a torrential shower it was amusing to watch them, their wet bodies glistening like burnished copper, holding banana leaves as umbrellas to shield their heads from the sharp stilettos of the tropical rain. I saw the last of them with the wistful regret I always feel when returning from the freedom and fresh air of the wilds to the crowded concentration camps of civilization.

And once more I left Saigon, this time onboard the "Sphinx" of the Messageries Maritimes line, and sailed to Tourane, where I saw small round boats which reminded me of the strange craft of similar shape I had so often seen on the faraway Tigris. At this important port I disembarked, and motored to Hué, the capital of Annan, along the Mandarin Road, which is a reconstruction and extension by the French of the old route used by court dignitaries, mandarins in their palanquins, and royal messengers on foot or on horseback. It was, at first, a lovely drive thorough the Pass of the Clouds, the sun gradually sinking as we mounted; and, at the highest point, are remains of a fort, probably a relic of the Chams who were, for a considerable period, rivals of the Khmers, and erected many towers along this coast. On descending to the plain, we drove for miles through picturesque scenes of agricultural work and here I first noticed the curious but most practical rain capes made of palm leaves, from which all the water drips, leaving the wearer perfectly dry. During a drive in Indo-China one can see the whole process of rice cultivation, from the ploughing of the flooded land by buffaloes to the harvest threshing by these powerful animals with their hooves. Dotted here and there through the fields are structures like an enormous wicker armchair, against which the ripe sheaves are beaten in another primitive method of separating the grain from the chaff. I stopped for a while to watch a group of women cutting young shoots of the precious cereal and carrying them away in baskets suspended from a pole across the shoulders, which is the usual oriental way of carrying everything. I saw two little black pigs going to market in this fashion, and even two babies who looked as happy and comfortable as if they possessed the most expensive perambulator. Before reaching Hué I visited the wonderful tomb of Khai-Dinh, father of the present emperor and another of much earlier date. The royal tombs of Annam, as is customary in the cast, occupy a large space; and, though the various pagodas, statues, and monuments differ in each, they all have in the background a walled grove or wooded hill within which the sovereign is buried in a secret slot—so secret indeed, that, formerly, as in the case of the Mings in China, those who took part in the actual burial were beheaded! Far from striving to destroy, France has ever been zealous in preserving every vestige of this country's ancient culture, and the fact that Hué reclined its old traditions intact endows it with an indescribable charm. For many centuries Annam was a vasal state of Imperial China, its court modelled on that of the Dragon Throne. Picturesque ceremonies which disappeared in Pekin with the fall of the Manchus still

take place in Hué, the most important of which are the triennial sacri-
fices to Heaven and Earth offered by the emperor and his mandarins.
A long bridge spanning the river unites the two parts of the city; the
one European-looking, the other distinctively native. Like the Forbidden City in Pekin, the palaces are surrounded by high walls and the
grounds look neglected, chiefly because lawn mowers are evidently
unknown. The Throne Room is magnificent in red and gold lacquer,
with an awning of exquisite embroidery, and many works of art, which
are some colossal vases. A museum within the old palace contains a
collection of beautiful Annamite inlaid furniture, ceramics, sculpture,
costumes and jewellery. Outside one of the numerous buildings is an
imposing row of nine monumental bronze urns, each large enough
to dwarf a man standing beside it, and each one to commemorate
the founder of a dynasty . . . Some miles outside the town is an elevated point called the Belvedere, overlooking the River of Perfumes
winding its way through scenery, among the scented trees and shrubs
whence it derives its name. From this delightful panorama I drove to
a royal mausoleum which left on my mind an indelible impression.
Like the Pharaohs, the emperors of Annan constructed their tombs
during their lifetime, and this particular one seemed a place where in
life its owner loved to linger. On a country road I entered a gate in a
high wall, and the moment I did so I felt I had left the present age far
behind me. A rugged path led me to the edge of a little lotus-filled
lake, on the opposite shore of which rose a fantastic bathing pavilion,
the fragile daintiness of which was more suggestive of the court of
Oberon than that of a mere mortal king. On the other side of the
way a steep flight of steps led to the courtyard of a temple, within the
dim interior of which I was lured by the ruby light of what looked
like a sanctuary lamp. Farther on, another flight of steps brought me
to a stone platform with figures of mandarins, horses, and elephants
in front of two lofty pillars beside a pagoda. More steps meandered
down to a small circular pond, and then mounted up to the great wall,
with its sealed entrance, enclosing the green hill where the emperor
is buried. Everywhere was the haunting fragrance of frangipani trees,
their ethereal white blossoms so well named the "temple flowers"; and

everywhere too was an aroma of poetry I inhaled with every breath, and which sank, softly as a caress, into the very depths of my soul. With a desperation, begotten by the short time at my disposal, I tried to etch all the details on my memory, so that in years to come, my spirit might steal back, like a pilgrim, to this sequestered spot, as a place of refuge from a prosaic world . . . Soon after sunset I went for a sail on a sampan along the River of Perfumes. When darkness came I could see a hand at the back placing a lamp in the little saloon under its crescent-shaped roof and I was conscious that a family lived on board only because I heard, for a moment, a baby crying. I sat on a piece of matting at the prow, under the stars, the lights of the old town drifting slowly past, like echoes of its ancient splendour; and at last, despondently, I stepped ashore, to face the discomforts of a hot night in the train . . . At dawn a series of beautiful oriental paintings seemed to pass before my eyes, so finely drawn were the figures in fields and village markets, so soft the contours, so delicate the colouring of the landscape. Then came a country of strange conformation, reminiscent of the art of Gustave Doré.[15] Deep ravines winding in serpentine folds, rocks chiselled into monstrous shapes, mammoth boulders half covered with leprous vegetation; all huddled in chaotic groups, some rising, with startling abruptness, hundreds of feet above the plain—in fact, as I afterwards discovered, a replica on land of the famous Bay of Along.

My next stop was at Hanoi, the capital of Tonkin, where I found an elegant combination of East and West. Its most striking features are the two lakes set, like jewels, in the heart of the city. On the shore of the larger rises the Grand Buddha Temple; in the middle of the smaller lies the diminutive Isle of Jade, with its lovely pagoda, where I felt chilled by an eerie atmosphere on finding myself alone at night in its gloomy, mysterious inner sanctum. The flower market on the

15. Paul-Gustave Louis Christophe Doré (1832–83) was a French engraver, printmaker, and book illustrator, whose dreamlike illustrations were often imitated by later Romantic artists.

lakeside under the trees, with the sellers in their colourful costumes, makes an unforgettable picture. Silk merchants, embroiderers, lacquer workers, silversmiths, and many other craftsmen, all contribute to the animation of the native quarter, where whole streets are devoted to one particular trade, a universal custom of the East. The cathedral, one of the finest in Indo-China, resembles Notre Dame in Paris on a smaller scale; and among other notable buildings is the large museum, from which I had a view of an immense bridge, two kilometres long, over the Red River, across which I motored on my way to Haiphong. This is a busy port, the principal streets of which have a European appearance, but it has an extensive section exclusively native. Here I visited a temple in which were devout worshippers and many offerings; in fact, the display before the altar looked like a buffet lunch or slipper. A little roast pig; cooked chickens sitting upright, quite naturally, as if alive; various fruits and small pink cakes were some of the appetising things I noticed. A few miles from the town is an observatory, from which I enjoyed a beautiful view and, on this drive, I saw many of the extraordinary, flat Tonkinese hats, which are nearly as large as cart-wheels. The costume of the upper-class Annamite women, who have exceptionally slender figures, consists of a perfectly cut tunic, which may be of any colour but is usually of black ciré satin, reaching to the knees, slashed at each side to the waist, with high collar, long close-fitting sleeves and fastened with tiny ball buttons on the shoulder. This is worn with narrow white trousers and the picturesque lamp-shade hat, so characteristic of the country. Unfortunately many of the lower class indulge in the disgusting habit of betel chewing, which has the disfiguring effect of making their teeth quite black . . . I left Haiphong in the early afternoon on a small steamer and sailed down the Red River for a cruise on the Bay of Along, which cannot be navigated by large vessels. With many other passengers, I was to be picked up by the "Sphinx" before sunset that evening. This marvellous bay is indeed a unique achievement of Nature in her most whimsical mood. Countless islands spring abruptly from the water, some green as emeralds, some grey colossal rocks, moulded, as if by a Titan's hand, into such spectral and grotesque shapes that I felt I had drifted into the bewilderingly fantastic dominion of Walt Disney.[16] No wonder Chinese mythology placed here the den of its legendary dragon of the sea. There are grottoes with amazing stalactites, navigable subterranean labyrinths where the boatman seems no other than Charon[17] himself; and, rising sheer from opalescent depths, a monumental monk in eternal contemplation, companioned by a gigantic toad and a most realistic unicorn. One island, larger than the others, had a miniature golden beach lapped by little sapphire blue, diamond-spangled waves; and a tiny house, surely the home of a nymph or a mermaid, clung, as if for protection to the brilliantly hued skirts of a towering cliff. Cascades of sunshine poured down like molten gold; every nook and fissure in those rocks was revealed by a light, ruthless in its microscopic power; on all sides was form, clear-cut as cameo, and colour, prodigal in its wealth . . . Then, suddenly, I shivered as at the touch of cold, clammy fingers; the sun was extinguished as if by an electric switch; and everything was enveloped in the stygian folds of a dense fog . . . The steamer stopped at once; to move in such surroundings would bring certain disaster. Even sufficient seating accommodation was not available for the large number on board, most of whom had only tropical clothes like myself; and the total contents of the larder consisted of a limited quantity of bread, a still smaller supply of fruit, and half a ham! The hours crawled slowly on . . . I was interested in studying my fellow sufferers, whose expressions had changed almost as dramatically as that of the landscape. They were huddled together here and there, like sacks of merchandise, when something, sudden as a trumpet-blast, galvanised them into life. It was the announcement, by the skipper, that one of the crew, in a desperate effort to solve the food problem, had succeeded, with much difficulty, in catching a large fish. We were also informed that dinner would follow in due course . . . The piece of ham had disappeared long before my turn

16. Walt Disney's animated musical *Fantasia* (1940) features a number of such scenes.

17. In Greek mythology, Charon is the ferryman of Hades who transports the recently dead across the rivers Styx and Acheron.

came, but I was the first to be presented with the platter on which reposed a weird vertebrate of quite unknown species. Hunger whetting my knife, I made a bold attempt to detach a morsel, but I might as well have tried to carve a slice from one of the granite cliffs outside. In despair I passed the dish on and saw that others, whose moral and physical strength were greater than mine, eventually secured possession of some unappetising chunks. I was lucky to capture a banana and a lump of hard bread. After the meal everybody tried to settle down for the night. This was no easy matter, owing to lack of space. Before midnight I wandered about, and came on pathetic groups in every passible attitude of discomfort, some even lying on the floor with a box for a pillow; but all appeared to be sleeping placidly . . . Then, before dawn, the peaceful stillness was rudely broken by the reverberating boom of a siren. Springing up at once, we rushed to the side of the boat to find the fog considerably cleared. There, shining through the gloom, were the lights of the "Sphinx," which, alarmed for our safety, had come in search of us. We were taken quickly to the comfort of our cabins; and, with a shrill cry of farewell to the companions left behind, we soon turned south, bound for Manila.

Usually, when I sailed away from a foreign country, I stood at the stern of the boot until the last faint blur was blotted out by distance; but my departure from Indo-China was abrupt and in darkness. And it was fitting thus to leave the scene of such strange sights and startling contrasts. Architecture seemingly the work of gods rather than of men; pagan temples and Christian churches; opium dens and cocktail bars; sacred white elephants and shaved French poodles; naked savages and chic Parisiennes; palaces apparently inhabited by a Midas, and houseboats where the floating population live and die; tiger-haunted jungles and flower-studded parks; stately villas and palm-thatched shacks; oxcarts, rickshaws, and Rolls Royce cars; lepers in the last stage of human deformity and torsos worthy of the chisel of Michelangelo; magnificence raised to the superlative degree beside the crudest and starkest simplicity. Yes, it was fitting to leave such scenes as one leaves a theatre. The curtain went down suddenly; and, with reluctance, I stepped out from a land of dreams into the grey light of a commonplace world.

COLUMBIA

ECUADOR

BRAZIL

PERU

■
LA MERCED

BOLIVIA

PACIFIC
OCEAN

1939

6. Map for Chasing the Chunchos, Brian Bixby, 2020.

5

Chasing the Chunchos

Ever since childhood when the finding of the first primrose was a thrilling annual event and foxglove petals on my fingers brought direct contact with fairyland, the humble blossoms of field and hedgerow have had a warmer place in my heart than the haughty blooms of garden or greenhouse. Memories of the blue-belled woods of May tarnish for me the brilliance of June's herbaceous borders and rose-trellised pergolas; and the sight of a gypsy caravan camped by the roadside fills me with an exhilaration, which even Keats's "beaker full of the warm South"[1] would be powerless to produce. And so, what I may call the wildflowers of humanity—the Bedouins of the desert,

This travelogue, published in the *The Capuchin Annual* for 1955, details another of Murphy's efforts to encounter what she calls the "wild flowers of humanity," those peoples who have remained, at least according to her understanding, largely untouched by the influence of modernity. In the Quechua language of Peru, *Ch'unchu* or *Chuncho* is a derogatory term, equivalent to "barbarian," for the indigenous peoples of the Amazon rainforest, though it is not clear that Murphy intends to use it in this deprecating sense. Rather, for the Irish traveler, the people identified with this term represent a human curiosity, which stimulates her abiding primitivism, holding in high regard what is considered simple or unsophisticated by some. It is evident that she commences the trip in a spirit of adventure, willing to risk any anticipated dangers in order to pursue her goal; but the measures she takes to overcome these threats, naïve as they are, also lead Murphy to become the object of her own deprecating humor. Undertaken in 1939, this would be her last major journey for many years due to the intercession of the war and the effective cessation of international travel. Reproduced with permission from *The Capuchin Annual*.

1. John Keats, "Ode to a Nightingale" (1819), line 15.

the Lapps within the Arctic Circle, the Caboclos of the Amazon, the Kabyles of the Atlas Mountains, the Mois of Indo-China, the Igorots of the Philippine Islands, and the Indians of the Andes—all these true children of nature, who dwell along the remote byways of the world, their "clouds of glory" undimmed by "shades of the prison-house,"[2] aroused in me, during my wanderings, a far deeper interest than did their sophisticated brethren who tread the crowded highways of civilisation.

It was then with a decided quickening of the pulse, even while I was under the spell of Peru's lovely capital, that I first heard of a primitive tribe called the Chunchos, who inhabit part of that immense, and largely unexplored, territory about the headwaters of the Amazon. I doubt if cannibalism, common in other regions, is practised at all by any of the residents of this particular area, but the ferocity of many is such that a traveller amongst them is not merely risking his life, but selecting a novel form of suicide. However, I was assured that the Chunchos were harmless, peaceful, and friendly to strangers; and, though Colonel Fawcett[3] once referred to them as being "on the war-path," military demonstrations on their part were probably provoked by aggressive neighbours. Anyhow, I determined to go in search of them but soon found that this project was not quite so simple as it seemed. Fortunately it was possible at that time, in 1939, to go practically the whole way by car, instead of on mule or horseback, as would have been necessary only a few years before; and a journey which formerly occupied months could then be accomplished in as many days. The need for direct communication between the scattered elements of such a vast country as Peru grew urgent in an era of mechanical transport; but, owing to the mountainous character of the land, this problem was only partly and very slowly solved by reviving the

2. William Wordsworth, "Ode: Intimations of Immortality from Recollections of Early Childhood" (1807), lines 65 and 68.

3. Percy Harrison Fawcett (1867–1925) was a British artillery officer, geographer, and explorer of South America, who disappeared during an expedition in search of an ancient lost city he called "Z."

principle of "road conscription,"[4] which originated in the Roman Empire, and was adopted by the Incas to link the far-flung portions of their great dominions by highways, reckoned by Humboldt[5] among the most stupendous achievements of man. These had been allowed to degenerate during the colonial period and, like the Roman roads over Europe, can now be judged only by a few isolated fragments. I confess my enthusiasm for exploration waned a little when I found only two chauffeurs, one a German, the other an Italian, willing to undertake my proposed trip. The reason for this seeming cowardice was the natives' dread of the *soroche*, or mountain sickness, caused by want of oxygen, from which even mules are not immune; and my programme included, not only a road considered the most dangerous in the world, but at least two of the highest passes in the Andes; resembling, in fact, a switchback ride on a colossal scale, one day rising to 16,000 feet in a frigid temperature and the next dropping abruptly to the sweltering atmosphere of the jungle.

I had come a long way since that dark morning before dawn when, having traversed the pampas of Argentina, I sat on the side of my bed in a hotel in the foothills, waiting impatiently for the car in which to make my first Andean crossing, torn between the thrill of what I was about to do and terror at the possible result of doing it, and of dying on the summit of the pass—a foreboding almost realised when an Indian in the backseat, suddenly seized by the *soroche*, clutched the driver's arm on the very edge of an abyss. Fear gripped me once more when I crossed another pass near the Bolivian frontier, having got a detailed description of all the symptoms, and even the approximate hour of the seizure, from an American engineer who worked in the

4. The Road Conscription Act of 1920 (*Ley de conscripción*, vial no. 4113) established compulsory road construction and maintenance duties in Peru for all males between eighteen and sixty years of age.

5. Alexander von Humboldt, in full Friedrich Wilhelm Heinrich Alexander, Freiherr (baron) von Humboldt (1769–1859), was a German naturalist and explorer who travelled extensively in South America between 1799 and 1804, later publishing the first modern scientific account of the continent in a massive multivolume study.

mines. Still vivid is my memory of that night of intense cold, which compelled me to leave my berth occasionally and walk along the corridor, in a desperate effort to keep my blood above freezing point, and to obtain a short respite from the harrowing experience of listening to an unfortunate passenger, who moaned incessantly, and complained that "a hammer was pounding her head." With considerable courage, which rapidly dwindled as I mounted, I faced the still greater heights between Bolivia and Peru; and when the rivers, apparently flowing backwards, proved me to be on the Continental Divide, I felt so vigorous that I bitterly regretted the lunch I had sacrificed as a precautionary measure. But now, when contemplating my expedition to the Chunchos, terror paralysed me again at the persistent vision of passes much higher than those I had already survived, knowing that some limit must be fixed to my endurance. Never in my life before had I realised how true it is that, in certain circumstances, ignorance is bliss. If only I did not know so much about the *soroche*; if only everybody I met, and every book and newspaper I read, did not insist on pouring information on the subject down my throat! Somebody who spent only one day in a sierra town was found dead in bed next morning; a party of American marines who had recently gone a short distance up the Central Railway were taken, unconscious, off the train, their ears bleeding and their fingernails turned black; a woman on another mountain railway was carried out of her compartment, suffering from violent hysterics. Such were the items of news thrust upon me in the most cruel example of forcible feeding possible to imagine; and the last upset me more than anything else I heard, having always had a horror of hysteria. Finally, however, love of adventure, and the imperious call of the wild, triumphed; mind conquered matter; and one morning, before sunrise, Fritz, the German chauffeur, and I left the lotus land of Lima, bearing, in a most literal sense, a banner inscribed "Excelsior."[6]

Soon after leaving the city, on a road opened only in 1933, the ascent began, and continued hour after hour through a few widely

6. [Latin] "ever upward."

separated villages, the largest of which was Canta, until at last we stopped on top of the Pass of La Viuda, at an altitude of 15,748 feet, and I felt as placid as the lake, fringed with snowcapped mountains, that lay, like a mirror, before me. Descending gradually we reached one of the table-lands called "punas," usually ranging from 11,000 to 14,000 feet, which are peculiar to the Andes, and are sometimes inhabited by shepherds. If this particular one had inhabitants, they would need to be of titanic stature to escape being dwarfed by their extraordinary setting. It was known as the Rock Forest and was strewn with gigantic boulders grouped in fantastic formation, reminiscent of Montserrat in Spain, but on an incomparably grander scale. The only living thing visible was a flock of llamas, which seemed scarcely larger than lambs against their awe-inspiring background. The appalling loneliness which broods over all these Andean heights became here almost tangible; and I was chilled by a sense of contact with hostility to man, characteristic of the Andes, in strong contrast to the friendliness of the Alps and Pyrenees.

Our next stop was at Cerro de Pasco, noted for its copper mines, where I visited an interesting Indian market; and from there we descended to Huánuco, founded by Gomez Alvarado[7] in 1539 and still retaining a Spanish atmosphere, with its balconied houses and picturesque plaza, in a site so close to the mountains that they appeared to rise sheer from the ends of the streets. The local inn had a square covered courtyard overlooked by a veranda, from which opened a double row of windowless bedrooms, in which the light, if not religious, was decidedly dim. I had hoped to secure two of these rooms so that I could sleep in the outer one, and thus have at least an illusion of fresh air; but, as the place was crowded, I had to occupy the first floor back and give the front to Fritz. When I retired I discovered that the upper half of the communicating door was made of glass, and that it

7. Gómez de Alvarado y Contreras (1482–1542) was a Spanish conquistador and explorer from Extremadura who traversed Cuba, Mexico, Guatemala, El Salvador, Ecuador, Peru, and Chile.

was impossible to close because it possessed no lock, bolt, nor handle; two problems effectively solved by transforming a quilt into a curtain, and erecting a barricade with all available weight, including a heavy washstand. When I quenched my candle, I was in pitch darkness, but my environment was not exactly an antidote to insomnia, and, luckily, I was wide awake when what would otherwise have seemed an earthquake occurred in the middle of the night. A hair-raising rumble reverberated through the outer room, as if walls and ceiling had collapsed; and, despite my fortifications, some living thing, which sounded more like a hippopotamus than a man, burst through my door with such terrific force that I narrowly escaped being bombarded by a cascade of furniture and getting a much-needed shower bath from a flying jug. I screamed like a howler monkey; and, with loudly muttered apologies, the obviously panic-stricken intruder withdrew, colliding with all the objects he had missed during his tempestuous entry. An almost incredible feature of the episode was the fact that my bodyguard slept soundly the whole time, quite unaware of any disturbance!

Cocaine is manufactured in this town, and coca—the sacred plant of the Incas—from which it is obtained, is grown throughout the district; and so universal is its use that a coca pouch is as essential a part of the Indian costume as the flowing cloak they call the poncho. I had heard so much about the amazing feats performed under the influence of this powerful stimulant, and was so eager to test its efficacy that, when in Bolivia a short time before, I asked my Indian landlady to administer a dose. Addicts mix it with lime and chew it like betel nut in the East; but, unable to face this ordeal, I drank it in the form of an infusion, unfortunately just before going to bed. Never shall I forget the frustration I suffered that night, nor my contempt for the mighty deeds of Samson[8] and Polyphemus.[9] Not only could I lift rocks and

8. Judges 13–16.

9. Polyphemus, son of Poseidon and the nymph Thoosa, is the most famous of the Cyclopes in Greek mythology.

pull down temples, but I felt I could literally move mountains when, unhappily, I was confined within four walls; and not only did the drug murder sleep, but firmly convinced me I had conquered that weakness for life.

In Huanuco I learned that the road in course of construction from there to the upper reaches of the Amazon was completed far beyond Tingo Maria; and the thrill of travelling on this route tempered, for the moment, my ardent desire to see the Chunchos, and I decided to make a detour involving the crossing of the Carpish Pass, a mere 10,000 feet, which now caused me no misgivings. Here, at wide intervals, were heavily thatched adobe cabins, oblong or circular in shape, lighted only by the open door, and with outdoor ovens similar to those I had seen in highland huts in Chile. As we ascended we met gangs of labourers still working on the road, and, on rounding a curve, I was horrified to see our passage blocked by a rock, almost as colossal as one of the famous Incan monoliths. It was impossible to turn the car as we were on the edge of a cliff which continued for miles, and equally impossible to proceed. The workers greeted us cheerily, and we were informed that if the obstacle were needed for pavement we must wait until it was broken up; but if they had sufficient material to dispense with it, then it would be hurled over the precipice. A prolonged discussion followed, during which the speakers gave an acrobatic display of expressive gestures; and eventually they all gathered together, and very, very slowly, inch by inch, and with tremendous exertion, their crowbars moved the ponderous mass a few feet until it overbalanced, and fell with a crash like a peal of thunder. Near the end of this tedious process a big lorry arrived and halted behind us: and I was surprised to see that it contained a large Japanese family—father, mother, and numerous children, ranging in age from youths of eighteen and twenty to toddlers and an infant in arms; and with them were all their worldly goods and chattels. Descending carefully along the untrodden way, we came to the densely wooded banks of the Huallaga, where many trees were the hosts of beautiful orchids, and were plentifully hung with weaver-birds' nests, which resemble

Christmas stockings after the departure of Santa Claus. This river, which unites with the Ucayali and the Marañon to form part of the headwaters of the Amazon, now escorted us to our destination.

Tingo Maria is a scattered cluster of shacks in a clearing in the jungle, and I was a little depressed at the prospect of another sleepless night when the innkeeper conducted me to my "room," and I realised that the whole sleeping accommodation consisted of a long row of tiny cubicles, with wooden partitions reaching only about a yard above the beds. I understood then why a certain Andean caravansary had acquired the name of "Hotel Silence," owing to its acoustic properties. That day at dinner I discovered I was in the neighbourhood of some mine, judging from the fact that the majority of my fellow guests were unmistakably miners. The dining room was the most spacious I had ever seen. A platform about fifty feet square was raised on piles six feet high, and at each corner a massive tree-trunk supported the palm-thatched roof; and on all sides were such wide open spaces that, when one of the customers ordered a lemon, the attendant simply plucked the fruit from a branch growing beside one of the tables. A major portion of my meal consisted of boiled cassava root,[10] the chief attribute of which is a complete lack of flavor—an immeasurable advantage when one is obliged to eat whatever is offered or starve.

Starting to explore the vicinity, I found an unfinished two-roomed shack which, though at some distance, was apparently part of the "hotel," and the sight of this gave me a sudden inspiration. I begged the proprietor to allow me to spend the night there and, though evidently astonished at my request, he readily consented. Feeling much happier at the prospect of what the immediate future held in store, I turned away from the inhabited quarters and found an irresistible path through the jungle, fortunately forgetting my shock in Brazil when I followed a similar trail and, suddenly hearing a rustle

---

10. *Manihot esculenta*, also called manioc, mandioca, or yuca, is a tuberous edible plant cultivated throughout the tropical world and consumed in boiled form or grated for use in breads, tapioca, and laundry starch.

in the undergrowth, jumped backwards to avoid a large snake, writhing across a few feet in front of me. It is a vice of mine never to think of danger until it is well past; in other words, I always leap before I look; and to this characteristic I owe many of the "purple patches" in my life. No serpent marred the paradise of that delightful walk, and I returned to find one apartment of the shack transformed into a bedroom; simply but adequately furnished with a camp bed and a chair, on which was placed a candle, a tin basin, and a jug of water. A banana tree grew within reach; and on the river bank behind was moored a dug-out canoe, which recalled my one experience of this typically Indian craft, when, in an Amazonian swamp, I went in search of the famous *Victoria Regis* lily[11] and, being warned by my *caboclo* boatman that the least movement would upset us, I scarcely dared to breathe, knowing that the water was swarming with hordes of the dreaded piranha, or man-eating fish.

Soon the full moon rose, and I sauntered along the gleaming white road, listening to the nocturnal orchestra of the jungle. The glory of the night and the romance of my strange surroundings made me reluctant to turn back and, when at last I did so, I lingered long on my balcony, draining every drop of the beauty and wonder of the scene. My movements were misinterpreted by mine host who, unknown to me, had been watching from a distance; and, concluding that panic had seized me at the thought of remaining alone in such a solitary abode, he came to urge me to return to the inn. At the moment, fear was so far from me that it would be no exaggeration to declare my state of mind ecstatic, feeling, as I did, something akin to that intense emotion described by the inventor of the aqualung for divers, which he has so well named "rapture of the depths." Even when I decided to retire, and lighted my candle, I stepped outside once more, rebellious against losing precious hours in sleep; and then made the startling discovery that when a light is placed within a house built of

---

11. *Victoria Regis* lily, also known as *Victoria amazonica*, is the largest of the Nymphaeaceae family of water lilies, with leaves up to ten feet (three meters) across.

bamboo poles, the occupant becomes as conspicuous as a bird in a cage. Life was simplified still further by this fact, rendering, as it did, all artificial illumination superfluous. Like all jungle dwellings, mine was raised on piles as a protection against wild beasts, but the space beneath also served as a dormitory for all the domestic animals of the neighbourhood, judging from the din which emerged from my basement to greet the dawn. It was a most effective alarm clock, and I lay awake looking at the amusing antics of a monkey perched on a tree a few yards from my pillow. Suddenly, from the back, came a sound distinctively human and, before I could grasp what was happening, two men were gazing at me through the yawning gap left in the partition; and, as if it were a most natural thing to find me there, they were bowing gracefully like a pair of hidalgos[12] and wishing me "good morning." The explanation flashed across my mind that my visitors were carpenters who had come to finish the building, and for half an hour I listened to their busy tools, wondering how to solve such an unexpected problem. Fortunately, at the end of that time, they needed more material for their work, and when both departed to fetch it, I sprang immediately out of bed, and quickly draped a sheet and some old newspapers between the two apartments.

After breakfast I set out to explore the new road and had penetrated several miles into the wilderness when, in a recent clearing, I was amazed to see my Japanese friends of the day before, all active as ants, engaged in founding their new home. The father and sons had already formed the skeleton of a commodious shack; the mother was cooking a substantial meal; and the children were frisking like kittens, boisterously delighted with their novel playground. The little man ran towards me with an overwhelmingly warm welcome, evidently assuming me to be a prospective neighbour, and pointing to a refrigerator leaning against a mahogany tree, begged me to advise him what to do with such an unwieldy "white elephant" in the absence of electricity.

12. In Spain, from the late medieval period to the modern era, a knight or member of the gentry.

My admiration for these brave pioneers was tinged with reverence; and during the terrible years so soon to follow, I often thought of them with envy, realising that, in that peaceful haven so sequestered from the world, they probably heard little, if anything, of the horrors of war. I continued about forty miles further until the road came abruptly to an end; and so thrilled was I at being the first to blaze the trail that I regretted not having an Irish flag to plant on the spot.

When I returned to my hotel in Huanuco I was greeted as an old customer, and told that the suite of two balcony rooms was placed at my disposal. Feeling very tired, I went upstairs early and, on opening the door, found two men leisurely removing their boots and, quite unembarrassed by my appearance, they politely made way for me to pass into the inner room. I went at once to the proprietor, and telling him I would sleep on a bench in the courtyard, promptly occupied that position. With rolling eyes he swept up the stairs like a tornado, and a niagara of fiery language flowed down, but he failed to dislodge the invaders who had taken possession of the beds and refused to budge. Snorting and fuming he entered a stygian cavity on the ground floor and soon prepared a bunk where I spent the night, more comfortably then in the black hole of Calcutta.

Next day, after many hours in the mountains, during which we passed the great lake of Junin at 12,940 feet, we reached a richly cultivated region where copper and silver are mined and grain and potatoes grow abundantly. The scenery had become much less rugged, and I saw one large clump of wild arum lilies,[13] not the sickly, pallid green plants of our woodlands, but stately and resplendent as the products of a European conservatory. Flocks of llamas with their colourful drivers, so picturesque against the sierra background, were a familiar sight on this part of the route; and, through an avenue of eucalyptus trees, we entered the town of Tarma. In the hotel there I got a room much superior to what I had been accustomed, but its stone floor caused an

13. Arum lily, also known as the calla or white arum lily, is a robust, dark green species of herbaceous, perennial, flowering plants.

extra drop in the temperature, already far too low for my taste. The owner—an American, but a citizen of the world—was literally a host in himself, so inexhaustible seemed his supply of adventurous tales.

The highlight of the following day's journey was the Carpapata Road, reputed the most dangerous on earth. Like a giant reptile, it writhes in constant acute hairpin bends along cliffs over a thousand feet high; is only eight feet wide, without wall or fence of any kind; and at one point, above a drop of fifteen hundred feet, six parallel levels are visible, one directly below the other. On emerging from this precarious labyrinth we arrived at the village of La Merced, situated in the lovely Chanchamayo Valley, close to the homeland of the Chunchos. The only inn was also a general grocery and provision store, and my meals were served at a small table in full view of all the customers, who were numerous because it was the eve of a great market. To reach my bedroom I had to cross a yard and mount a ladder over what I believed was a stable, judging from the sounds I heard under me during a night of almost intolerable heat. A large gathering of Chunchos was expected there next morning, but, being anxious to see them in their real environment, I started that afternoon into the jungle on a rough track, which for many miles could be negotiated by a motor car. I was now at the beginning of the Pichis Trail, by which Iquitos on the Amazon is reached in about three arduous weeks; ten days by mule and the rest by boat. Mails were dispatched there twice a month, and I was lucky to see the departure of a "mail train," consisting of a long string of mules, with their *arrieros* or drivers on foot. As we crawled along, I saw beside the way a patch of blue so brilliant that it reminded me of an Alpine slope carpeted with gentians. Suddenly it disintegrated and took flight, setting the gloom of the forest aglow with the intensity of its colour; and I knew I was looking at Peruvian butterflies almost as large and beautiful as the famous morphos of Brazil.[14] All this time I was on the fringe of the Chuncho country,

14. The blue morpho, with iridescent wings that span up to eight inches or twenty centimeters, is among the largest butterflies in the world and the most emblematic of Amazonian species.

but so elusive were they that I was obliged to stalk them as warily as though I were chamois hunting; and I secured my first sight of one by concealing myself in the brushwood beside a river, where a stalwart member of the tribe was fishing with dynamite on the opposite bank. Bow and arrow fishing, which I had seen on the lower Amazon, is difficult owing to the refraction of light by water, and the fact that arrows penetrate only about a foot below the surface; but the dynamite fisherman, while requiring no special skill, would need to be a diver to retrieve the greater part of his catch. I continued for several miles, seeing through the foliage many habitations but few inhabitants, except a crowded raft which the current swept past me; and so I turned back, feeling somewhat disappointed at the result of my quest. I could, therefore, hardly believe my eyes when, about twenty miles from La Merced, I suddenly saw two Chunchos, a man and a woman, a few dozen yards in front of us. In frenzied excitement, I stopped and tried to speak to them, but, finding their knowledge of Spanish too limited, I made more progress with signs. Fritz objected to giving them a lift on the ground that they were too dirty, but I overcame his opposition by assuring him that since I left Lima I had only had a pint of washing water each day, and consequently any reflection of mine on the sanitary condition of my friends would be a glaring instance of the kettle calling the pot black. These people, who were both very young, were going to the market, and I had much difficulty in making them understand that I wished to bring them there free of charge. When I refused to take some of the goods they carried for sale, they offered me money; and, when finally they understood that the drive would be a gift, their joy was delightful to see. No Roman general leading his triumphal procession ever felt more elated than I returning that evening with my two "captives"; and, when I found in the plaza of La Merced a large camp containing hundreds of their kin, I spent the early hours of that night availing myself of such ample opportunity to study them at close quarters.

The most striking and curious thing in connection with these jungle-dwellers was the fact that, in 1939, I found all the men with tonsured heads, their hair cut like mediaeval monks, and wearing loose brown robes, in imitation of the Franciscans who had brought them Christianity many centuries before. They carry satchels with leather straps like schoolboys and, as ornaments, wear jaguar teeth and dead humming birds attached to a scarf; and a few were distinguished by a peculiar headdress or hat, but this was so rare that it might be part of a ceremonial uniform, or a symbol of authority similar to the elaborately mounted staffs I had seen proudly displayed by some Indians of Pisac. In common with all savage women, the Chunchos make lavish use of cosmetics, the chief of which is the juice of the achiote berry, which the forest supplies free, and which has very much the same effect as the costly lipstick and rouge of their civilised sisters.

And now, having accomplished my task, the prospect of facing the Carpapata Road once more reminded me of having read about two American scientists who crossed the continent from the mouth of the Amazon to the coast of Peru. They had frequent encounters with headhunters and narrow escapes from drowning in whirlpools; but when one of them wrote an account of their adventures he declared that the most dangerous part began at La Merced, as they had "more to fear on this route than on the rest of the entire trip." In various parts of the globe I have motored much on mountain passes, ranging from one where the driver whirled round each hairpin bend at the pace of a ballet dancer's pirouette, to another, where at each curve the car seemed to plunge over the chasm and draw back only at the eleventh second; I have even survived on two occasions a wheel actually going over the edge; and whether it was due to this intensive training or to my absorption in the magnificent scenery, I felt no nervousness whatever, either on the outward or return journeys, until Fritz, in reprisal for my insistence on a lift for the Chunchos, stopped the car, and bade me look down to where a mutilated lorry lay on the river bank, a thousand feet below. However, it was, in my opinion, infinitely less nerve-racking to motor over the Carpapata than to negotiate it on a mule. Whenever I have found myself on the back of one of these animals on a steep trail, their vaunted surefootedness has always been discounted for me by their incorrigible habit of doggedly treading the very brink of the precipice, where each stumbling step, each dislodged stone, proved to me the truth of Shakespeare's dictum that "cowards die many times before their death."[15]

Deciding to return to Lima by the Central Highway, I left Tarma next day and drove through a bleak, desolate land leading to another pass, where, beside a lake, were large flocks of sheep, which are not native to Peru, but were introduced by the Spaniards. All this part of the country is closely associated with the Spanish Conquest; and it was at Jauja, which was visited by Francisco Pizarro[16] on his way to take Cuzco, that the conquerors received seventy loads of gold for the ransom of the last Inca. Soon after leaving there we passed San Jerónimo with its fine church and pretty plaza and arrived at Huancayo, one of the most attractive of the sierra towns, where, from my bedroom window, I watched a religious procession, rendered strikingly picturesque by troops of Indians in their gorgeous costumes.

Awaking next morning to the prospect of spending the final stage of my journey on the world's highest road would be a thrilling experience, were it not that the gibbering wraith of the *soroche*, which had haunted me for so long, became aggressive once more; and I feared that this famous highway might well be the last straw. It was indeed a day of superlatives, so many of the sights I saw were described as such; and Oroya, the first place of importance we reached, boasts of possessing one of the largest smelting works and the loftiest chimney in the world. The landscape in the locality is so austere and forbidding that when I got a glimpse, through a gash in the mountains, of this tall white shaft, graceful as a lily, etherealised by an auriole of bluish mist, and belching columns of dense smoke—it seemed the very chimney of hell itself—a fancy fostered by the fact that as we drew near I had to cover my nose and mouth with a scarf to avoid being overcome by the fumes. This was so unpleasant that I scarcely noticed our progress until suddenly we stopped, and, much to my surprise and joy, I

15. *Julius Caesar*, act II, scene 2.

16. Francisco Pizarro (1475–1541) was the Spanish conquistador of Peru who took Cuzco, then the capital of the Inca empire, in November 1533.

saw the Anticona glacier close on my right, and straight in front, on a snow-covered patch, a sign-post inscribed with, what were to me, the magic words "La Cima, 15,862 feet." I walked along the road, revelling in *looking down* at Ticlio Station, the summit of the Central Railway, which is the highest of standard gauge in the world, and in which I had been tempted to travel this section of my trip, because the trains always carry oxygen. However, contradictory as it may seem, the fact that the road is higher and that in a car I could stop and stare at will prevailed over my ever-recurring fears, now, happily, proved groundless.

This wonderful railway which, for a considerable distance, was my constant companion, is two hundred and ninety-eight miles long, has sixty-five tunnels, sixty-seven bridges, and countless zigzags. Eight thousand workmen were employed, and as at the Great Wall of China, many sacrificed their lives in its construction. Even now the territory through which it runs, with its landslides, floods, and torrents, is a battlefield for constant war between natural forces and human skill. The most spectacular part of the line is the *Infiernillo* or Infernal Gorge, a narrow cleft between sheer towering cliffs, where the spectator stands breathless with admiration for the daring engineer, who conceived the idea of piercing the path of a mighty machine through an obstacle, defiantly flung down by nature to bar the passage of man. The road here seemed literally to get entangled with the railway; so often did I find myself above and below and beside and between the innumerable tunnels and bridges that I felt like a fly caught in a spider's web. I had hardly recovered from this bewildering experience than I plunged impulsively into another of a totally different kind, which was even more upsetting to my mental and physical equilibrium. My passive mood of silent wonder, engendered by that marvellous feat of engineering, was rudely shattered, and my mind switched back abruptly many hundreds, perhaps thousands, of years, by the sight of one of those ancient suspension bridges I had long been eager to see, and which I had always cherished an ambition to cross. Constructed from a species of osier lashed together with thongs, it was about four feet wide, with a single rope handrail at one side only, and spanned an apparently bottomless ravine. My chivalrous companion insisted on going over first, and he began valiantly, but his second step produced a tremor, his third a sickening sway; and when he had tottered a few yards, the whole structure behaved like a bucking bronco, and flinging himself face downwards, he crawled back as slowly and ignominiously as a snail. I reached a point even less advanced, but succeeded, with much difficulty, in remaining erect; and was photographed there filled with esteem for the commonsense of the mules that resolutely refuse to set foot on such contraptions, except when blindfolded. Notwithstanding the wildness and sullen grandeur of these regions, they are a botanist's paradise, so rare are the floral treasures found on those seemingly arid slopes; and as we descended, the landscape grew softer and greener; and, after skirting a rich mining district, and passing the charming tree-lined village of San Mateo, with its well-known medicinal springs, I bade goodbye to the llamas, knowing that their dainty feet would disdain to tread the dust of lower altitudes. These lovely animals feed themselves; bear heavy loads on tracks no goat or donkey could travel; can walk up and down an almost perpendicular wall beside a precipice; and are as indispensable to the Indians of the Andes as are camels to the Arabs of the desert. Rapidly descending, we passed Surco, noted for what are claimed to be the best violets in the world, and arrived at Chosica, a favourite summer resort.

Having now a distant view of the capital, I turned off the main road to visit the ruins of Cajamarquilla, so striking a contrast to the modern chalets and bungalows of that neighbourhood. And it was a fitting place to stop and meditate on the wonders of Peru. As I lingered in the solitude of those deserted acres, eloquent stones spoke to me of a past so remote that I was overwhelmed with a sense of antiquity, such as I felt in Ur of the Chaldees, when I reflected that Abraham was one of its comparatively modern inhabitants.[17] The people conquered by the Spaniards were themselves conquerors of the older cultures, which had vanished centuries before the Spanish invasion. The ancient

17. Genesis 11:28.

Peruvians excelled in architecture; were expert workers in gold and silver; some of the most exquisite specimens of the weaver's art have been found in their tombs; and samples of their pottery are among the most cherished possessions of the British Museum. To that unsolved mystery of the Andes, the ruined city of Tiahuanaco, some scholars have assigned an age of ten thousand years; and yet excavators have discovered there two stone wheels, six feet in diameter, and with axle holes; objects which would have been as great a novelty to the Incas as were the horses of the Spaniards. With good reason the archaeologists of today trace the Aztec and Mayan cultures to a common prehistoric source and locate in Peru the cradle of American Indian civilisation. And now, so close to the end of my journey, as I looked down on Lima, my thoughts crept back to the condor I had seen a few weeks before near Cuzco. I had long wished to see this majestic bird in its solitary native haunts, soaring exultingly above all other living things; but, to my sorrow, I saw only a miserable captive behind iron bars. I too had breathed the rarefied atmosphere of those sublime heights; I too had hovered above those terrifying gorges, and spread my wings across those boundless plains; and now I realised poignantly that to one who had lived even a fleeting hour of such glorious freedom, any city on earth, however beautiful, would be forever afterwards—a cage.

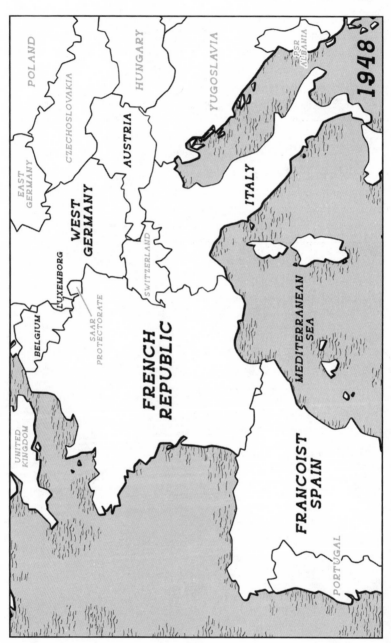

7. Map for Benedictine Byways, Brian Bixby, 2020.

6

Benedictine Byways

Ever since I fell under the spell of Gregorian chant many years ago at San Anselmo's in Rome, I have been occasionally lured to some remote monastery of the Benedictines,[1] who are universally acknowledged its greatest exponents. Thus one day in the spring of last year I found myself winging in a cable car above awe-inspiring precipices and across yawning chasms as I made the hair-raising ascent to the famous Abbey of Montserrat. I had come there from the ancient city of Tarragona, the capital of Roman Spain, where I had assisted at the sublime ceremonies of Holy Week and seen the torchlight precession of Good Friday—"the funeral of Christ"[2]—at which the heartrending

Published in the 1956–57 issue of *The Capuchin Annual*, this travelogue recounts Murphy's pilgrimage across Europe—from Spain eastward through France, Italy, and Austria and northward as far as Luxembourg and Belgium—in order to visit a series of Benedictine abbeys. The extended journey is a Catholic Grand Tour of sorts, which offers her readers a glimpse of noteworthy religious sites that they too might visit one day. Murphy highlights the attractions of these sites with abundant historical detail and some of her most poetic prose, often venturing into florid ekphrasis, elaborately describing the artwork and architecture to be found in the abbeys. In this way, she casts her "tourist gaze" across the Continent, directing attention to objects of historical and aesthetic interest for her middle-class Irish Catholic audience and helping to construct a series of expectations for their own possible travels. Reproduced with permission from *The Capuchin Annual*.

1. The Order of Saint Benedict is a monastic religious order of the Roman Catholic Church following the precepts of Benedict of Nursia (ca. 480–547).

2. A Holy Week ceremony that persists only in some relatively isolated parts of the Catholic world, most notably in the Franciscan rites at the Church of the Holy Sepulchre in Jerusalem.

notes of a Dead March accentuated the intense silence of what was to me, aesthetically and religiously, one of the most impressive spectacles I had ever witnessed. I had come from the island of Majorca, where I had gone to follow the footsteps of that wonderful man and great mystic, Ramon Lull,[3] from his cave on Mount Randa to his tomb in Palma's lovely church of San Francisco. And my mind was attuned to a mood keenly appreciative of the chant, which, for some days, I heard sung with outstanding perfection, in the midst of scenery surely among the rarest and most spectacular on earth. And yet, sensitive to my environment as an Aeolian harp to the wind, I found there a note out of tune with the austerity of the music, and something exotic, almost barbaric, in the splendour of the church, illuminated by votive lamps from all nations. Then too, in spite of its isolation from the beaten track, its atmosphere of other-worldliness, the halo of sanctity and poetic mysticism radiating from that strange mountain, which, in the Middle Ages, caused it to be revered as the shrine of the Holy Grail, and, in the ninth century, attracted innumerable hermits, the world was too much with me in Monserrat. Every afternoon, cars and coaches disgorged thousands of visitors, whose divers tongues turned the limited space around the abbey into a Tower of Babel, from which I fled to the rugged paths high up amid gigantic rocks, where I was enveloped by a solitude, as it were at the dawn of creation, in which God and I were the only existing beings. Lulled by that blessed peace and quiet, my thoughts wandered back to the days when pilgrims arrived here footsore and weary; when, from this hallowed spot, a monk[4] accompanied Columbus on his voyage of discovery to the New

---

3. Ramon Lull, also called Raymond Lully (Latin: Raimnudus Lullus) (ca. 1232–ca. 1315), was a Catalan mathematician, philosopher, poet, and Franciscan tertiary, as well as mystic, who is remembered for producing the first great works of Catalan literature and inventing the "art of finding truth" to underwrite the Roman Catholic faith.

4. Juan Pérez (dates unknown) was a Spanish friar of the Conventual Franciscans, who sailed with Columbus on his second voyage to the New World in 1493, after blessing the explorer and his fleet for their first voyage the previous year.

World; and when Ignatius of Loyola,[5] in the flaming fervour of repentance, climbed these precipitous heights to lay his sword and his heart on the steps of the altar. It was only at night when the throngs had dispersed, and I stood alone outside the closed door of the church, listening to the melodious voices within, while the moonlight blanched those eerie, pitch-dark peaks with an unearthly radiance, and the valley far below seemed an uninhabited wilderness, it was only then I found something of what I sought. Agreeing with Plato that the fitting abode for a beautiful soul is a beautiful body, I left Montserrat with an enthusiasm that kindled a longing to find for Gregorian chant a setting in which my eyes would convey to my soul a message of beauty similar to that conveyed there so eloquently by my ears. And this wish led my feet once more to the open road on an unusual pilgrimage, during which I visited many Benedictine monasteries in various countries.

Liturgists differ in assigning a date of origin for the plainchant,[6] but all agree on its antiquity. The exclusive music of the Church till the ninth century, it was well developed during the fourth in the monasteries of Syria and Egypt, and in the West, particularly by Saint Ambrose,[7] in Milan, continuing to develop until the reign of Pope Gregory the Great,[8] to whom is ascribed its final arrangement, and with whose name it has ever since been associated. But, in its simplest and most elementary form, it was probably sung in the catacombs; and sometimes in the awful silence of the desert I have heard a lonely camel rider chanting notes which, like drops of water in the tiny stream that eventually swells into a mighty river, have seemed to me

5. St. Ignatius of Loyola (1491–1556) was a Spanish theologian who founded the Society of Jesus (Jesuits) in 1534.

6. Another name for the Gregorian chant.

7. St. Ambrose (Latin: Ambrosius) (339–97) was bishop of Milan and a biblical critic whose ideas about church-state relations made him one of the most important ecclesiastical figures of his time.

8. St. Gregory the Great, also called Saint Gregory I (540–604), was Pope from 590 until his death.

the primal source of the flood of melody I afterwards heard surging through monastic aisles.

A suitable starting point for my journey in search of an ideal was the city of Bruges, founded more than a thousand years ago, with its art treasures, its canals mentioned in Dante's *Inferno*, its love of culture demonstrated by its public monuments, and its picturesque medieval appearance so jealously preserved by its present inhabitants. Only a few miles distant I attended Vespers in the Abbey of Steenbrugge, founded in 1084, destroyed in the French Revolution, and restored in 1879. The far more imposing Abbey of Saint André at Lophem, also in the neighbourhood of Bruges, has a similar history. Founded in 1100, it too was destroyed in the eighteenth century and restored in 1901 for the primary purpose of saving the life of the Benedictine Order in Brazil, which Pedro II[9] had menaced by closing the novitiates. The Brazilian Congregation is now in a flourishing and self-supporting condition. Important missionary work has been carried out from here also in Poland, the Belgian Congo, and China. A former Chinese Minister of External Affairs joined the order, and became eventually an abbot. Exemplifying the Benedictine motto, "*Ora et Labora*,"[10] there is here a large secondary school; the monks publish no fewer than nine reviews; and the sale of their missals, which are known all over the world, provided the funds for building the daringly original modern Church. A striking and deliberate embodiment of the Ultramontane doctrine as opposed to Gallicanism,[11] its walls enclose seven churches in one, representing the seven basilicas of Rome, and specimens of the

9. Pedro II, originally Dom Pedro de Alcântara (1825–91), was the second and final monarch of the Empire of Brazil.

10. [Latin] "pray and labor," usually associated with the *Rule of Saint Benedict*, a book of precepts written by Saint Benedict of Nursia in 516.

11. Ultramontanism (from the Latin *ultramontanus*, "beyond the mountains") in Roman Catholicism put a strong emphasis on the powers of the Pope and on centralization of the church, while Gallicanism, associated with the Church of France (Gallican Church), stressed limitations on papal authority across the wider church.

architecture and religious art of the Christian era from its origin down to the present day. The central chapel, with its high altar dedicated to Saints Peter and Andrew, is in Roman style, its apse richly decorated with frescoes. Saint Sebastian's, reminiscent of the catacombs and containing some of their relics, is identified by the design, in its mosaic pavement, of bows and arrows, the instruments of that saint's martyrdom; while Saint Mary's, with its Byzantine cupola, is dominated by Charlier's[12] fine statue of the Mother of God. Then comes the small chapel representing Santa Croce, externally surmounted by a cross-crowned globe and, in the right aisle, the Romanesque chapel of Saint Lawrence, followed on the left by Saint John's in Gothic and Saint Paul's in the style of the Italian Renaissance. All the chapels are grouped around a platform under an octagonal lantern-tower and, despite the heterogeneous elements of its component parts, the entire church appears a single whole. The eminent quality of the Vespers I heard chanted there deepened the impression it inevitably gives of dignity and magnificence.

The next monastery I visited was Termonde, an ancient foundation, of which the present building, owing to its chequered history, preserves no trace. The only relic of antiquity I saw there was an image of Our Lady made from some of the shattered fragments of the original, which was miraculously associated with Saint Bernard.[13] I was shown a similar statue in Afflighem, which was founded in 1075 by six repentant knights converted by a Benedictine, and which became the mother-house of many monasteries; it acquired so great a reputation for sanctity that when Saint Bernard came there in the twelfth century, he declared he found a community of angels. The old church was destroyed during the French Revolution, but found intact among

12. Guillaume Charlier (1854–1925) was a Belgian sculptor, many of whose works are displayed in the Charlier Museum in the suburbs of Brussels.

13. St. Bernard of Clairvaux (1090–1153) was a major reformer of Benedictine monasticism, founder of the abbey of Clairvaux, and important early influence on the Cistercian order.

the ruins and removed to its successor was the imposing tomb of Eleanor of Brabant, daughter-in-law of William the Conqueror and wife of
Henry I of England.[14]

From the pleasant little town of Dinant, built on both sides of
the Meuse River, I visited the well-known modern Maredsous Abbey,
where Dom Marmion[15] spent much of his life, and wrote many of his
books. The church is Gothic, but with none of the asceticism characteristic of that style; its mellow brick-red columns and walls are covered with frescoes, presumably an attempt to recapture the spirit of
the thirteenth and fourteenth centuries when the churches were the
Bibles of the people. From here was founded the Priory of Glenstal in
Ireland, and Mont César near Louvain, where the first thing I saw was
a specimen of the brilliantly blue morphos butterfly, which advertised
the fact that these monks have missions in Brazil. The abbots had evidently been connoisseurs, judging from their "parlours," which were
full of works of art of various kinds, including some good paintings.
Later, in war-ravaged Louvain, my melancholy mood was somewhat
relieved by finding in the remnant of the ruined cathedral, which is
now used for divine service, a lovely triptych by Dirk Bouts.[16]

Situated on a hill, "far from the madding crowd,"[17] is the Priory of Chevetogne, founded in 1926 to promote reunion with the
eastern churches. Originally a chateau, the architecture is obviously
French, and it contains both Latin and Greek chapels. In the latter is
used the Slavonic rite, the intricacies of which were most interestingly

14. Eleanor of Brabant, better known as Adeliza of Louvain, later Adeliza Louvain of Brabant (ca. 1103–51), was the daughter of Godfrey I, Count of Louvain and
reigned as Queen of England from 1121 to 1135.

15. Columba Marmion (formerly Aloysius Marmion) (1858–1923) was an Irish
Benedictine monk and, from 1909 until his death, the third Abbot of Maredsous
Abbey in Belgium. Many of his books, including *Christ, the Life of the Soul* (1917)
and *Christ in His Mysteries* (1924), are regarded as spiritual masterpieces.

16. Dirk Bouts, also spelled Dieric, Dierick, or Dirck (ca. 1415–75), was a
northern Netherlandish painter about whom very little is known.

17. *Far from the Madding Crowd* (1874) is the fourth novel by Thomas Hardy.

explained to me by an ethereal-looking Australian monk. I had often been in Orthodox Greek churches and was rather surprised to find most of their familiar features in this chapel—the exotic note in the decoration, the massive, lavishly gilded screen, the numerous icons, and the concealed tabernacle, here in the form of a silver dove.

I was now in the country so intimately associated with Saint Hubert, Apostle of the Ardennes,[18] who was born about the middle of the seventh century. It was in this forest, as a pleasure-loving court-ier, he indulged his passion for the chase; and in later life, no less eager in his pursuit of souls, he penetrated its darkest recesses, at great personal risk, to abolish the last lingering vestige of paganism. In the National Gallery in London hangs a picture by the artist known as the Master of Werden,[19] representing the legend of the Saint's conversion. The painter immortalized the moment that the young knight, on a Good Friday, was hunting a stag, when suddenly the animal turned, and the hunter saw a crucifix between its antlers. Renouncing his birthright to the Duchy of Aquitaine, and distributing all his goods to the poor, he became a priest and made a pilgrimage to Rome, dur-ing which the Pope, acting on divine inspiration, appointed him to the See of Maastricht, from which eventually he was translated to become first Bishop of Liège. About a hundred years after his death his body was brought to the Abbey of Amdain, henceforth called Saint Hubert's. It had been founded about 706 for Canons Regular and became Benedictine a century later; but it is now no longer a mon-astery. The Place de l'Abbaye, as the cathedral square is still called, is flanked by private houses, which once formed part of the abbey, and the present church, begun in 1526, is built on the site of several oth-ers and has undergone many alterations; but it still retains traces of its predecessors. The façade belongs so emphatically to the eighteenth century that it is almost bewildering to find a Gothic interior, which,

18. Saint Hubert or Hubertus (ca. 656–727) became Bishop of Liège in 708.

19. The Master of Werden (German: Meister von Werden) is known for four pictures attributed to him in the Abbey of Werden, which are believed to date from the fifteenth century.

however, has no touch of coldness or severity. The delicate pastel tints of natural stone—grey-blue, yellow ochre, burnt umber, muted jade, pale rose—blend harmoniously and shed a warm glow on the slender columns of the spacious nave. But the blatant Renaissance style of the high altar, and two side altars in front of the choir, notwithstanding their many excellent features, conflict so violently with their Gothic setting that they marred for me the harmony of what would otherwise be a beautiful church. Best preserved of the ancient chapels is that of Saint Hubert, with its magnificent altar of carved wood, on which relics are occasionally exposed, the most precious of these being the Holy Stole of the Saint, made of white silk and gold thread, probably woven in the eighth century. The finely sculptured tomb presented by Leopold I[20] is empty, because the body was hidden when the monk departed, and the last abbot died without disclosing the secret of its hiding place.

As one approaches Luxembourg the landscape becomes more severe, until suddenly on a high hill, among dark pinewoods, dominating the narrow valley where the town nestles, the red-tiled roofs, picturesque gables, and soaring spire of Clervaux Abbey seem like a blare of trumpets. At the beginning of the century, a group of monks from Solesmes restored the monastery of Saint Maur, near Angers, one of the oldest in France, but they were soon banished from their country by a hostile government, and the exiles, assisted by wealthy benefactors, founded Clervaux in 1910. Often confused with its celebrated French namesake, the twelfth-century Cistercian Abbey of Saint Bernard, this new foundation developed rapidly, and when Pius XI, continuing the work of his predecessor, wished to establish a monastery in Rome in connection with the revision of the Vulgate, it was to the monks of Clervaux this task was entrusted, and they now occupy the Abbey of Saint Jerome in the neighbourhood of the Vatican. In 1940 the Germans invaded Luxembourg and took possession

---

20. Leopold I (French: Léopold-Georges-Chrétien-Frédéric) (1790–1865) reigned as the first king of the Belgians following the nation's independence in 1830.

of the monastery for nearly five years, during which in an attempt to transform it into a school for Hitler Youth, it underwent a course of systematic mutilation that earned for it the title of the "martyred abbey." When the monks returned in 1945 they found their old home quite unrecognisable, but the Benedictines have always been builders, and, with indomitable courage, they set to work, and now they have restored the huge building, not perhaps to its former glory, but at least they have obliterated all traces of the Nazis' sacrilegious hands.

Crossing the German frontier to the Saar, I visited Tholey, founded in the seventh century, suppressed in the eighteenth, and restored in 1950. Built on the site of a Roman villa, it has an interesting collection of antiquities, amongst them a Gothic *Mona Lisa*, the stone statue of a woman with a fascinating smile. The very modern church has a remarkable carved wooden pulpit resting on the shoulders of an heroic figure in the crouching attitude of Atlas supporting the globe, and with hair and beard even more luxuriant than those of Michelangelo's *Moses*.[21]

A drive through the valley of the Neckar River brought me to the charming little twelfth-century Priory of Neuburg, cradled among trees and looking down along a green gorge to the nearby roofs of Heidelberg. Wandering about this delightful spot, I opened a door in a high wall and found myself in the cemetery. Inevitably my thoughts crept back to the mound of earth, with its primitive wooden cross, that marks the grave of Newman on the lonely hillside of Raynal,[22] for these tombs are far more impressive than his, even in their utter simplicity. Suddenly I was startled by a voice which put an abrupt end to my reverie by politely ordering me to leave the enclosure,

21. Michelangelo Buonarroti, *Moses* (ca. 1515), based on a description in Exodus 34, depicts the biblical figure with a long beard and horns on his head.

22. John Henry Newman (1801–90) was an influential English writer and theologian who became the first rector of the Catholic University in Dublin. He was buried alongside his lifelong friend, Ambrose St. John, in the cemetery at Rednal Hill, Birmingham.

because I stood on forbidden ground. Realising, for the first time, that my interpretation of the word "cloister" had been too narrow, I left reluctantly, filled with resentment against the rule which excluded me so rigorously from those sacred precincts, particularly from the great libraries that are such an essential part of these monasteries, and that often contain many priceless books and manuscripts. To a Benedictine, study and prayer are complementary elements in the act of divine worship, and he approaches his library with a reverence generated by the belief that "when we read God speaks to us, and when we pray we speak to God."[23] In a most unedifying mood I entered the whitewashed chapel, which had all the attractive intimacy of a village church, and my inferiority complex and rebellious emotions vanished completely at the stimulating sight of what seemed to me, in every sense, its dominating feature, an ancient carved stone figure of a mitred abbess, firmly grasping a crozier, the symbol of her authority, and standing rampant on the back of a couchant lion.

Stopping on my way to see the almost incredibly humble birth of the Danube at Donaueschingen, I crossed into Switzerland to visit the Abbey of Einsiedeln, which, like Montserrat, is a popular place of pilgrimage owing to its celebrated shrine of the "Black Virgin." Meinrad, Count of Hohenzollern,[24] seeking a hermitage, came to this locality as the most inaccessible and desolate he could find, his only companions two ravens and a sacred image presented to him by a holy nun. He lived here in peace and poverty, until, in 861, he was murdered by robbers, who thought he possessed hidden treasure. His faithful birds betrayed the murderers by following them to Zurich, shrieking around their heads. An oratory was built above the saint's grave and pious men came to live in the vicinity. Gradually a monastery arose on the spot and, in course of time, the village of the

---

23. The Latin, *"Oras: loqueris ad sponsum; legis: ille tibi loquitur,"* is attributed to St. Jerome.

24. Saint Meinrad, also known as Meinrad of Einsiedeln (ca. 797–861), of the family of the counts of Hohenzollern, was a Benedictine monk who is sometimes referred to as the "Martyr of Hospitality."

present day. In 946 the Bishop of Constance[25] arrived to consecrate the church, but at midnight on the eve he heard there the music and all the offices of the ceremony, and from this legend originated what is known as "the Angelic Consecration," the feast of which is held annually in September, as is also the performance of a mystery play, which attracts spectators from all over the world. Paracelsus[26] was born in the neighbourhood while his father was physician to the monastery, and Zwingli,[27] the founder of the Reformation in Switzerland, who challenged the priority of Luther, preached here for some years. A star of the first magnitude in the Benedictine firmament, Einsiedeln, ever famous for the erudition of its monks, has always fostered the study of music and letters. In the thirteenth century Rudolf of Hapsburg[28] created the abbey and its dependencies an independent principality, over which the Prince Abbot exercised both temporal and spiritual jurisdiction, and this continued until the French Revolution. It has become the mother-house of many American monasteries, which have sprung up in the footsteps of the band of missionaries sent out from it about a hundred years ago to work among native Indian tribes. Fire has repeatedly wrought destruction here, and the present buildings are the sixth or seventh since its foundation, but the venerated image has always been spared and is enthroned in the original little chapel now encased in marble, which stands inside the great church, like the Portiuncula at Assisi, and the Holy House at Loreto. The church has often been rebuilt, the last time in the eighteenth century, and

25. Saint Conrad of Constance (ca. 900–975), son of Count Heinrich of Altdorf and a member of the powerful Welf (Guelph) family, was Bishop of Constance from 934 until his death.

26. Paracelsus, byname of Philippus Aureolus Theophrastus Bombastus von Hohenheim (1493–1541), was a German-Swiss physician, astrologer, and alchemist whose pioneering work established the role of chemistry in medical science.

27. Huldrych Zwingli (1484–1531).

28. Rudolf I (1218–91) was the first German king of the Habsburg dynasty, ruling as Count of Habsburg from about 1240 and King of Germany from 1273 until his death.

the style is pure baroque. An offspring of the Counter-Reformation, fiercely antagonistic to all puritanic gloom, this architecture, in form and colour, in construction and decoration, strives, not merely to be expressive of an exuberant mood, but to be the very embodiment of joy; and this fact alone renders it, in my opinion, an uncongenial setting for Gregorian chant. Sin-stained, repentant man, overwhelmed with gratitude for the tenderness and mercy radiating from the tabernacle, feels himself an alien in surroundings in which there can be but faint echoes of the chant, which is essentially a wail of sorrow welling from a contrite heart. A baroque church is a fitting place of worship only for the Fra Angelicos[29] of life, the lustre of whose faith is never tarnished by doubt or distrust, who never see God as the stern judge, but always as the loving Father, those childlike souls "unspotted from the world,"[30] whom Francis Thompson[31] so beautifully tells us to look for, after death, "in the nurseries of Heaven."

Passing through Schaffhausen, where I lingered beside the Falls of the Rhine, I entered Germany once more and descended the steep side of a wooded valley, in which were situated the vast building of the important Abbey of Beuron, founded in the eighth century, when Saint Boniface[32] was preaching the faith in Bavaria, and destroyed two hundred years later by the Huns. Soon rebuilt, it was occupied by the Canons of Saint Augustine[33] until 1031, when the Benedictine

---

29. Fra Angelico, byname of Guido di Pietro, also called Fra Giovanni da Fiesole and Beato Angelico (ca. 1400–1455), was a celebrated painter of the early Italian Renaissance whose works are distinguished by their serene religious outlook.

30. James 1:27.

31. Francis Thompson (1859–1907) was an English author, mystic, and opium addict. His tombstone is inscribed with the final line of his poem, "To My Godchild" (1891): "Look for me in the nurseries of Heaven."

32. Saint Boniface (Latin: Bonifatius) (ca. 675–754) was born Wynfrid or Wynfrith in Devon, England, and became a central figure in the Anglo-Saxon mission to the Germanic regions of the Frankish Empire. He is often called "the Apostle of Germany."

33. The Augustinian Canons, or Augustin Canons (in full the Canons Regular of Saint Augustine), whose constitution was based on the Rule of St. Augustine, were a Roman Catholic religious order that combined ministry and contemplation.

Rule was revived, and throughout the Middle Ages it was renowned for learning and piety suppressed by the government in 1802; it was finally restored in 1863 by Princess Katherine Hohenzollern[34] and two German Fathers from Saint Paul's in Rome, who had been entrusted by Pope Pius IX[35] with the reestablishment of their order in their native land. The church is baroque, profusely decorated with "Beuron Art,"[36] the product of a school which owes its origin here, in 1880, to an artist who had become a member of the community, and many specimens of which I had already seen at Saint André and Maredsous.

Spending the night in the attractive little town of Sigmaringen, with its ancient houses surmounted by the imposing castle of the prince, where I saw some exquisite tapestries, I stopped at Ravensburg to see Fugel's *Stations of the Cross*,[37] before continuing my journey to Weingarten. The original monastery was destroyed by fire in the eleventh century, but Guelph III of Bavaria,[38] whose descendants are buried here, presented one of his castles to the monks. This was burned several times, but always rebuilt, and, having been suppressed in 1802, it served for a time as a barrack but was restored in 1922. The present church, dating from 1715, and containing a relic of the

34. Princess Katharina of Hohenlohe-Waldenburg-Schillingsfürst (German: Katharina Wilhelmine Maria Josepha, Prinzessin von Hohenlohe-Waldenburg-Schillingsfürst) (1817–93), was the second wife of Charles, prince of Hohenzolern-Sigmaringen. She purchased the former Augustine abbey for the order of Saint Benedict.

35. Pope Pius IX, born Giovanni Maria Mastai Ferretti (1792–1878), was head of the Roman Catholic Church from 1846 until his death.

36. The Beuron Art School was founded by a group of Benedictine monks, including the first abbot of Beuron Archabbey, Maurs Wolter (1825–90), Father Desiderius Lenz (1832–1928), and Gabriel Würger (1829–92).

37. Gebhard Fugel (1863–1939) was a German painter who painted a large number of murals and altarpieces for churches in Germany, Switzerland, Austria, Italy, and the United States.

38. Guelph, also spelled Guelf or Welf, III (ca.1007–55) was Margrave of Verona and Duke of Carinthia from 1047 until his death.

Precious Blood which is carried in an annual procession accompanied by two thousand horsemen, is a brilliant example of baroque. The bold sweep of its arches, its uplifting sense of space, its vibrant vitality, and the Venetian richness of its colouring, all unite to produce an overpowering effect of grandeur and magnificence. "Baroque at its best," commented my monastic guide, but in a coldly critical tone that lacked enthusiasm, and I was about to agree with him, when I was suddenly confronted by the pulpit. In his statue of *Daphne and Apollo*, in the Borghese Gallery in Rome, Bernini, seized by a frenzy for realism, represents the former, in the course of her flight, actually being transformed into a laurel. Similarly in this pulpit, instead of undergoing a gradual process of evolution, baroque flings aside all restraint, wildly leaps over all barriers, and, in a violent paroxysm, becomes rococo. It is as if a hurricane had swept through the church, hurling the various angelic figures, with their swirling draperies, into such precarious attitudes that they seem in imminent danger of crashing down on the heads of the congregation. The colossal angel beneath the rostrum might well be described as hanging on by the skin of his teeth, were it not nearer the truth to say, by the nails of his toes. As evangelical symbols, the ox and the lion are common subjects of ecclesiastical decoration, but here both animals are represented with their mouths wide open, presumably as a stimulant for the preacher. Even now when time and space have tempered the harshness and blunted the edges of crude impressions, it is not the majesty, I might almost say the sublimity, of that stately edifice which haunts my memory but, rather, what made it impossible for me to pray there, the exasperating presence, so audible to my inner ear, of that roaring lion and that bellowing bull.

After a night at Ulm, where I had an unforgettable vision of a floodlighted cathedral with the loftiest spire in the world, I arrived at the Abbey of Neresheim, founded at the end of the eleventh century, suppressed in 1802, and restored in 1920. The church, which recalled that of the great Bavarian monastery of Etta, is a striking monument of baroque; with marble-framed, sculptured backs to the numerous side altars, and a frescoed ceiling reminiscent of Tiepolo.[39] So exultant was the note of joy loudly ringing through its flamboyant interior that it became to me distinctly strident, producing such violent discordance with the chant, that I could appreciate the beautiful Vespers only by closing my eyes. It was as if the "Funeral March" of Chopin[40] were played on an organ simultaneously with a Liszt "Rhapsody"[41] on a violin.

Travelling through open country, with pretty, typical German villages' harvesting scenes and ox-drawn carts, I slipped back to the Middle Ages during a delightful interlude in the enchanting town of Rothenburg and reached the Abbey of Münsterschwarzach, founded in the ninth century, twice suppressed, and, finally restored in 1945. The church, in exceptionally severe Romanesque style, with roughly plastered walls, is quite modern. An enormous copper paschal candlestick, inlaid in brass with scenes from the Old Testament, is the work of one of the brothers, as are also the stone statues on the side altars, among which is a fine Saint Benedict,[42] notable for its serene dignity, with stylised beard and thickly pleated robe, like the famous charioteer at Delphi.[43] Musicians, who are so essential to a Benedictine community, are not the only artists to be found there. Painters, sculptors, wood-carvers, metal workers have all a prominent position, as well as various kinds of skilled artisans; indeed it is common to find, as here, a complete collection of ecclesiastical furniture, the product of

39. Giovanni Battista Tiepolo (1696–1770) was an Italian painter whose luminous ceiling decorations exemplify the lightness and elegance of the rococo style.

40. The third movement of Frédéric Chopin's *Piano Sonata No. 2 in B-flat Minor* was published in 1840.

41. Franz Liszt composed nineteen *Hungarian Rhapsodies* between 1846 and 1853.

42. Saint Benedict of Nursia (Latin: Benedictus Nursiae) (ca. 480–ca. 543) was founder of the Benedictine monastery at Monte Cassino and father of western monasticism.

43. The *Charioteer of Delphi*, also known as *Heniokhos*, a life-sized bronze figure in full-length robes, is regarded as one of the finest examples of ancient Greek statuary.

a labour of love by the monks themselves. Designed deliberately by its architect so that every line of the impressive interior, like each ray in a searchlight, converges directly and is focussed on the huge crucifix suspended above the high altar, this church is an ideal place of prayer for a repentant sinner. Its classic restraint, its stark simplicity, the harmony of its minor key, the absence of garish colours or grotesque forms, all combined to produce for me an overwhelming, but most soothing, contrast to days of undiluted baroque. It was as though I had suddenly entered a land of cool shadows after long exposure to dazzling tropical sunshine; and, in my opinion, its newness alone disqualified this building from being an admirable setting for Gregorian chant.

Driving through the Black Forest I passed castle-crowned Wurzburg, the scene of Saint Norbert's first miracle,[44] and one of the many German cities whose medieval seals are imprinted with the figure of the Irish Saint Kilian,[45] first apostle of Christianity in this region. Still treasured here is a copy of the Bible in Latin, which, according to tradition, was found, about the middle of the eighth century, in the saint's tomb. Arriving in Cologne, I was saddened by the tragic changes wrought by war since I last visited the cathedral, the memory of which, after seeing innumerable examples of the style, I had ever cherished as the greatest Gothic of them all. Hideous modern buildings seemed almost blasphemous in the presence of those wonderful twin towers, and, though the restoration has been most successful, I missed some of the former splendour, sensed a dimness of the ancient glory, and was scarcely cheered by finding there, as at Louvain, a lovely triptych by Stefan Lochner.[46]

My next stop was at the eleventh-century Abbey of Siegburg near Bonn which, like so many of the others, was suppressed under

44. On Easter Sunday 1126, Saint Norbert (1080–1134) restored the sight of a blind woman by breathing on her eyes. The act came to be known as the "Miracle of Wurzburg."

45. Saint Kilian (ca. 640–ca. 689).

46. Stefan Lochner (1410–51) was a German painter recognized as the greatest exemplar of the medieval Cologne School of religious painting.

Napoleon. It was restored in 1914. Situated on the summit of a lofty hill, with the town clustering round its feet, it dominates the surrounding country. The entrance, from a precipitous roadway, through a tree-shaded courtyard, with a beautifully curved outside stone staircase, is most picturesque. The whole structure was extensively bombed during the last war, and the church is now temporarily replaced by a simple chapel. A holy abbot of this monastery was the spiritual director of Saint Norbert after his conversion, and it was here he made a forty days' retreat after ordination to the priesthood before celebrating his first Mass.

Following the Rhine for many miles into a Wagnerian realm of fantasy, I was suddenly awakened from my dreams by an abrupt turn leading to a steep road, which seemed long and lonely in the deepening twilight, until at last I reached Maria Laach, remote, majestic, nestling among densely wooded hills, beside a placid lake. Founded in 1093 by Count Palatine Henry II of Lorraine,[47] who is buried in the Gothic sarcophagus in the west apse of the church, this abbey, despite its turbulent history, has ever remained an abode of learning, a hive of literary and artistic activity. Another victim of the secularising movement of 1802, which paralysed for nearly a century all normal Benedictine life, Maria Laach was occupied for a decade by the Jesuits, but in 1892 reverted once more to its original owner, having been acquired by a group of monks of the Congregation of Beuron. Eager to explore my surroundings, I rose before dawn, and, a short distance from the hostel, I passed under an arch crowned by scarlet geraniums, flowers which I have always associated with Oriel College in Oxford, and which in both places contrasted delightfully with the dark grey stone. Descending a cobbled road I arrived in a courtyard, flanked on one side by some of the main buildings, and on the other by a massive church, which, through some subtle resemblance, recalled my first breathtaking view of that other eleventh-century monastery of Melk,

---

47. Henry of Laach (German: Heinrich von Laach) (1050–95) was the first count palatine of the Rhine and a follower of the Holy Roman Emperor Henry IV.

suddenly towering above my boat on the Danube, and seeming to me, at that moment, the creation of another world, indeed nothing less than Valhalla itself. A flight of shallow steps led me into a small cloister, in the centre of which is a lion fountain reminiscent of the Alhambra, as was also the pale amber-tinted patina of its columns, the whole so flawless a gem that I almost exclaimed aloud at its loveliness. When I entered the church I had again to suppress an exclamation of delight. A Romanesque masterpiece confronted me, so exquisitely proportioned that I sat there, as I had done in the Parthenon at Athens, spellbound by the "frozen music"[48] of its architecture. Here at last was the ideal setting for the plainchant; and later on, during High Mass, I realised that my quest was ended. Soul and body were fused into a complete whole, no jarring note fretted the serenity of the atmosphere; all was harmony even in the most minor details; from the elegant thirteenth-century *baldachino*[49] over the high altar to the smallest statue lovingly carved by monastic hand; from the graceful, delicately synchronised movements of the monks to the mellow lighting of the choir stall by lamps of so unusual a colour that each seemed formed of "one entire and perfect chrysolite."[50]

After Vespers and Compline that evening I remained in the church until slowly, almost imperceptibly, the congregation ebbed away, leaving me alone. With ghostly footsteps a monk glided through the shadows and played the organ so softly that the notes fell tenderly as a caress on those dim-lit aisles. Untrammeled by time, my universe bounded by those ancient walls, my thoughts no longer a flight of wayward birds flouting my will, but caged contentedly in effortless concentration, I lived through one of those "moments eternal" so rare in this mortal life. The world fell from me like a plaything from a tired child, and my soul was filled with the peace that lay on the Sea of

48. "Music is liquid architecture, architecture is frozen music," attributed to Johann Wolfgang von Goethe.

49. A *baldachino*, also spelled *baldachin* or *baldaquin*, is the canopy over a tomb or alter, supported on columns.

50. William Shakespeare, *Othello* (1603), act V, scene 2.

Galilee at the command of the Master. No articulate words passed my lips, but were not the emotions enkindled in that holy place, the spiritual exaltation, the white flame of faith, the rapture of silent worship, the overwhelming sense of gratitude for so priceless a privilege—were not all these the most perfect prayer a weary pilgrim could utter? One by one the lights went out, quenched by an unseen hand, and at last in darkness, guided by the sweet sound of falling water, I groped my way through the cloister. On merging from the gloom, I was dazzled by a sudden flood of glory, as a full moon burst through the clouds, transmuting the granite church towers to silver . . . Next morning, sad and reluctant, I left Maria Laach; but so indelibly etched on my mind is that peaceful sanctuary, where I spent such precious hours, that ever since, in the midst of the turmoil of a great city, I hear again the murmur of that monastery fountain, and the superb chanting of those monks, with a nostalgia poignant as that of the poet Yeats, when, on "pavements grey" he longed for his loved Isle of Innisfree.[51]

51. W. B. Yeats, "The Lake Isle of Innisfree" (1890), line 11.

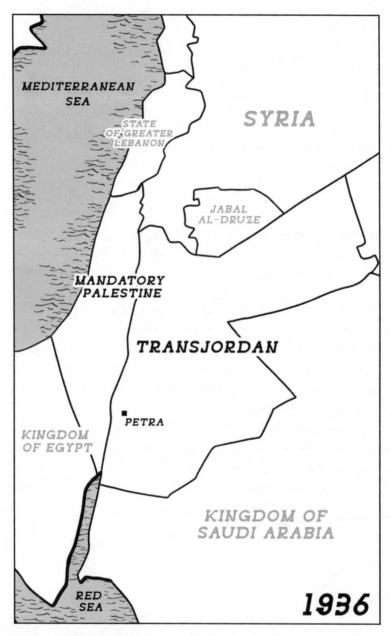

MEDITERRANEAN
SEA

SYRIA

STATE
OF GREATER
LEBANON

JABAL
AL-DRUZE

MANDATORY
PALESTINE

TRANSJORDAN

PETRA

KINGDOM
OF EGYPT

KINGDOM OF
SAUDI ARABIA

RED
SEA

1936

8. Map for Requievi in Petra, Brian Bixby, 2020.

7

Requievi in Petra

The prayer of Isaias "Send forth, O Lord, the lamb, the ruler of the earth, from Petra of the desert, to the mount of the daughter of Sion,"[1] seemed to be fulfilled on that peaceful Easter Monday of 1936, when I set out from Jerusalem on the strenuous two days' journey to what an obscure poet became famous by describing as "the rose-red city half as old as Time."[2] Ascending the lower slopes of Mount Olivet, I was soon surrounded by the wilderness of Judah, the desolation of which became quickly peopled by ghosts of the past, as the pages of sacred and profane history turned slowly and distinctly before my eyes. Passing on the right the Inn of the Good Samaritan, surmounted by the

Published in the 1958 issue of *The Capuchin Annual*, this travelogue tells the story of Murphy's pilgrimage to the Holy Lands in 1936, though "requievi" ([Latin] "I rest" or "I repose") is a misnomer here. Once the center of an Arab Kingdom during the Hellenistic era, the ancient city of Petra lays adjacent to the Valley of Moses in southwest Jordan. But Murphy makes her way to a number of other biblical sites throughout the region, providing her readers with abundant geographical and archaeological details along the way. Although the travelogue is full of allusions to biblical history, putting Murphy's religious learning on display, it also records her awe at encountering these sites in person after so much study. The article concludes with her departure from Jerusalem, but the story of her travels through the Middle East does not end there: rather, "Requievi in Petra" was the first in a trilogy of articles about the region that Murphy would publish in the *Annual*. Reproduced with permission from *The Capuchin Annual*.

1. Isaiah 16:1.
2. John William Burgon, "Petra" (1845), line 14.

ruins of a fortress of the Templars[3] and, on the left, the remains of a Roman aqueduct, I was led by a rapid descent to an immense cleft in the mountain, where, clinging like a bird's nest to the side of the abyss, is the Greek monastery of Koziba, where Saint John the Kozibite[4] lived in the fifth century. Still descending the steep road between tawny, sandstone cliffs, I reached the lowest spot on earth, twelve hundred and ninety-two feet below the Mediterranean, from where the whole valley of the Jordan lay stretched out before me, like a patched and well-worn carpet. Far away, but dominating the scene, is Mount Hermon with its crown of perpetual snow, the site of a temple to Baal, and once believed to be, like Olympus, the seat of the gods. Human history in this area began about 100,000 years ago, when it was the home of prehistoric Palestinian man, whose skeleton was discovered near Mount Carmel in 1932; and the tusks of elephants he hunted have been found along the banks of the Jordan. This turbulent river, one of the swiftest in the world, leaps from a cave at the foot of Hermon, flows across the blue lake of Galilee, burrows through a deep fissure in the earth's crust, and, like a wild animal caught in a trap, frantically twists and turns in numerous whirlpools, rapids, and cascades, until at last, weary and vanquished, it falls into the turbid depths of the Dead Sea. The thicket through which it winds part of its way was known in Biblical times as "the Jungle of the Jordan,"[5] and, though no longer the haunt of lions, as in the days of Jeremiah, it is still the home of jackals, scorpions, vipers, and other exceptionally venomous snakes. Above the salt-saturated waters of the Dead Sea, in which no fish can swim and no flesh can sink, rises the prominent peak from which the dying eyes of Moses gazed on the Promised Land, and on whose slopes lies hidden and unmarked the great patriarch's lonely

3. Templars, also called Knights Templar, were a Catholic military order established during the Crusades in ca. 1119.

4. John of Thebes, canonized as St. John of Choziba or Koziba (ca. 445–ca. 525), was a monk born in Egypt who founded the monastery of St. George of Koziba around 480 and later became bishop of Caesarea.

5. Jeremiah 12:15.

grave. Those silent mountains of Moab, their harshness tempered by the morning mists, once echoed boisterous sounds of revelry, when, among their shadowed folds, Herod feasted and Salome danced, in sight of the hallowed spot where John baptised One "the latchet of Whose shoes he was unworthy to loose."[6]

More than seventy towns, many founded more than five thousand years ago, have been discovered in the Jordan valley, which, in Genesis called "a garden of God," has now degenerated almost into a desert, like Eden and other Biblical sites. Near the southern end of the Dead Sea are some oddly shaped saline formations, one column of which, according to local tradition, is Lot's wife;[7] and in this locality French archaeologists have long searched, without success, for traces of Sodom and Gomorrah.[8] Here too is the place where the ashes of "Dead Sea fruit"[9] are transmuted into gold by the extraction from the water of many minerals and fertilisers that give life to these arid lands. The Egyptians valued highly the asphalt found here for its embalming properties, the word "mummy" being derived from the Arabic name for that substance. On the left of the road rises the Mount of Temptation, its side honeycombed, since the days of the crusaders, with the cells of anchorites, and, in its shadow, the site of ancient Jericho, represented by a mound about seventy feet high, where, as at Ur of the Chaldees, the spade of the archaeologist has forcibly corroborated the pages of the Bible. In the adjoining area, rendered fertile by the still-existing spring purified by Eliseus,[10] many settlements arose, from the Neolithic city, where excavation has resulted in finding even the skulls of some of its inhabitants, to its almost impregnable successor of the Middle Bronze Age, which Abraham may have seen in his wanderings:[11] from the Canaanite stronghold burned by Joshua about

6. John 1:27.
7. Genesis 19:26.
8. Genesis 18–19.
9. Defined as something that appears full of promise but turns out to be rotten.
10. 2 Kings 2:21.
11. Genesis 12:1–9.

1400 BC[12] to the favourite winter residence of Herod the Great,[13] with its splendid public buildings and gardens, which Vespasian[14] and Titus[15] destroyed in the first century of the Christian era. Specimens of the art of the Hyksos period, about 1700 BC, as well as seals bearing the names of their leaders, have been found in the tombs and palace precincts; and from this fact it is believed that Jericho served as a base for the successful invasion of Egypt by these people, to whom is attributed the invention of chariot warfare.

Rapidly turning the leaves of the Old Testament I soon reached the place where the Israelites crossed the now placid Jordan,[16] and the site of their camp in Galgala where Joshua erected twelve stones to mark the scene of the miracle,[17] and where the manna ceased to fall after they had eaten unleavened bread made from the corn of the country. Here again the waters divided to give passage to Elias and Eliseus,[18] and a second time to the latter after the former, leaving his mantle to his disciple, ascended to Heaven in the fiery chariot. Along this route, as do the peasants of the present day in harvest time, went Naomi of Bethlehem with her husband and sons, and returned with Ruth, the faithful Moabite, destined to become the ancestress of the royal house of David.[19] Crossing the Allenby Bridge, I entered Transjordan, which, except for a narrow, fertile fringe beside the river, is mostly a barren land, composed of chalk and sandy soil. The Biblical pageant had passed vividly before my eyes, and then vanished, like a mirage, leaving a landscape empty as a stage after the last act of a

12. Joshua 6:1–27.

13. Herod the Great (74 BCE–4 CE) was a Roman-appointed King of Judaea.

14. Vespian (Latin: Titus Flavius Vespasianus) (9–79) was Roman Emperor from 69 until his death.

15. Titus (Latin: Titus Flavius Caesar Vespasianus Augustus) (39–81), succeeded his father as Roman Emperor in 79 and ruled until his own death two years later.

16. Joshua 3:11–17.

17. Joshua 4:1–11.

18. 2 Kings 2:14.

19. The book of Ruth 1–4.

great drama. Gradually the face of nature became so stern and repellent that it engendered a melancholy which seeped into my very soul, and in a desperate effort to climb out of such a veritable Slough of Despond, I sought in vain for some foothold on those inhospitable heights until, suddenly, like the rosy gleam of a flamingo's wing in the desert, flashed along the roadside for many miles the lovely pink blossoms of the oleander. Buoyant, refreshed, my spirits mounted with the car into a hilly region, where grazing cows, a rare sight in Palestine, green patches of wheat, and the black tents of Kedar, combined to form a picturesque scene on which the customary Arab salute, "Peace be on you," seemed to rest like a benediction. The Bedouin calls his home "the house of hair,"[20] which, made from the shearings of black goats, is the same coarse, prickly stuff as the sackcloth of the Bible and the shirt of the modern saint. Slowly we passed large flocks of sheep and lambs, which, according to oriental usage, are always led but never driven, and the plaintive notes of the shepherds' pipes, falling softly as raindrops on the parched soil, have ever remained for me an abiding memory of all those eastern lands.

Companioned still by the ghosts of the past, I drove through the town of Salt, built in terraces of sand-coloured houses, and reached Amman, where I slept that night in a room facing an almost intact Roman theatre. The Rabbath Ammon of the Bible, called after the son of Lot,[21] progenitor of the Ammonites, it is now the capital of Transjordan. Captured by David,[22] who celebrated his victory by atrocities as great as those of modern times, it was rebuilt by Ptolemy Philadelphus of Egypt, who named it Philadelphia, "the City of Brotherly Love."

Next morning, the beginning of my route lay through cornfields dotted with numerous clumps of purple iris, and then the seemingly interminable desert so overwhelmed me that I felt inclined to sing a

20. Arabic: *bait al-sha'ar*.
21. Genesis 19:37–38.
22. 2 Samuel 12:26–29.

Te Deum[23] at the welcome sight of a little hut occupied by a member
of the Desert Patrol, which, organised by Glubb Pasha,[24] their com-
manding officer, is an aristocratic corps of the famous Arab Legion
founded by Captain Peake.[25] Gladly accepting an invitation to eat my
packed lunch inside, which was impracticable out-of-doors owing to
the gale blowing with a force against which it was impossible to stand,
I recalled an unusual experience I once had of finding myself locked
by mistake within a Carthusian monastery, and realised that the life
of one of these monks is gay and luxurious compared to the stark simplicity and appalling loneliness of my host's existence. The one small
room had no furniture except a camp bed and a stove, the former
being the only seat, and from the latter some cooking utensils were
hastily removed, proving, to my embarrassment, that I had intruded
on the preparation of a meal. Stimulated by such a pleasant reprieve,
I resumed my journey with renewed fortitude, which gradually dwindled as the monotony of mile after mile of the wilderness weighed
heavily upon me, deepening my sympathy with the Israelites who, in
this locality, had murmured against Moses for having brought them
out of Egypt into "this wretched place which cannot be sowed";[26]
and no child of Israel could be more parched with thirst than I when
I eventually reached the rock of Ain Musa, from which the great leader's rod struck the life-saving water.[27] It was from this neighbourhood
too that he sent messengers to the King of Edom asking permission to
pass through his territory,[28] the refusal of which obliged the Chosen

23. [Latin] from its incipit, *Te deum laudamus* ("Thee, O God, we praise"), a
Christian hymn composed during the fourth century.

24. Glubb Pasha, byname of Sir John Bagot Glubb (1897–1986), was a British
army officer who commanded the Arab Legion from 1939 to 1956.

25. Arab Legion (Arabic: *al-Jaysh al-'Arabi*) was a police force formed in 1923
by Lieut. Col. Frederick Gerard Peake, who served with T. E. Lawrence and the Arab
forces in the First World War.

26. Numbers 20:5.

27. Numbers 20:9–11.

28. Numbers 20:14.

People to go round another way and come to Mount Hor, now called Jebel Harun, where Aaron died.[29] All the country between here and Suez is dominated by the personality of Moses, many Arab names and traditions perpetuating the memory of the mighty wonderworker "whom the Lord knew face to face."[30]

At last we arrived in the village of Eljeh—a collection of sordid hovels—where horses awaited us, and, escorted by an armed Arab police officer, my driver, interpreter, and I started on the last lap of our journey. Descending the valley, we followed a rugged trail on which our mounts slipped and stumbled, and where huge rocks of most fantastic shapes rose up menacingly, as if intent on barring our progress. Passing many tombs, the most remarkable of which is embellished by four obelisks, we rode through the dried bed of a river for a considerable distance till we were suddenly confronted by a stupendous cliff, which looked so literally the end of the world that, in the gloom, it seemed to be riven asunder before my eyes, from top to bottom, as by some breathtaking Biblical miracle. Entering this gigantic cleft, so narrow in parts that it might be spanned by a man's outstretched arms, we left the light of day behind us, and I seemed to see those grim portals illuminated by the fiery letters of the infernal inscription, "Abandon hope all ye who enter here."[31] Slowly and cautiously over shelving boulders, which still showed traces of the original pavement, we moved along the dim crevasse, called by the Arabs "El Sik," which, for two miles, at a depth of 1,200 feet, writhes like a colossal snake through that narrow chasm, lighted only by a ragged ribbon of intense blue sky, so far above our heads that, to a watcher on the summit, we seemed mere insects crawling on the bottom of the abyss. It was impossible to see far ahead, because of the numerous twists and turns, and remembering, in my eerie surroundings, a mediaeval torture machine I once saw in a German castle, I imagined myself

29. Numbers 20:22–29.
30. Deuteronomy 34:10.
31. The inscription at the entrance to Hell in Dante Alighieri's *Divine Comedy* (1320).

crushed to death between the stealthily closing jaws of those terrible cliffs, which were suffused with a lurid glow, as if, within their stygian depths, smouldered an unquenchable fire. Gloomier and gloomier grew the rock-strewn way, the hooves of the horses seemed muffled like a funeral drum, the dismal chant of the Bedouin guide was strangled into a heart-piercing wail; stifled by the serpentine folds of that awe-inspiring atmosphere, my other companions had lapsed into an almost tangible silence; and then suddenly, on rounding a corner, a flood of sunshine burst through an opening above, and revealed a vision which, once seen, could never afterwards cease to gild the greyest pages of memory. Carved with mallet and chisel from the towering precipice, the temple of El Khazna, with which I found it impossible to associate long and arduous labour, seemed as though it appeared instantly at the waving of a wand, or at the imperious command of a sorcerer. A work of magic, apparently beyond the power of mere human achievement, its lovely rose-petal colouring merging imperceptibly into highlights of glowing gold and soft purple shadows, its richly sculptured columns, the symphonic harmony of its proportions, the exotic character of its situation, all combine to cast a spell over the spectator, who approaches on tiptoe, hardly daring to breathe, lest the whole ethereal fabric dissolve in the cruel mockery of a dream. Still feeling dazed and overcome by a sense of unreality, I mounted my horse and reluctantly entered once more the sombre canyon; but, like the pillar of fire before the Israelites, my way was now lighted by the never-fading remembrance of that revelation of supreme beauty; and when eventually I emerged, I found myself in the ruins of a city which surely must have been the strangest and most secluded on earth. Hidden deep in the sterile mountains of Arabia, the site of Petra has furnished to archaeologists abundant proof of human habitation in the late Chellian period,[32] millenniums before the dawn of history, but

---

32. Chellian was the name (now antiquated) given by the French anthropologist Louis Laurent Gabriel de Mortillet (1821–98) to the lower Quaternary period in which the earliest human remains are discoverable.

its first recorded appearance is found in the Bible. Who can doubt that the fulminations of Jeremiah, in a paroxysm of righteous anger, were directed against the inhabitants of Petra when he cried out, "Thy arrogance hath deceived thee, and the pride of thy heart. O thou that dwellest in the clefts of the rock, though thou shouldst make thy nest as high as the eagle, I will bring thee down from thence, saith the Lord"?[33] The surrounding country was the Mount Seir of the Old Testament, where Esau dwelt and became the ancestor of the Edomites, who were driven out by the Nabateans, a Bedouin tribe descended from the "wild man," Ishmael.[34] Here these people established their capital which, about 600 BC, became a rich caravan city with extensive trade routes, over which passed the products of many, far-distant lands; and, though raided by Persians, Macedonians, and Romans, who coveted their wealth, the Rockmen, for many centuries, maintained their supremacy, and even extended their territory, as is proved by inscriptions found in the Sinai peninsula. Their prestige was greatly enhanced during the war between Augustus and Mark Anthony, when they completed the overthrow of Cleopatra by destroying the Egyptian Red Sea fleet.[35] Finally, in AD 106, the Emperor Trajan[36] reduced their wonderful metropolis to the status of a Roman province, and for a long time afterwards its flourishing trade continued to pour gold into the gaping coffers of Rome. Then, like another great eastern city, like fabulous Angkor, or the famous fortress of the Incas in the solitary foothills of the Andes, Petra was mysteriously abandoned and forgotten by the outside world for about twelve hundred years. At the

33. Jeremiah 49:16.

34. Genesis 16:12.

35. The last civil war of the Roman Republic (32–30 BCE) pitted Roman military leader and politician, Mark Anthony (83–30 BCE), and the last ruler of the Ptolemaic Kingdom of Egypt, Cleopatra VII Philopator (69–30 BCE), against the Emperor of the Roman Empire, Augustus, also known as Octavian (63 BCE–14 CE).

36. Trajan (53–117) was Roman Emperor from 98 until his death, seeking for much of his reign to extend the boundaries of the empire to the east.

beginning of the nineteenth century it was rediscovered by the Swiss traveller Burckhardt,[37] disguised as a sheik, but he did so at the risk of his life, because by then it had become so sacred to some fanatic Arab sect that death menaced any "infidel" who dared to defile its sanctity. Even at the time of my visit I was allowed to make the journey only under the protection of an armed patrol, and the moment I arrived I was assigned a special bodyguard of two stalwart Bedouins, with a formidable array of knives in their belts and, slung across their shoulders, loaded rifles obviously ready for action.

The ancient city is situated in an oval space more than a mile long, completely encircled by precipices about a thousand feet high, and, though nearly all traces of the buildings that once covered this plain have disappeared, an almost imperishable Petra remains, carved from the solid rock of the rose-red cliffs. The only edifice still standing, the only one constructed entirely of masonry, is a large Roman temple surrounded by great clumps of oleander which grows in profusion throughout the ruins and, pitched amid the pink blossoms, was a cluster of white tents destined to be our domicile in the wilderness. At sight of this camp, a wave of keen disappointment swept over me. The wonderful journey, the thrilling ride through El Sik, the atmosphere of enchantment, the feeling of having left the material world and entered a realm of dreams; and now, after all this, I was doomed to occupy a sleeping-place which I might easily have had in my own garden at home. In as casual a tone as if I required one of the best bedrooms in a hotel, I asked the Arab attendant to show me one of the most comfortable tombs. He looked startled, but immediately conducted me to the foot of a precipice, up which we climbed about thirty feet until we reached a jagged rent leading into a cave, which, when I retired that night, I found furnished with a bed, a chair, a tin basin, a jug of water, and a candle. It seemed an ideal place of residence for a colony of bats,

37. Johann Ludwig Burckhardt (1784–1817) was a Swiss explorer who became the first modern European to visit Petra and to reach the great Egyptian temple at Abu Simbel.

my life-long horror of which has been intensified a hundredfold since I visited the island of Bali, the inhabitants of which believe them to be evil spirits, whom a primitive people's instinctive desire to placate has inspired a temple dedicated to these loathsome creatures, where, like swarms of bees, they hang in thousands suspended from the roof. This was a gruesome memory to haunt me in such weird surroundings, where my candle, unlike Shakespeare's, threw its beams only far enough to accentuate the large area of "darkness visible"[38] that enveloped me closely as a shroud. But nothing whatever ruffled the placidity of my night, except the intermittent howling of jackals in the valley below, and next morning I experienced the most poetic awakening of my life. The sun rose exactly opposite my abode, and the slim fingers of its rays, penetrating through the narrow entrance, touched my face tenderly as a caress. I opened my dazzled eyes, and lay there for some minutes, revelling in my abnormal situation; and then I heard the distant sound of whistling, gradually approaching nearer and nearer, until suddenly, the picturesque figure of an Arab glided gracefully towards me, bearing on his head a pitcher of hot water, an amenity all the more appreciated because so unexpected in a tomb. Like the sun, my attendant had chosen a most charming and soothing substitute for an irritating knock on a closed door. In my unconventional apartment it was not only commendable but absolutely necessary to arise on the right side of the bed, because on the left lurked a sudden and certain death in the abysmal depths of a great gash in the rugged floor, yawning to swallow its unwary victims. Descending from my eyrie to breakfast in the camp, I found my guide and guards ready to escort me on my two days of exploration, which I soon discovered was exceptionally arduous, owing to the fact that the greater part involved much climbing, occasionally so steep that, during the descent, my only foothold was the outstretched palm of one of my companions.

There are altogether about a thousand monuments in Petra, only twenty-five of which were erected after the advent of Greek and

38. John Milton, *Paradise Lost* (1667), book I, line 62.

Roman influence, and of these, the most striking is the fine amphitheatre which provides accommodation for an audience of five thousand, including special seats for the king and his court. The highest of the thirty-three tiers is occupied by a semicircle of tombs, forming part of the strange city of the dead which completely surrounds and dominates that of the living. Like the ancestor worship of the Chinese, there was nothing gloomy or morbid in this curious cult, founded as it was on the belief that after death the soul lingers beside the body, as a sort of guardian angel; so that, working or playing, in peace and in war, the Petreans enjoyed the constant ghostly companionship and protection of their departed families and fellow tribesmen. The decorative value of the natural stone colouring, ranging from pastel shades to those of intense vividness—pink, primrose, mauve, purple, emerald, scarlet, flame—all marbled, striped, or fantastically patterned, renders these burial chambers absolutely unique; producing in them the effect of being hung with priceless tapestries, or curtained with rich silks and gorgeous brocades. Dazzled by the rare beauty and luxurious splendour of those reserved for kings, nobles, and merchant princes, I realised that my own habitation was situated in the plebeian quarter, its Spartan severity proving that its former occupants were mere humble members of the proletariat. In the various architectural styles of these amazing tombs we can read the history of Petra's Golden Age. Here are pylons reminiscent of Egyptian temples, sculptures recalling Persepolis, delicately chiselled capitals whispering of Greece, and majestic columns proudly proclaiming Rome; but here too is something daringly original, something essentially Nabatean,[39] which may, perhaps, be the first sprouting of the creative spirit that blossomed in full flower in the patios of the Alhambra, or in the exquisite mihrab of Cordoba's multipillared mosque.

Scattered all over Petra, near tombs, beside pathways, and in temple niches, just as the cross is placed by Christians, are black monoliths

39. The Nabateans were an ancient people who lived in the southern Levant and northern Arabia.

which are symbols of the sun god, Dusares,[40] whom these people worshipped. The Black Stone of the Kaaba in Mecca, the kissing of which is part of the Mohammedan ritual, is similar to those held sacred by the Petreans which some ancient Semitic tribe long reverenced as the dwellings of deity. A difficult climb leads to the Great High Place of Sacrifice where, on one of the altars, the sacrificial animals were slain, and still plainly visible, is a channel through which the blood was caught and poured as a libation before the image or emblem of the god. The rite of the whole burnt offering was comparatively seldom practised even by the Hebrews of the Old Testament, the victim being usually cooked and eaten at the sanctuary; and this was the universal custom of paganism, exemplified here by the spacious court surrounded by raised seats reserved for those who partook of the feast. Even to this day the Samaritans of Nablus[41] sacrifice the Paschal Lamb on Mount Gerizim, cook and eat the flesh there, and sprinkle the blood on the foreheads of their firstborn and on the doorposts of their tents.

Nearly six hundred feet above the city is the classical temple of Ed Deir, near which are many proofs of its having been formerly much frequented. The Petrean stonecutters worked from the top downwards, without the aid of scaffolding, and the outstanding interest of this monument springs from the fact that it was necessary to remove a whole section of the mountain to create a cliff in which to carve the vast edifice; the large flat space in front demonstrating the extent of the excavation. That it was once used by Christians is suggested by the two red crosses painted on its interior, while another magnificent temple has a Greek inscription of the year AD 447, bearing the name of a bishop. Christianity came to Petra in the fourth century, and a small portion of the ruins is called the Christian Quarter because so many of its dwellings and doors are distinguished by a carved cross. Prominently situated on a ledge of a lofty peak is a still more eloquent

40. Dusares, also spelled Dushara, is a pre-Islamic Arabian god worshipped by the Nabataeans at Petra.

41. A small minority population of Samaritans, descended from Israelites of the Ancient Near East, still inhabit the West Bank city of Nablus today.

testimonial to the extraordinary skill and stamina of the Nabatean workmen, who hewed away the whole solid rock of the summit to leave standing two enormous obelisks facing Mount Hor, where Aaron is buried;[42] and over his grave the Arabs have built a white-domed shrine, so holy that no non-Moslem dare enter or even approach its precincts. Close to the camp was the mysterious columbarium, which consists of two rock-hewn chambers, the walls of which are covered with a network of cavities about ten inches square. It owes its name to its resemblance to ancient Roman burial vaults, but archaeologists have no certain evidence of its sepulchral origin and no reason to believe that the Nabateans cremated their dead.

It was only on my last morning's stroll that I appreciated the fidelity of my bodyguard, which, up to that time, I had strongly resented. Believing that I and my companions were the only human beings in this isolated region, I came, most unexpectedly, on a group of caves occupied by the remnant of a wild, degenerate race, living almost at animal level, who are believed to be the descendants of Israelites abandoned by Moses during his march to the Promised Land.[43] Had I made the acquaintance of such undesirable neighbours soon after my arrival, my rest in the tomb would certainly have been less peaceful. But Petra that morning was indeed the "dove's nest"[44] of the Bible, and nothing dimmed the glorious light of that early dawn, which transmuted every rock and pinnacle into glowing jewels, set in a scene of unearthly beauty that fettered the departing feet of anyone fortunate enough to possess an "Open Sesame" to that enchanted spot.

I rode again through El Sik, and was no longer haunted by jinns and demons, but seemed to hear the sweet tinkling of camel bells, echoed from those far-off days when caravans laden with all the treasures of the East wended their leisurely way along this tortuous ravine. I stopped again at the beautiful temple, where, according to ancient

---

42. Numbers 20:23.
43. Numbers 20:14–20.
44. Jeremiah 48:28.

custom, all wayfarers, before facing the desert, offered prayers for a safe return; and I, for whom there would be no return, tried, with a passionate eagerness, to bring back to the prosaic world of everyday life, the lines and curves, the form and colour, that fused into the perfect poem of that exquisitely carved façade, engraved indelibly on my memory.

Riding once more over the rocky road to Eljeh, where we bade goodbye to horses and guides, we passed the adobe village of Ma'an, surrounded by palms and fig trees, and plunged again into the dreary wilderness with its terrible wind, fierce enough to inspire the punishment of Dante's second circle and sharp enough to pierce like needles into the very marrow of my bones. At last a warm welcome awaited me from the cheerful legionary and the hospitality of his hut, where, as I sat on the hard bed in that bare little room, all the events of the past few days seemed to be transfigured into adventures in the magic land of the *Arabian Nights*. Next morning in Amman I explored some interesting Roman ruins and saw the residence, rather a stately villa than a royal palace, of the Emir Abdullah,[45] who became king in 1946 and was assassinated in 1950 on the steps of a mosque in Jerusalem. Lawrence of Arabia,[46] known only as an archaeologist and classical scholar until he set out to free this land from Turkish domination, fought in the First World War with the future ruler of Transjordan and his brother, Faysal of Iraq,[47] who has been described as the outstanding Arab of recent centuries. The present sovereign, Hussein,[48] while

45. Abdullah I, in full Abdullah I bin Al-Hussein (1882–1951), was the first ruler of the Hashemite Kingdom until his assassination by a Palestinian nationalist on July 20, 1951, a year later than Murphy indicates.

46. Lawrence of Arabia, byname of Thomas Edward Lawrence (1888–1935), famously wrote of these activities in *The Seven Pillars of Wisdom* (1926).

47. Faysal, also spelled Faisal, I (1885–1933), was king of Iraq from 1922 until his death. He became a prominent advocate of Arab nationalism during the First World War.

48. Hussein bin Talal (1935–99) was a member of the Hashemite dynasty who reigned as king of Jordan from 1952 until his death.

a student at Harrow, was called to the throne by the abdication of his
father after a brief reign, and already, despite his youth, shows signs of
having inherited the moral strength characteristic of his family.

Palestine had been for so long a highway on the caravan route
between its neighbouring countries and the Far East that the realisation by the Romans of the need for public security is testified by
a long line of strongholds built to protect their frontiers. Amongst
these is Jerash, formerly called Gerasa, an important member of the
Decapolis, a league of ten cities with Graeco-Roman culture; and, as
the ruins of this interesting place lay not very far from the direct route,
I decided to make this detour on my return journey. In doing so, the
desert soon became a nebulous memory, as we entered a land of milk
and honey, shaded by olive trees and evergreen oaks, vivified by the
flight of birds, some of quite unknown species, and carpeted with an
abundance of wild flowers. Descending a steep road, we arrived at the
ford of Jeboc, where Jacob met Esau and wrestled with the angel;[49]
and then ascending on the other side of the river, we soon reached our
destination. Under an imposing triumphal arch, an avenue bordered
by sumptuous mausoleums leads to the city gates where, outside the
walls, is an immense stadium in which horse races once took place, but
which could be flooded for the miniature naval battles so dear to the
Roman populace. Near the entrance are the well-preserved remains of
the Forum, and on every side rise ruins of magnificent buildings, temples, theatres, fountains, public baths, and among these relics of pagan
times, two Byzantine churches. In Jerash I was impressed by evidence
of a refined simplicity of taste, an elegance, an ethereal quality, a joyous
and serene atmosphere, entirely lacking in other ancient Roman cities;
an effect partly, if not wholly, attributable to the exceptional number of
columns, crowned by Corinthian or Ionic capitals, which is so striking
a feature of the place that I still cherish a memory, clear-cut as a cameo,
of one long sunlit street lined with exquisitely proportioned pillars,
white against an azure sky, lovely and graceful as lilies.

49. Genesis 32:22–32.

Once more regaining the main road, I commenced the final stage of my journey. Along this historic route had marched the armies of many nations: Assyrians, Babylonians, Egyptians, Israelites, Greeks, Romans, Moslems, conquerors and invaders, Alexander the Great[50] and Allenby.[51] Here, too, had passed the greatest Conqueror of all, Whose kingdom was not of this world, and Whose footsteps I followed, as He went for the last time from beyond the Jordan to Jerusalem and the Cross of Calvary. Somewhere here the rich man, so eager to attain perfection but barred by his great possessions, turned sadly away; nearby grew the sycamore from which Zaccheus "made haste to come down"[52] to receive his divine Guest; and further on, by the roadside, sat the beggar, Bartimeus, whose persistent begging brought light to his darkened eyes, because "his faith hath made him whole."[53]

After leaving palm-shaded modern Jericho, the Dead Sea, sizzling under a pitiless sun, lay on my left; and, on its northern shore, deep in shadow, rise pitch-dark cliffs, punctured by numerous caves in which were hidden the famous scrolls found in 1947, and the still more sensational discovery in 1952 of Hebrew manuscripts inscribed on strips of copper,[54] so precious that no archaeologist for years dared, by unrolling them, to risk their damage or destruction. Mounting ever higher from this desolate plain, the way is soon shut in between grim precipices and meanders for miles through the barren hills of Judah, then so infested by robbers that a traveller, as in the time of the New Testament, was still in danger of falling among thieves.

50. Alexander the Great, also known as Alexander III or Alexander of Macedonia (356–323 BCE), was conqueror of the Persian empire and king of the ancient Greek kingdom of Macedonia from 336 BCE until this death.

51. Edmund Henry Hynman Allenby, 1st Viscount Allenby (1861–1936), was a British field marshal who directed the Palestine campaign in the First World War.

52. Luke 19:5.

53. Luke 17:19.

54. The Dead Sea Scrolls, ancient Hebrew manuscripts written on parchment and papyrus, were first discovered in a cave on the northwestern shore of the Dead Sea. Subsequent excavations unearthed the Copper Scrolls in another cave near Khirbet Qumran.

On my last day in Jerusalem I made a farewell pilgrimage to the holy places before lingering to admire once more the marvelous dome of the Mosque of Omar, which seems a colossal jewel, a masterpiece created by magic, like the Petrean temple; an iridescent bubble blown by a Titan rather than the product of human hands. Standing beside an adjoining wall, I looked down at the Valley of Josaphat, and, from its serried ranks of Jewish tombs, my eyes were drawn, as by a magnet, to a spot directly beneath me, where I seemed to see a majestic Figure crossing the Cedron, and, with unfaltering steps, ascending to the Garden of Gethsemane for His lonely night of agony.[55]

Early next morning, on the summit of Mount Scopas, where the army of Titus once camped, I stopped the car to get a parting glimpse of Jerusalem, recalling inevitably the touching Gospel story of how Jesus wept when contemplating the same scene. I, too, would weep could I have known that this was the last peaceful day the sacred place was destined to enjoy for many unhappy years. A British Commission sent to Palestine in 1936 had recommended a drastic partition of the country, which involved the separation of farmers from their fields, orange growers from their groves, and villagers from their wells; and to this arrangement both parties were naturally antagonistic. On the very morrow of my departure, fierce riots broke out to usher in the long war between the Jews and Arabs, which, culminating in a reign of terror, reached its apex of horror in 1948,[56] when screaming bombs shattered the joyous bells that heralded the Resurrection, and the glory of Easter was tarnished by the stain of blood. Never since then has the message of the angels at Bethlehem found an echo in the hearts of its inhabitants, nor the dove of peace a resting-place in the hostile atmosphere of the Holy Land.

55. Mark 14:31; Matthew 26:36; John 18:1.
56. The First Arab-Israeli War began immediately following the end of the British Mandate for Palestine on May 14, 1948, when a military coalition of five Arab nations invaded the territory of Palestine.

BLACK
SEA

USSR

TURKEY

PERSIA

SYRIA

BAGHDAD

IRAQ

JABAL
AL-DRUZE

TRANSJORDAN

KINGDOM OF
SAUDI ARABIA

RED
SEA

1936

9. Map for An Eyeful of Iraq, Brian Bixby, 2020.

8

An Eyeful of Iraq

Like the response of an orchestra to the first beat of a conductor's baton, the moment the rays of the rising sun dropped on the stillness of a newborn day, loud calls to prayer rang out simultaneously from all the minarets of Damascus, stimulating me as I started on the lonely road to Baghdad. Meandering for a considerable distance along the fringes of the city, I bathed my eyes in the intensely vivid green of its gardens to strengthen my sight for many weeks of wandering through some of the most arid regions of the globe. Suddenly the car swerved to the right, and, with startling abruptness, plunged into the desert, our caterpillar wheels clinging desperately to the faint tracks other wayfarers had left in the sand. The spirit of adventure, which for some time had burned fiercely within me, gradually smouldered as the seconds crawled into minutes and the minutes into hours, but it was never wholly extinguished during the 538 miles of that memorable journey. Steadily we travelled over an illimitable plain without making

The second in Murphy's trilogy of travelogues about the Middle East, "An Eyeful of Iraq," was published in *The Capuchin Annual* for 1959. This installment finds the Irish traveler driving long hours through sparsely populated expanses of desert, which severely test her sense of daring. But Murphy keeps that adventurousness alive, and works to stimulate it in her readers, with attention to the potential dangers to the contemporary traveler, as well as to the age-old romance of the *Arabian Nights*. In doing so, Murphy adopts a series of common orientalist tropes, portraying her surroundings as exotic, colorful, sensual, somehow fixed in time; but she also displays her detailed historical and archeological knowledge of the region as she adds to her extensive itinerary of biblical sites. Reproduced with permission from *The Capuchin Annual*.

any apparent progress. For the greater part of the way no living thing
cast a shadow on the awful solitude; no sound fretted even the surface
of a silence, deep as that of the world before the creation of life. Occasionally a string of camels, or an isolated rider was etched against a
nebulous background, always so distant that they seemed to traverse
the sky rather than the land. At last the monotony was shattered, as by
a trumpet-blast, when the setting sun split the very atom of colour,
and all the shades of the spectrum, with their innumerable gradations,
flooded the pallid earth. Then, as at the close of a magnificently staged
drama, a thick curtain fell on the apocalyptic scene, and, in the cool
companionship of night, we arrived at Rutba Wells. Here, two hundred miles from anywhere, the resting place of caravans since time
immemorial, we had a short pause for dinner; and when we emerged
beneath myriads of stars glittering with unusual brilliance, the large
block of buildings, which in daylight was probably ugly and commonplace, assumed the glamour of an enchanted castle, where I longed to
linger, even under a spell. A nocturnal crossing of the desert bears a
strong resemblance to a voyage at sea. Dwarfed to the dimensions of
an insect by boundless space, the big car lurched and rolled, sand was
churned against the windows like spray, and, after some time, the
similarity grew so great that we seemed to be floundering helplessly
amid mountainous waves. A stertorous chant reverberated from the
seven men of various nationalities who were my fellow passengers, but
for me the exotic nature of my surroundings effectively murdered
sleep. In the midst of dunes, which we were taking in our stride with
a sickening switchback motion, so obviously were we revolving in cir-
cles that, with a pang of terror, I realised our driver had lost the way.
Becoming still more panic-stricken at the sight of a cluster of black
tents, thrown into relief by flickering camp fires, I recalled having read
that this particular part of the route had once been so dangerous that
many travellers had met a tragic fate here at the hands of hostile Bedouins. With raucous cries and wild gesticulations, tall draped figures,
carrying lanterns, rapidly approached, and, coward that I am, this was
one of the many times I died before my death. Soon, however, my
fears dissolved under the glow of friendly faces, and expert guides, full

of pity for our plight, conducted us back to the trail from which we had widely wandered. My companions speedily resumed their interrupted slumber, but I remained abnormally wakeful until we reached Ramadi, the frontier of Mesopotamia, now called Iraq, where we were welcomed by a dawn which seemed to me a mirage, because of its breathtaking beauty. After a delay at the customs-post for a prolonged scrutiny, we crossed the Euphrates, a broad river with a swift current that reminded me of the "arrowy Rhône,"[1] and continued through the desert, until at last, at the end of twenty-six hours, we arrived at our destination. I remembered distinctly how I had trembled with excitement when I first saw the distant lights of Rome; the enthusiasm that swept through me like a flame when my boat rounded a Grecian promontory and I glimpsed the Acropolis of Athens; how Constantinople, flushed with the splendour of sunset, seemed to me a supernatural vision; and the feeling of unreality that thrilled me as my train glided slowly past the walls of Pekin. But now I might have been a robot for all the emotion I felt, except an acute sense of isolation of which I had never before been conscious, even in my tomb at Petra, or in my shack in the jungle of Peru. Where was the magic city so familiar since childhood, the scene that inspired the tales of Sheherezade[2] and the midnight rambles of Harun al-Rashid? Where was the great metropolis of the Arabian Empire which, from the ninth to the twelfth centuries, flourished as one of the world's most famous citadels of learning? Through what streets had strolled the philosophers who had exercised so profound and enduring an influence on European thought? Where were the homes of those scholars who, when a knowledge of Greek had almost vanished from the West, had translated Plato and Aristotle into Latin[3] and thus supplied themes for the

---

1. Lord Byron (George Gordon), *Childe Harold's Pilgrimage* (1812–18), Canto the Third, LXXI, line 3: "By the blue rushing of the arrowy Rhône."

2. Sheherezade, also spelled Scheherazade, is an important female character and narrator of the *Arabian Nights*.

3. Texts by Plato (ca. 428–348 BCE) and Aristotle (384–22 BCE) were translated into Arabic and then, beginning in the fourteenth century, into Latin.

disputations of medieval thinkers and textbooks for the pupils of Duns Scotus[4] and Saint Thomas?[5] Disillusion coiled round me with its serpentine folds, and I sauntered along the two-mile main street, where everything seemed shabby and sordid, in a mood of the deepest depression. Dodging buckets of water flung on the pavement by street-cleaners, utterly oblivious of passing pedestrians; narrowly escaping collision with Kurdish porters staggering under burdens, ranging from grand pianos to four-poster beds; picking my steps through the overflow from densely crowded coffee-shops, in which outsized Victorian sofas furnished seating accommodation, I at length found myself facing a signpost pointing the way to a Catholic church. Following this, I soon gazed incredulously at my surroundings, where, with bewildering abruptness, I was swept back to the age of the *Arabian Nights*, as Baghdad, like a beautiful Mohammedan maiden, dropped her veil, and revealed to me an indescribable charm, which has never been effaced from my memory. Wandering through a labyrinth of narrow, cobbled streets, redolent of romance and mystery, their houses painted in various pastel shades, dark eyes peering through overhanging latticed windows, I followed the footsteps of the adventurous caliph through scenes which must still be haunted by his ghost. On a flat roof a slender woman in a saffron-yellow dress stood motionless against an azure sky; a group of girls in rose and jade-green frocks chatted with a man in the flowing robes of a Bedouin; a gaily caparisoned milk-white mule, laden with orange bricks, jostled a stately Jewess in Tyrian purple, who raised a visor like that of an ancient knight, to return my friendly stare; and round every corner I met women wearing the lovely garment known as the "izzar," which transformed them into living flowers. Plunging into the depths of the dimly lit bazaars, I stopped before a veritable forge of Vulcan, watching the coppersmiths hammering and burnishing their vessels, some of which

4. Blessed John Duns Scotus, byname Doctor Subtilis (1266–1308), Scottish philosopher, Franciscan friar, university professor, and Catholic theologian.

5. St. Thomas Aquinas, byname Doctor Angelicus (ca. 1225–74), was an Italian Dominican theologian and the foremost medieval Scholastic.

were capacious enough to conceal the portly forms of the Forty Thieves.[6] In these tortuous arcades I met familiar figures at every turn, from rich merchants and proud viziers to carpet-weavers loudly proclaiming their wares and whining beggars bewailing their woes; from an Aladdin grown wistful without his wonderful lamp[7] to a radiant Sindbad rid of his intolerable load.[8] Extricating myself with difficulty from this picturesque throng, I passed to the silent precincts of a mosque belonging to the Sunnite sect of Moslems, which contained the tomb of Abdul Kadir, who lectured in the schools in the fifteenth century and was renowned for his learning and sanctity. In a street unchanged by modern life I lingered in the workshops of the Amarna silversmiths, who claim relationship to Saint John the Baptist. Members of a guild as old as Nebuchodonosor,[9] they possess a secret process for engraving hand-beaten silver, the key to which was probably the primitive electric battery found in recent excavations, and which was used for gilding by Arabian jewellers nearly two thousand years before electrolysis was rediscovered by Galvani.[10] Towards sunset I crossed the pontoon bridge named after Sir Stanley Maude,[11] who commanded the British forces when they arrived here in 1917, and I found this such an interesting experience that afterwards it became a daily habit. To and from in endless procession passed people of all nations, creeds, and classes; desert nomads and dwellers in palatial

6. From "Ali Baba and the Forty Thieves," one of the tales that comprises the *Arabian Nights.*

7. Aladdin, a protagonist in the *Arabian Nights*, temporarily loses his magic lamp and its wish-granting genie to an evil sorcerer.

8. Sinbad, or Sindbad, the Sailor, is a hero in the *Arabian Nights*, whose story opens when a poor porter, also named Sinbad, rests his heavy load to listen to the tale of how the rich Sinbad became wealthy during his seven wondrous voyages.

9. Nabuchodonosor, or Nebuchadnezzar, II (ca. 634–ca. 562 BCE), was the king of the second Babylonian Empire from 605 until his death. He is portrayed in several books of the Old Testament.

10. Luigi Galvani (1737–98) was an Italian physician, biologist, and physicist who made early advances in the study of electricity.

11. Lieutenant General Sir Frederick Stanley Maude (1864–1917).

homes; a sheik mounted on a restive Arab steed swerved to avoid the Greek patriarch in his gorgeous raiment; scantily clad coolies collided with resplendent figures in rainbow-tinted silks; veiled women in garments black as night accentuated others clothed in the radiance of dawn; complexions dark as ebony or delicate as magnolia petals; water-sellers straight from the pages of the Bible; schoolchildren in charge of white-coifed Sisters of Charity; camels, donkeys, goats—all fused into a riot of colour and movement to dazzle the eyes of a painter and drive him to fling down his palette in despair. As if by a wizard's wand, everything squalid and commonplace was banished, and, though few traces of its former glory remained, Baghdad, at that hour, became an enchanted city. I had secured a room in a hotel which, though primitive according to European standards, won a lasting place in my heart when luxurious establishments are long forgotten. Its many defects were, in my opinion, amply atoned for by the fact that it possessed, on the bank of the river, a few palm trees and a patch of anaemic grass, which, though completely devoid of flowers, rejoiced in the courtesy title of "garden." From my apartment, monastic in its austerity, an outside staircase led to this spot, and, after the heat of the day, I used to relax in a deck chair, greeted by the croaking of frogs, and occasionally disturbed by a flight of locusts, and enjoy many delightful hours beside the moonlit Tigris. Every night I was companioned by an abnormally patient fisherman anchored in a diminutive gufa, which claims to be the oldest form of boat in existence. Described by Herodotus,[12] and illustrated on ancient Assyrian monuments, this perfectly round, flat-bottomed, wicker-work coracle, coated with bitumen, ranges in size from the diameter of a clothes-basket to the dimensions of a Noah's ark, which is believed to have been merely a roofed specimen of this strange craft.

Accustomed as I had been in other countries to enter mosques freely and frequently, I found the refusal to admit "infidels" to those

12. Herodotus (ca. 484–ca. 425 BCE) was a historian known for *The Histories*, a detailed inquiry into the origins of the Greco-Persian Wars.

of Iraq a keen disappointment, all the more so as their exteriors were so attractive, with their turquoise-blue cupolas always dappled with snow-white doves. But when I visited Kadamain, with its twin domes sheathed in pure gold and its four gleaming minarets, I felt like a peri outside the gate of Paradise. Controlled by the fanatic Shia sect, the place was too dangerous to approach alone, and I took the precaution of going there under the protection of an armed policeman and a native, who conducted me to the verandah of an adjoining house, from which there was an excellent view of the whole building. I walked round the walls and peeped furtively into the spacious courtyard through the four open gates, barred by massive looped chains, brightly polished by the kisses of the faithful. The principal entrance, from the threshold of which I kept a respectful distance, was embellished with crystal stucco work, and the piers encased in iridescent tiles. The whole formed a magnificent shrine for the silver mausoleum of two saintly Imams, descended from the family of the Prophet, who were buried here in the ninth century and were still so venerated that thousands of pilgrims came on foot from the most remote parts of Asia to offer prayers beside their tomb.

From this splendid embodiment of permanence and vitality I went to the opposite extreme by visiting the ruins of Ctesiphon, standing gaunt and clear-cut against the desert, visible for many miles in all their tragic grandeur. The wealth and luxury of this proud capital of the Parthian Empire,[13] Rome's powerful Asiatic rival, tempted the cupidity of Roman emperors for centuries. Trajan, Severus, Caracalla, Caius, Julian,[14] and eventually Saad,[15] the Islamic conqueror, plundered its treasures and carried off rich booty; vast quantities of jewels and gold, from the king's throne to the contents of his armoury, all wrought from the precious metal. Part of the main façade and

13. The Parthian Empire, also known as the Arsacid Empire (247 BCE–224 CE), was the foremost political power in ancient Iran.

14. Roman emperors who ruled between 12 and 363.

15. Sa'd ibn Abi Waqqas (595–674) was one of Mohammed's companions, best known for his leadership in the conquest of Persia in 636.

the famous arch alone remain to testify to the beauty of the White Palace, which was the pearl of Sassanian architecture, and was built in the sixth century by Chosroes I.[16] As I stood beside the mighty structure, trying to imagine the pompous scenes of bygone days, the flowers and fountains, the temples and monuments that once transformed this terrible wilderness, a shade of melancholy seeped through my thoughts and became articulate, as softly, through my dreams of the past, trickled an eerie sound. It resembled the drowsy murmuring of a bee on a summer afternoon, but, instead of a mean-ingless drone, it took the form of a sweet melody, infinitely plain-tive, quite unlike anything I had ever heard. For some time I failed even to locate it and could hardly believe in its reality. Then I saw a shepherd squatted in an obscure corner, playing a primitive instru-ment made of sheepskin, with strings of asses' hair and a bow like a violin. That strange, sad music still lingers in my memory as the voice of the desolate city lamenting its long-lost glory. The demolition of one wing of the hall provided material to build a neighbouring vil-lage, which contains a mosque where the barber of Mohammed is buried;[17] and farther on, at Lancashire Bridge, is a memorial to the soldier of the regiment of that name who fought a battle there in 1917. Situated on the bank of the river opposite Ctesiphon is the site of Seleucia, founded by one of the generals of Alexander the Great, but it has never been excavated. Driving along a road bordered with oleanders in full bloom, I raced the setting sun to avoid getting into trouble with the police for failing to complete my journey before sunset. The Iraq government disapproved of lone ladies travelling outside the city's orbit; and, with a paternal solicitude for my welfare,

16. Khosrow, also spelled Khosrau, Khusro, or Husraw, I, byname Khosrow of the Immortal Soul (died 579), was a generous patron of the arts and sciences, as well as ruler of the Sasanian empire from 531 until his death.

17. The village of Soleiman-Pak ([Persian] "Solomon the Pure") is named for the companion and private barber of the prophet Mohammed, also known as Salman al-Farsi ([Persian] "Salman the Persian").

subjected me to all sorts of rules and regulations. To attain the honourable status of being "accompanied," it was essential for me to have as fellow traveller "a European or American member of the male sex." For obvious reasons this was impossible, and my only companion on my trips from Baghdad was Abraham, my excellent Arab chauffeur, who proved a tower of strength in all emergencies, but whose "too, too solid flesh" unfortunately melted in my company, rendering him officially invisible. Consequently I had to promise "to keep in close touch with the British Administrative Inspector, and to accept the advice of any responsible government authority in regard to my movements."

Early next morning, in a state of tense excitement, I started for Babylon. Literally a name to conjure with; of all the cities of remote antiquity this stands supreme in its power to evoke the grandeur of a past civilisation. The book of Genesis records it earliest history when the "mighty hunter," Nimrod, went forth to "the land of Shinar,"[18] which was Sumeria, later called Babylonia, and there founded the capital of his kingdom. In the long struggle for supremacy between Babylonia and Assyria, so complete was the destruction of the city by Sennacherib[19] in the seventh century BC that almost every brick found in the ruins of the present day is inscribed with the name of Nebuchodonosor. One of the greatest builders of all time, the conqueror of Jerusalem who led the Jews into captivity, he was a comparatively modern ruler of a metropolis noted for learning and culture in 2200 BC, in the reign of Hammurabi,[20] the famous law-giver. Herodotus visited the place in the fifth century, and from him and

18. Genesis 10:9–10.

19. Sennacherib, Akkadian Sin-akhkheeriba (died 681 BCE), was king of Assyria from 705 BCE until his death. He made Nineveh his capital, built a palace there, and greatly expanded the city.

20. Hammurabi, also spelled Hammurapi (died ca. 1750 BCE), ruled the Amorite dynasty of Babylon from ca. 1792 BCE until his death. He is remembered for his law decrees, once considered the oldest in human history.

other classical writers, such as Pliny[21] and Strabo,[22] we get descriptions of its wealth and magnificence, and learn that its walls were three hundred feet high, eighty-seven feet thick, were crowned by two hundred and fifty fortified towers, and, like Thebes, had a hundred brazen gates. Captured by Alexander the Great, who died there, little of the city remained towards the beginning of the Christian era, and what "hath been a golden cup in the hand of the Lord"[23] was shattered, and the doom, prophesied by Jerenuah and Isaias, fulfilled. The site, though never lost, degenerated into a vast, chaotic mass of mounds and ditches, where all that appeared above ground was the roughly blocked basalt statue of a lion mauling the prostrate figure of a man, which is believed to be a Hittite war trophy. Unlike the Assyrians, the Babylonians, owing to lack of stone, were obliged to build their cities almost entirely of mud-brick, either sun-dried or burned, a fact which rendered the task of excavating such places slow and laborious, because of the difficulty of distinguishing ruined walls from the surrounding earth. Several archaeologists, when faced with this problem at Babylon, abandoned the attempt in despair, but in the early years of this century it was undertaken by a group of Germans, led by Professor Koldewey,[24] and accomplished with such efficiency that all the chief monuments of Nebuchodonosor's capital were discovered, with little doubt of their identity, so convincing was the evidence revealed by the spade. In abysmal silence, feeling myself an intruder in a world of shadows, I wandered along the Sacred Way, where the solid

---

21. Pliny the Elder, Latin in full Gaius Plinius Secundus (23–79), was an ancient Roman nobleman, historian, and author of the celebrated *Naturalis Historia* (*Pliny's Natural History*).

22. Strabo (ca. 64 BCE–21) was an ancient Greek geographer and historian, whose *Geography* provides an account of the peoples and countries known to Greek civilization during the period.

23. Jeremiah 51:7.

24. Robert Johann Koldewey (1855–1925) was a German architect and archaeologist who is best remembered for his meticulous excavation of Babylon.

gold image of the god, Marduk,[25] had once been borne in procession "to the sound of the trumpet, the flute, the harp, the sackbut and the psaltery."[26] Passing through the Gate of Ishtar, decorated with coloured reliefs of animals on enamelled tiles, an art in which the Babylonians excelled, I entered the banqueting hall of the palace, where Balthasar quailed before the writing on the wall,[27] and stood beside the foundations of the Tower of Babel, striving to imagine that gigantic eight-tiered structure "reaching unto Heaven."[28] The hanging garden which had consisted of a series of balconies, diminishing in size as they mounted to a height of 350 feet, planted with rare trees and flowers, were irrigated by an ingenious method, the discovery of which provided a key to the identification of the ruins. Finally, I climbed to the summit of the mound on which had been lighted the funeral pyre of Hephaistion,[29] Alexander's young friend, traces of which still remained, and the flames of which, reflected in the Euphrates, must have been visible for miles. Descending from this lofty perch, I was lured into a network of narrow passages, and it was while exploring these that an oft-expressed wish of mine was most literally realised, when the earth did indeed open and swallowed me. I walked across an apparently solid patch of ground which suddenly collapsed in the middle, leaving me trapped exactly like a wild elephant captured by a hunter. Fortunately the local guide saw me disappear and hastened to rescue me, none the worse for my unique accident. Of the many things associated in my mind with Babylon, the only one I failed to find was the lion's den, and I like to think that my mishap may have occurred on the very site of Daniel's ordeal.[30] During the years following the

25. Marduk was the chief god of the city of Babylon in Mesopotamian religion.

26. Daniel 3:5.

27. Daniel 5:7–17.

28. Genesis 11:4.

29. Hephaestion (ca. 356–324 BCE) was a Macedonian aristocrat and a general in the army of Alexander the Great, who was devastated by the king's sudden death.

30. Daniel 6.

departure of the Germans, the whole area gradually lapsed into its former condition, and I now appreciate the inestimable privilege of having witnessed its brief but wonderful resurrection.

Rapidly turning back the pages of history, my next excursion was made to Kish, which Professor Langdon,[31] its excavator, has proved to be at least seven thousand years old. Of outstanding military and political importance, it was for centuries a great religious centre and was the original capital of the Sumerian people, who brought to Mesopotamia a civilisation, the earliest of which we have historical knowledge, and a culture, dating from before 3000 BCE, which has been compared to that of Athens in the age of Pericles.[32] In architecture they have given us the arch, the vault, and the dome; and the influence of their art, which was at its zenith in the fourth millennium BC, has flowed through Assyrian, Phoenician, and Cretan channel until, in its full vigour, it reached as far as the frieze of the Parthenon. Their army was invincible because of the superiority of their weapons, their organisation, and methods of warfare; and it was from them that Alexander the Great borrowed the phalanx which made him conqueror of the world. Credited with being the inventors of writing, their cuneiform tablets predating Egyptian hieroglyphics, they discovered the use of the wheel, and the oldest two- and four-wheeled vehicles were found in the tombs of Kish. This mysterious race, whose origin is unknown, is believed to have migrated from mountainous country into the plains of Iraq, and, growing weary of the flat monotony of their environment, they erected artificial hills called ziggurats to replace the sacred mounts, or "high places," on which they had been accustomed to worship their gods. I first saw one of these at Borsippa, near Babylon, and, as it was covered with vegetation, I mistook it for a work of nature, until, on a closer survey, a gash in one side

31. Stephen Herbert Langdon (1876–1937) was a professor of Assyriology at Oxford University who carried out excavations at Kish between 1923 and 1933.

32. Pericles (ca. 495–429 BCE) was an influential Greek statesman responsible for the Golden Age of Athens, when the city became the cultural, military, and political center of Greece.

betrayed the underlying brick. These primitive structures developed later into massive multistaged towers, of which that of Babel was the most celebrated example; and this yearning for height, characteristic of mankind, finds material expression, not only in the architecture of the Sumerians, but in the Gothic spires of the Middle Ages, and in the skyscrapers of the present day. Excavated at Kish are abundant remains of many temples, chiefly dedicated to Ishtar, goddess of love and war; ramparts and fortifications; and an enormous palace, a fragment of whose richly decorated walls, inlaid with mother-of-pearl, is preserved in the museum of Baghdad. So remote and isolated is this once superb city, and so impossible is it to approach by car, that I was obliged to finish my journey there on foot. Entering through what seemed a stupendous gate, leading to a maze of narrow streets, I was immediately assailed by an army of birds flying out from all the clefts and crannies in the walls and angrily protesting against my intrusion. They were of various kinds, large and small, including flights of a lovely green species, flashing in the brilliant sunshine like living jade. The effect of their shrill cries was startling, and almost terrifying in the tense silence, and, to escape from their attack, I climbed to the top of a steep pile, from which I saw, on all sides, a barren expanse of scorched clay, where straining eyes sought a horizon in vain. The only sign of life was a distant group of black tents huddled together, as if scared by the immensity of space; and, silhouetted against the reddening sun, a horseman slowly wending his solitary way. As I retraced my steps a frightened hare ran across my path, and a jackal slunk through a dark passage. The powerful city, the very name of which once signified "universal dominion," now deserted by man, had become a bird sanctuary, a home for the creatures of the wild.

The first time I applied to the Ministry of the Interior for permission to visit Ur, I was told it was quite impossible, as the government was "at war with the tribes," and a journey there would inevitably bring me within the danger zone. Some weeks later, when the conflict had developed into a situation "well in hand," I persevered again and succeeded in securing a permit, so reluctantly granted, that I determined to avail myself of it at once before the Minister had time to

change his mind. The following night I was the only European passenger on the train to Basra, which, obligingly, stopped on the way,
and let me off early next morning at the nearest point to my destination; by which time I had accumulated so many layers of dust that I
resembled something disinterred from one of the ancient tombs.
Along the line the presence of soldiers, sandbags, and all the grim
trappings of war had warned me that I was approaching the area of the
"trouble with the tribes," but these gradually disappeared, and when
the train stopped, I jumped out on the sand and looked round at what
Sir Leonard Woolley, despite its proximity to the Garden of Eden,
called "the most desolate spot on earth."[33] Bewildered for a moment,
I started to walk in the direction of the ruins, which were visible in the
distance, and, just as I had decided that I was the world's last surviving
inhabitant, I saw, coming towards me, a dark-skinned son of India
who told me he was the caretaker of the "rest house." This seemed a
rather pompous title for what proved to be a mud hut containing a
kitchen and bedroom, extremely severe and simple, but a most welcome refuge from the already burning sun. After breakfast my attendant procured for me a bodyguard in the form of an armed policeman,
and a decrepit Ford car belonging to the railway company, the driver
of which nearly kissed the hem of my garment when he heard I was
Irish, as his mother was a native of Galway. At the excavations I was
received by an Arab guide, carrying a rifle, but, although thus amply
protected, my companions were so tactful that eventually I became
unconscious of their presence, and was allowed perfect freedom to
explore, though, doubtless, never out of their sight. As in all Sumerian
cities, the dominant feature is the well-preserved ziggurat, a solid mass
of brickwork, with a triple staircase leading to the summit, on which
was formerly the shrine of the god. The façade was originally painted

33. Sir Leonard Woolley (1880–1960) was a British archaeologist whose excavation at Ur significantly advanced knowledge of ancient Mesopotamian civilization.
In the opening paragraph of his book, *Excavations at Ur* (1929), he writes that to
the west of the railway line that joins Basra to Baghdad was "desert blank and unre-
deemed. Out of this waste rise the mounds which were Ur."

in symbolic colours, and the graduated terraces were planted with trees, like the "hanging gardens" of Babylon. The whole was an architectural masterpiece in which an optical illusion created straight lines, of which there were none, from cleverly concealed curves, proving that its architect, in 2300 BC, possessed exactly the same secret as the builder of the Parthenon. The Temple of Nannar, the moon-god, of which the tower forms part, is the largest of many in this quarter, where another, dedicated to the same deity, is noted for its fine arched doorway. Three streets have been excavated, in one of which is shown the house of Abraham,[34] whom I had always imagined living in a tent, but found, to my astonishment, that the home of his youth closely resembled the residence of a modern merchant of Baghdad and contained many comforts and amenities which, for thousands of years afterwards, were unknown in the West. In that area, too, were factories, workshops, schools, and libraries and, not far off, the cemetery where sovereigns and their consorts were buried, and where Sir Leonard Woolley made one of the most spectacular discoveries in the whole history of archaeology. Here are the "death pits," or outer chambers of the stone-built tombs, in which were found, not only the royal occupants themselves and their treasures, but their whole retinues; the court ladies with their elaborate head-dresses, the soldiers of the guard, household servants, government officials, chariots adorned with lions' heads in pure gold, ox-wagons with grooms and drivers, musicians with various instruments, including a pathetic figure with her hand still across the broken strings of her harp. There is abundant evidence to prove that all these victims entered the tombs alive, then drank poison, and died peacefully; and there is strong probability that their sacrifice was voluntary, considering that Sumerian kings were deified during their lifetime, and, consequently, companionship with them implied a blissful abode in the world beyond the grave. With these gruesome relics were also discovered the marvellous objects I had already seen in the British and Baghdad museums. Amongst these

34. Genesis 11:27–31.

are a ram's head carved in black steatite; a bull's head modelled in gold; vessels in copper, silver and alabaster; fluted gold tumblers; two lions' heads in silver; a beaten gold helmet in the form of a wig; several lyres, exquisitely fashioned; innumerable miniature gold animals; a gold dagger with solid lapis-lazuli hilt and filigree sheath; and the unique mosaic known as the "Standard of Ur," which is one of the priceless possessions of the British Museum. Both these last outstanding works of art date from 3500 BC and prove that the Sumerians were consummate artists at a time when the Egyptians were a barbarous nation, and Europe was still immersed in the darkness of the Stone Age. The most characteristic feature of the excavations at Ur is their abnormal depth. It was a place of human habitation for thousands of years, each generation building on the debris of the last, so that successive layers preserved intact the history of the site. I descended at a part even deeper than the rest, and was gazing with wonder at the numerous stratifications, with their respective specimens of pottery, so precious in the sight of an archaeologist as a means of establishing the date of different cultures. Suddenly my eyes rested on a line abruptly terminating a particular section, below which was a stratum of clean clay, about eight feet thick, obviously the deposit left by a great inundation. Dazed by an overwhelming emotion, the words of Genesis bashed through my brain, and I realised why the name of Leonard Woolley will be forever associated with Ur; not for his discovery of the royal tombs and their fabulous contents, not for the light he has shed on the origin of civilisation, but for his supreme achievement in having laid bare an irrefutable proof of the Flood . . . About four miles away is the mound of El Ubaid, where excavation has revealed remains of the pre-Sumerian, antediluvian inhabitants of this country, and proved them to have been a people who lived in pitch-covered reed huts, and used stone implements, but produced excellent painted pottery. The discovery of a small temple built here by a king of Ur about 3000 BCE was the first revelation of the wonderful architecture of the early Sumerians. The British Museum possesses some of its rich decorations, including a frieze depicting a pastoral scene believed to have symbolic significance; some lovely columns inlaid with rose-tinted shell and mother-of-pearl; and a large copper relief with the heraldic design of a lion-headed eagle grasping two stags with its talons, which was the emblem of a local god.[35] As I drove back from here, the burning wind blew sand into my face like sparks from a furnace, and the heat had become almost intolerable when, suddenly, I was refreshed by the sight of a strange mirage. Looking across the desert I saw Ur transformed into an island set in the midst of a placid lake, the dark mass of the ziggurat clearly reflected in the blue depths of the water. This unexpected scene fortified me until I reached the "rest house," which I now considered had a most appropriate name. After lunch I was left alone, and retired to my bedroom for a much needed siesta; and when, at the end of a couple of hours I looked into the kitchen I was astonished to see, writing at the table, a man in European clothes, who evidently shared my astonishment, for he stared at me as if I were a ghost. He was an English engineer living in Basra, who came here occasionally on business, and finding his own accommodation, some distance away, too hot for work, came to mine, which he believed unoccupied, hoping it might be cooler. I had expected that my attendant would spend the night on a mat spread on the kitchen floor, in oriental fashion, but, to my amazement, having served my supper he hastily departed, turning back for a moment to say, quite casually: "Last year we had an awful time. The tribes broke in one night, and we had to fly for our lives." To what shelter the inhabitants of these few scattered huts had fled, I could not imagine, surrounded, as they were, by a vast expanse, level as a billiard-table, where even the best binoculars could hardly find cover for a mouse. About an hour afterwards I was standing at the outside door, which had neither lock nor bolt, enjoying the welcome shade of the deepening twilight, when an Arab boy and two fierce-looking tribesmen, armed to the teeth, strode towards me. Paralysed with terror, I tried to look delighted to see such unusual visitors, and made no defence when the youth pushed me

35. Excavated in 1919, *The Imdugud Relief* displays a symbol of the ancient Mesopotamian god Ningirsu.

aside, and boldly entered. But when he emerged, and I saw in his hand
my indispensable bar of soap, impossible to replace in present circumstances, all fear vanished, and I wrenched my property from the thief's
grasp and succeeded in looking so formidable that he and his companions disappeared. I had arranged to leave at five o'clock next morning,
but, being unable to sleep, I arose much too early and was out in the
desert long before sunrise. On my way to the train I met the engineer,
who gave me a most amusing explanation of the mysterious raid on
my premises. He had arrived only a short time before, and, on unpack-
ing his luggage, found he had forgotten to bring soap. His young
servant immediately promised to procure some, but returned empty-
handed, without disclosing the reason for his failure.

Again at five o'clock next morning I left Baghdad by car for the
long journey to Mosul. The route lay through the burial-ground
of many of the world's greatest capitals, the battlefield of numerous
races and dynasties ages before the dawn of Christianity, and through
which had swept, in the thirteenth and fourteenth centuries of our
era, the Mongol hordes of Houlagon[36] and Tamerlane.[37] An endless
waste of baked clay, broken only by remnants of old irrigation systems,
or mounds concealing the skeletons of ancient cities, became so dull
and monotonous that when I saw, in the distance, a huge ball, like
the westering sun, I mistook for a mirage the famous golden dome of
Samarra. In the ninth century AD this city, which had been founded
thousands of years before, was made the capital of the Abbasid caliphs,
who enriched it with many beautiful buildings, which rapidly decayed
when their builders, at the end of fifty years, returned with the court
to Baghdad. Now only a picturesque walled town, it is surrounded by
most impressive ruins, which extend for twenty miles along the Tigris.
Unfortunately I found myself on the opposite bank, and there was no
bridge and no ferry. In my desperation, I leaped before I looked, and

36. Houlagon, also known as Hulagu Khan or Hulegu (1218–65), was a Mongol ruler who conquered large areas of western Asia.
37. Tamerlane or Tamburlaine ([Turkish] "Timur the Lame") (1336–1405),
was a Turkic conqueror, remembered for the extent and barbarity of his conquests.

accepted the services of two youths who found a derelict boat without oars, and, while the water mounted almost to their necks, towed me with the current, until, with a dexterous twist, they sent me skimming across to where I was safely caught by a man who swam out from the other side. As Samarra is one of the holy cities of Islam, I went straight to the police station to ask for an armed escort, who led me to a roof close to the mosque, which looked like an enormous jewel, with its multicoloured Persian tiles and dome of beaten gold glittering under a vivid blue sky. According to tradition, the tomb of Julian the Apostate[38] is situated in the outskirts of the town, and there is no doubt that he died somewhere in this neighborhood. All round the walls are extensive remains of streets and houses, balconies and colonnades, palaces and prisons; but the outstanding feature is the strange tower, two hundred feet high, with a spiral outside ramp leading to the summit. It is believed to be a ziggurat surviving from Babylonian times, and was adopted as a minaret by the immense mosque, now in ruins, built at its foot. There is no railing or protection of any kind on this corkscrew pathway, and I quickly abandoned my climb when I found, as I had been warned, that the constant circling movement at the edge of a precipice, caused a dizziness, most dangerous in such a situation. I came to the conclusion that the muezzin, whose duties obliged him to go up and down that pinnacle for the call to prayer three times a day, must have been a singularly levelheaded man! Despite its romantic appearance, there was something sinister about Samarra, an eerie atmosphere that troubled my peace, an echo, perhaps, from the days of the caliphs, when the whispers of intrigue and treachery floated through its silent courtyards, and hatred and murder crept stealthily through its darkened streets. Looking back there for the last time I felt I was awakening from a wonderful dream, but a dream whose glamour was slightly tarnished by the chill touch of a nightmare.

---

38. Julian (Latin: Flavius Claudius Julianus) (331–63) was Roman emperor from 361 until his death. His rejection of Christianity, in favor of Neoplatonic Hellenism, led him to be remembered as Julian the Apostate.

My next stop was at Ashur, the earliest capital of Assyria, and the centre of the worship of the war-god of that name, the ziggurat of whose temple dominates the excavations. Perched on a rocky hill, with its massive forts and battlements, it reminded me of a ruined Carcassonne.

I left the car and walked some distance to the well-preserved and most imposing ruins of the great Parthian city of Hatra, which flourished about AD 300. I heard later that a police permit was necessary for visiting this secluded spot, where nothing living, neither bird, nor beast, nor man, shared with me its awful loneliness, nor disputed my right there to be "monarch of all I surveyed."[39] The journey of two hundred and seventy miles "dragged its slow length along" a road so abnormally bad that I was constantly shaken like a pebble-filled gourd in a South American jazz band. This discomfort, coupled with the sweltering heat and the drab scenery, generated an intense longing for the first sight of Mosul, and when at last it came, the rest house there was indeed well named. This city lies in the midst of an agricultural district, and the surrounding country in spring is aflame with wild-flowers, but so fugitive is this season that at the end of May, when I was there, all verdure had already been wilted by the pitiless sun. Rising in tiers above the river, Mosul, which gave its name to muslin, was an ancient fortified city, the centre of all the old caravan routes, and the seat of the caliphs of Baghdad in the twelfth century. Among its citizens are a Latin archbishop and the Nestorian and Chaldean patriarchs; and it is the home of numerous sects and creeds, ranging from Jacobites, Gnostics, Maronites, and Mohammedans to Yezidis or devil-worshippers. These last are a singular people who acknowledge the inspiration of the Bible, the Talmud, and the Koran, who worship God, but also pay homage to Satan, whom, because of his emblem, they style the "Peacock King." A Chaldean priest acted as my guide to two interesting churches, one of which is reputed to be thirteen

---

39. William Cowper, "The Solitude of Alexander Selkirk" (1782), lines 1–2: "I am monarch of all I survey, / My right there is none to dispute."

hundred years old; and afterwards I visited a Moslem shrine of Saint John the Baptist, containing an exquisitely illuminated copy of the Koran in forty volumes. The oldest mosque has a beautiful fountain with fine carving, and a leaning minaret that rivals the tower of Pisa, and which, according to legend, bowed to Mohammed on his way to heaven. Another mosque is distinguished by having three balconies on its minaret instead of the orthodox two, an anomaly due to the fact that it was built by Christian masons who wished, in their work, to symbolise the Blessed Trinity. The bridge across the Tigris was always the scene of colourful and turbulent animation; heavily laden camels, flocks of sheep and goats, ox-carts, caravans, shepherds, hawkers, drivers, and, along the adjacent quays, groups of gaily clad women washing clothes and gossiping from morning till night. But this well-trodden way was something more than merely picturesque; it was the road that led to Nineveh, last and greatest of all the capitals of Assyria, situated on the river bank exactly opposite Mosul.

The traveller is apt to be disappointed on first seeing this historic spot, whose cyclopean walls were wide enough for four chariots to be driven there abreast, and whose palaces surpassed in splendour all those of ancient and modern times. Until discovered by Layard[40] in 1842, so lost to human knowledge was its site that when Xenophon[41] and his "ten thousand" marched past its remains, they believed them to be those of a Parthian city. At the present day no ruins whatever are visible; all the glory that was Nineveh lies buried beneath two mounds, one dreary beyond description, the other partly covered by a densely populated village. The former has been completely excavated, and its treasures removed to the museums of Europe; the latter has been left undisturbed, and is crowned by a graceful mosque which enshrines,

40. Sir Austen Henry Layard (1817–94) was an English archaeologist, art historian, collector, politician, and diplomat, best known as the excavator of Nineveh and Nimrud.

41. Xenophon (ca. 430–ca. 350 BCE) was a Greek soldier, philosopher, and historian who commanded a large force of mercenary units and later wrote numerous works of value for their record of classical Greece.

in its crypt, the tomb of Jonah. Looking down a deep well, lined with blue and green tiles, simulating the depths of the sea, I shared the common belief that I saw the last resting place of the great prophet, whose powerful preaching induced even the Ninevites to assume the sackcloth and ashes of repentance. I must confess, however, that a wave of scepticism swept over me when, at the exit, I was confronted by a fragment of the jawbone of a fish, professing to be a genuine relic of the whale; Nineveh was in existence millenniums before Sennacherib, in the sixth century BC, transformed it into the resplendent capital which, according to the prophet, Nahum, had "multiplied its merchandises above the stars of Heaven."[42] In the history of its excavation the most thrilling event was the discovery by Layard and Rassam[43] of the royal libraries, which consisted of thousands of clay tablets inscribed with cuneiform script. From these has been derived much information about every phase of Assyrian life, and the most precious of all is the Epic of Gilgamesh, a poem giving the Sumerian version of the flood, which, in all details, is almost identical with that of Genesis. The kings of Assyria probably originated the cruel practice of compulsory migration when they uprooted large numbers of people from their native soil and transplanted them far from the homes of their childhood. These tyrants welded their subjects into an invulnerable war machine, a juggernaut that rolled over smaller nations, reducing their cities to rubble, yielding an enormous quantity of loot and an inexhaustible supply of miserable captives, who produced the buildings that dazzled the imaginations of future archaeologists. The passion for immensity, which is characteristic of all ancient architecture, is exemplified in the excavated palaces, with their colossal man-headed bulls and lions guarding gates and doorways; and the walls of their innumerable apartments decorated with stone carvings, which are masterpieces of sculpture, seldom, if ever, surpassed for stark realism.

42. Nahum 3:16.

43. Hormuzd Rassam (1826–1910) was an Assyriologist who made several important archaeological discoveries, including a cache of cuneiform tablets at Nineveh.

The most magnificent of all these royal residences was the scene of the final extinction of Nineveh's glory. Besieged in 608 BC by the Medes and Chaldeans, and expecting no mercy from those to whom he had shown none, Sardanapalus[44] fired his palace, rather than submit to the humiliation of surrender, and, with all his priceless treasures, and all the members of his household, men, women, and children, perished spectacularly on the greatest of all funeral pyres.

I had reached the end of my journey through a land which had been the theatre of much of the world's drama, the cradle of the human race, and the grave of its earliest civilisations. I had passed through scenes where wealth and power had vanished like smoke before the wind; where haughty monarchs had fallen from gorgeous thrones, and mighty empires had crumbled into dust. My eyes had been seared by the aridity of a landscape once described as "a sea of verdure,"[45] and my footsteps had sunk into desert sand which once had "blossomed like a rose."[46] And now, as I stood beside the river at Mosul, and gazed for the last time at the mounds of Nineveh, imagining the awe-inspiring sight of that splendid palace in flames beneath the midnight sky, I realised that for many days I had been listening to a preacher, whose forcible words and striking illustrations had etched on the depths of my soul the text of a most eloquent sermon, "*Sic transit gloria mundi*."

---

44. Sardanapalus, also spelled Sardanapallus, is a legendary king of Assyria, who represents the characters and tragic fates of three different Assyrian rulers from the seventh century BCE.

45. Hon. George Curzon, *Persia and the Persian Question*, vol. II (London: Longmans, 1892), 110.

46. Curzon, *Persia and the Persian Question*, 2:359.

USSR

CASPIAN
SEA

TEHRAN ■

PERSIA

IRAQ

KINGDOM OF
SAUDI ARABIA

TRUCIAL
STATES

SULTANATE
OF
MUSCAT
AND
OMAN

GULF
OF
OMAN

1936

10. Map for Patches of Persia, Brian Bixby, 2020.

9

Patches of Persia

All lovers of literature have experienced the peculiar effect of certain lines of poetry, in which sound and sense are wedded in so perfect a harmony, and which possess such a magical and evocative quality that, once read, they ever afterwards haunt the reader's memory. The choice of these is a personal matter, varying with different individuals, and for me a striking example occurs in Marlowe's great tragedy, when Tamburlaine, "that fiery thirster after Sovereignty," arrogantly exclaims, "Is it not passing brave to be a king, and ride in triumph through Persepolis?"[1] These words produced in my mind, not merely a moment's aesthetic pleasure, but were written for years in letters of gold across the distant horizon of my dreams, serving as a clarion call to follow the conqueror, not imaginatively mounted on the charger of a haughty monarch, but, in grim reality, on a humble traveller's wayworn feet. Persia has been described by one of her poets as "a land

The final installment of Murphy's Middle Eastern trilogy, this travelogue was published in the 1960 issue of *The Capuchin Annual*. Perhaps provoked by the memory of her growing homesickness, Murphy makes several condescending remarks about the people she encounters in the region, even as she waxes poetic about the landscapes and bucolic scenes she passes. The account is also notable for her ekphrastic descriptions of the architecture and design, palaces and bazaars, she observes along the way: Murphy is particularly interested in entering the famous mosques she comes upon, though she is often frustrated in this desire. To be sure, she details the many challenges to travel in the region for a western woman, from access restrictions to unreliable modes of transportation and bureaucratic complications related to her passport. Reproduced with permission from *The Capuchin Annual*.

1. Christopher Marlowe, *Tamberlaine* (1588), act II, scene 5.

189

of roses"[2] and, while there, I inhaled with delight the fragrance they have wafted down the ages, but I soon learned that their fragile petals were amply protected by many thorns from my eager grasp. Rocks, rather than roses, were strewn on my way, and even before I reached the frontier I had a foretaste of the hardships the future held in store.

I left Baghdad at five o'clock one May morning, in a car driven by an abnormally tall Persian named Mohammed, whose luxuriant moustache was reminiscent of those depicted in his country's famous miniatures. He had advertised himself as "English-speaking," which, in my opinion, was an asset so much in his favour that I selected him from numerous competitors, but, on closer acquaintance, I found his language so predominantly "pidgin" that I understood a mere fraction of his fluent conversation. Later on, however, my wistful memories of his almost unintelligible chatter prolonged interminably the hours of monastic silence I was obliged to spend in the company of his successor, who spoke only the vernacular. During the first hundred miles through a drab, melancholy landscape, I was the helpless victim of a typical sample of the roads, over which I was doomed to travel for many days, literally from morning till night, because even the most primitive places of accommodation were few and far between, and I had no camping equipment. Gradually my mind was submerged by a wave of homesickness more tumultuous than the nausea which assailed my unfortunate body from being continually flung from side to side, backwards and forwards, like a shuttlecock. A welcome delay at the little desert town of Khaneqin afforded me time to recover from the latter, while the former evaporated completely at the sight, from here, of a range of mountains rising menacingly in the background, as if to protect from intrusion the glamour and mystery of the unknown. Emerging from the ordeal of customs and passport formalities, we left the plain of Iraq behind, and, through

---

2. The *Gulistan*, also spelled *Golestan* ([Persian] "The Rose Garden" or "The Land of Roses") (1258), is perhaps the most influential work of Persian prose and one of two major works by Saadi.

undulating country, reached Qassr Shirin, where extensive ruins are all that remain of the fabulous parks and palaces of Khosru II,[3] one of the last sovereigns of the Sasanian dynasty, which was overthrown by the Arab invasion in the middle of the seventh century. Passing the ancient village of Sarpol, in the neighbourhood of which are two rock carvings dating from 2800 BC, we ascended towards a plateau inhabited by Kurdish tribes, whose tawny, mud-walled huts were scattered haphazardly over the land, like withered, windblown autumn leaves. On the roadside is a small building known as Tagh Garra, the purpose of which has been the subject of much controversy; one historian maintaining that it was a halting-place for the king during his journeys through his dominions. I mounted the steps to peer into the dim interior and found, in undisputed possession, the prostrate form of a beggar, wrapped in a voluminous black cloak, fast asleep on the stone floor. Continuing to ascend through majestic scenery, we arrived at Shahabad, a large village which owed its prosperous appearance to the adjacent oil fields, and to the fact that it was the exclusive property of the shah. Here, for the first time, I was confronted by evidence of the latter's deplorable passion for westernisation. The architecture was an incongruous medley of old and new; the women had retained remnants of their national dress, but the men were pathetic figures, despite their grotesque resemblance to Charlie Chaplin,[4] in their shoddy, ill-fitting European suits, topped by bowler hats, inches too small, clamped on obviously unwilling heads. The road grew steeper as we approached the pass, and soon we became entangled in a series of zigzags and hairpin bends, as we were bewilderingly whirled round to face the jagged pinnacles towering above us, or switched to the edge of an abyss to catch a fleeting glimpse of the boundless plain far below. Triumphant at last in our struggle to escape from the chill

3. Khosru, also spelled Khosrow, II, byname Khosrow Parviz ([Persian] "Khosrow the Victorious") (died 628), was the Sasanian king of Persia, who ruled from 590 until his death.

4. Charlie Chaplin, in full Sir Charles Spencer Chaplin (1889–1977), was a British comedian and filmmaker.

embrace of those rocky peaks, we suddenly looked down on a tranquil, pastoral scene, soothing to mind and body, and, with the faint tinkling of distant camel bells in our ears, we glided down the white road to Kermanshah.

Dating from the fifth century AD, this place was often visited by Harun-al-Rashid, but all traces of a royal residence or any other objects of interest have disappeared. Its only claim to importance nowadays is founded on its close proximity to Tagh Bostan, the site of some remarkably fine specimens of the rock carvings so characteristic of Persia. At one end of a fertile valley surrounding the town, rises a barren mountain range, close to which lie the ruins of palaces and other buildings, overshadowed by a precipice, from whose base gushes a river which the natives call Shirin,[5] in memory of the heroine of a royal romance. In this secluded spot, excavated from the face of the cliff, two lofty arches or caves enclose a gallery of most imposing sculpture. Gigantic male and female figures clad in the military or court costumes of the period; an orchestra of various instruments; wild boar and stag hunts; archers seeking their prey; elephants with their riders crashing through the jungle; boats filled with harpists and lute players gliding gently to the rhythm of "unheard melodies"; scenes of violent action and idylls of peaceful harmony; all pent in a "moment eternal" by the magic wand of a true artist. The most impressive carving is the colossal equestrian statue of Khosru II, that formidable warrior who led his troops almost to the walls of Constantinople, but whose "vaulting ambition o'er-leaped itself,"[6] and was finally crushed beneath the heel of Heraclius.[7] Time has nearly obliterated the greater part of the inscriptions engraved on the first cave, but those of the second are mostly intact. The dominant figure here

5. Shirin (died 628) was a wife of Khosrow Parviz, the Sassanid Pearsian Shahanshah ([Persian] "King of Kings"). Centuries after her death she became a prominent heroine in Persian literature as an archetypal lover and faithful wife.

6. Shakespeare, *Macbeth* (1606), act I, scene 7.

7. Heraclius (ca. 575–641) was emperor of the Byzantine Empire from 610 until his death.

is that of Shapur II,[8] the illustrious ruler of the fourth century who, according to Gibbon, "was the only rival Julian deemed worthy of his arms,"[9] the proud emperor never dreaming that he himself was doomed to fall in his campaign against Persia, which ended in one of the most humiliating defeats ever suffered by the Roman army.

Continuing along this ancient route, which is flanked by a perpendicular mountain chain, we soon reached a place where caravans for untold ages have watered their beasts and where innumerable soldiers marching through Persia have quenched their thirst. At the foot of the precipice which rises vertically above this primeval spring I realised, with a sense of awe, a long-cherished wish to visit this remote site of one of the two most outstanding events in the advancement of historical knowledge. The Rosetta Stone in the hands of Champollion[10] became an "Open Sesame" to the treasure-filled cave of Egyptian history; on the Rock of Behistun, beneath which I stood, Henry Rawlinson[11] found the key to the cuneiform inscriptions that revealed the wonders of all the vanished civilisations of the Middle East. Chiselled here, high above the ground, is the story of the conquests of Darius I,[12] and, carved in relief, his life-sized figure receiving the submission of ten rival claimants to the throne, the great king being then at the zenith of his power, before his glory was eclipsed on the plain of Marathon. Fascinated by this interesting spot, and the memories it evoked, I lingered until the touch of twilight warned me that I had still many rugged miles to face before journey's end. Dimly at first, but stealthily

8. Shapur II (309–379) was king of the Sasanian Empire and brought it to the height of its power.

9. Edward Gibbon, *The History of the Decline and Fall of the Roman Empire*, vol. 2 (London: Harper, 1843), 49.

10. Jean-François Champollion (1790–1832) was a French historian and linguist who pioneered scientific Egyptology and the decipherment of Egyptian hieroglyphs.

11. Sir Henry Creswicke Rawlinson (1810–95) was a British army officer, politician, and orientalist, often referred to as the father of Assyriology.

12. Darius I, byname Darius the Great (550–486 BCE), was Persian king of the Achaemenid dynasty from 522 until his death. He conquered the Indus Valley, eastern Thrace, and European Sythia, but failed in several attempts to subdue Greece.

growing nearer, snow-capped mountains appeared like ghosts; the dogs of some isolated village shattered for a moment the dense silence; a shepherd standing by the wayside, far from human habitation, accentuated the oppressive solitude. While we crawled cautiously up the steep gradient, we felt the chill breath of night, and darkness coiled gradually round us, concealing the dangers of the road, but setting my imagination free to feel them with bloodcurdling intensity. Then, as we descended towards the valley, the moon rose, and, with its magical light, transformed into a scene of eerie loveliness the landscape that surrounded us until eventually we arrived in Hamadan.

Formerly known as Ecbatana, the builder of this old Median capital was Arphaxed, king of the Medes; and, judging from the magnitude of its gates, towers, and battlements, so meticulously described in the Bible, he undoubtedly "built a very strong city."[13] No trace whatsoever survives of the seven concentric walls mentioned by Herodotus, nor of the famous palace, once the home of Cyrus the Great who established the Persian Empire in 550 BC, and marched from here to liberate the Jews by the conquest of Babylon, and to raise his country to a position of supremacy in western Asia. Ecbatana was the birthplace, in AD 218, of Mani,[14] father of Manichaeism, that strange doctrine which became so firmly rooted for centuries even in remote quarters of the globe, casting a spell for several years before his conversion even on such an intellectual giant as Saint Augustine.[15] The summer residence of many royal dynasties, this city retained much of its splendour until it was captured in AD 644 by the Arab invaders, and it remained sufficiently attractive to tempt the cupidity of the Mongols who sacked it in the thirteenth century. One of the few

13. Judith 1:1.

14. Mani, also known as Manes or Manichaeus (218–ca. 274), founded a church in Persia advocating a dualistic doctrine that opposed a good spiritual world against an evil material world.

15. St. Augustine, also known as Saint Augustine of Hippo (354–430), was one of the Latin Fathers of the Church, who joined the Manichean sect in his teens, but spent much of his thirties writing works that attack its principles.

surviving relics of antiquity is the tomb of Esther and Mordecai,[16] but it is probable that this building is not their actual burial place, but merely a monument erected to their memory. As in Damascus, the constant sound of running water is a pleasant feature of Hamadan, a fact to which is due the numerous trees that adorn its streets, and the blossom-laden orchards and verdant wheatfields of the neighbourhood. Often next day I looked back wistfully to this green oasis as I lurched along a rugged highway, through a colourless land, ridged like corrugated iron or wrinkled like an elephant's skin. We passed many villages of mud cabins, and numbers of the tea-shops so characteristic of Persia, where they take the place of bars in other countries. It was difficult to associate "the cup that cheers"[17] with these depressing hovels, but the beverage they provided had a most delicious flavour, quite unlike anything I had ever tasted, and was always served in glasses, without milk. The bread, which was only about a couple of inches thick, was soft and flabby like a crumpet, but rectangular in shape; and could almost be sold by the yard, so enormous was each separate piece. I saw the entire stock of a baker hanging on lines outside his house, exactly like the family washing! On my only visit to a rural cafe, my midday meal consisted of tea and an omelette, but on my subsequent journeys I found it more appetising, for sanitary reasons, to lunch in the car on oranges and raw eggs, both of which were protected by their natural covering. My companion, who was not deterred by any squeamishness from satisfying his hunger, kept up at intervals a ceaseless chatter which, in such scenes of desolation, was as welcome to my ears, though almost as incomprehensible, as the twittering of birds at dawn on a spring morning. Towards sunset a duster of mountains, pink as the petals of a rose, "swam into my ken,"[18] and gradually leaving all the drab monotony behind, I shed my weary self

16. Esther 2:7,15.

17. William Cowper, *The Task: A Poem, in Six Books*, book IV (1785): "The Winter Evening," lines 39–40: "the cups / That cheer but not inebriate."

18. John Keats, "On First Looking into Chapman's Homer," lines 9–10: "Then felt I like some watcher of the skies / When a new planet swims into his ken."

like a threadbare garment on the threshold of an earthly paradise. Flooded with golden light in a sylvan setting of vivid emerald, the mosques of Ispahan rivalled the azure of the sky with their brilliant blue cupolas and minarets; and the call to prayer echoed along a wide tree-lined boulevard, where the exotic beauty of the buildings seemed to belong to another world. The hordes of Tamburlaine once swept through this city like a swarm of locusts, leaving such disastrous results that when Shah Abbas[19] ascended the throne, nearly two centuries later, he found here a scene of devastation which he resolved to transform into a capital, in which to establish a court emulating in magnificence that of his contemporary, Louis XIV of France.[20] The success of his ambition was proved by the fact that Elizabeth of England[21] and Akbar of Delhi[22] both sent missions to Ispahan, and many European travellers of various nationalities brought back from here tales of its wealth and splendour similar to those told by Marco Polo[23] about the "pleasure-dome"[24] of Kubla Khan. Judging from all that survives until the present day, we have no reason to doubt their truth, and little imagination is needed to people those quiet ways with the picturesque life illustrated in the old miniatures, and dominated by

19. Shah Abbas I of Persia, byname Abbas the Great (1571–1629), was shah of Persia from 1588 until his death. He expelled Ottoman and Uzbek troops from Persia and, in 1598, made Isfahan the capital, where he developed a reputation for promoting commerce, architecture, and the arts.

20. Louis XIV, byname Louis the Great (1638–1715), was king of France from 1643 until his death, hence his court did not influence Shah Abbas I.

21. Elizabeth I (1533–1603) was queen of England and Ireland from 1558 until her death.

22. Akbar, in full Abu al-Fatḥ Jalal al-Din Muhammad Akbar (1542–1605), is remembered as the greatest of Mughal emperors of India, reigning from 1556 until his death.

23. Marco Polo (1254–1324) was a Venetian merchant and explorer who traveled to Asia in 1271 and reached Kubla Khan's summer palace sometime before 1275.

24. Samuel Taylor Coleridge, *Kubla Khan; or, A Vision in a Dream: A Fragment* (1816), line 2.

the king, whose spirit still seemed to haunt the scenes of his former glory. We can see his gorgeously clad figure, surrounded by courtiers, looking down from his balcony at the polo tournament, held in a square, so spacious that it dwarfs all others, even the Place de la Concorde in Paris.[25] At one end of this impressive space a façade of fine painted pottery distinguishes the Yellow Mosque, near which, according to a custom older than Islam, colossal drums and trumpets thunder twice daily, a primitive, barbaric salute to the rising and setting sun. Close to the palace is the Royal Mosque, Persia's most treasured shrine, where the essence of all the blues in the world seems to be distilled into a colour of breathtaking beauty. A gigantic doorway leads to a vestibule where I was so overwhelmed by the richness of the decoration that to me the apartment appeared visionary rather than real: a ceiling studded with crystal stalactites; walls shimmering with liquid gold; enamels of every shade in the spectrum; carvings fine as lace; intricate embroideries worked by fairy fingers; carpets woven in magic looms; all suffused with a strange ethereal light; and, despite the number and variety of the parts, all fused into a whole of perfect harmony. The splendour of the inner sanctuary, of which this is the mere foretaste, can never dazzle the eyes of Christians, to whom its entry is forbidden, but I was allowed to wander at will through the lovely courtyards, where it was impossible to fret about "unborn tomorrow and dead yesterday,"[26] because, like Omar,[27] I found today so sweet. The chief feature of one royal residence is the "Hall of Forty Columns" which derives its name from the fact that twenty graceful pillars, with conventional lion bases, are reflected so clearly in the dark depths of a huge oblong pool that it is difficult to separate shadow

25. The Place de la Concorde is a major public square measuring nineteen acres (7.6 hectares) in area.

26. Edward FitzGerald, trans., *Rubáiyát of Omar Khayyám* (1859), LVII: "Ah, fill the Cup—what boots it to repeat / How Time is slipping underneath our Feet / Unborn tomorrow and dead Yesterday / Why fret about them if Today be sweet!"

27. Omar Khayyam (1048–1131) was a renowned Persian poet, mathematician, and astronomer.

from substance. This difficulty is indeed ever-present in a place where numerous ponds of still water surround one constantly with vivid reflections, and where a feeling of unreality is inevitably blended with a sense of wonder. Rows of lofty plane trees, pruned to produce the effect of a Gothic interior; masses of flowers of every species and colour, among which, according to Persian custom, the queenly rose was accompanied by her humble sister, the eglantine; fountains, terraces, pavilions, colonnades, all combined to provide a worthy setting for the palace, tragic in its frail elegance and desolation, gazing forever at its own fair image, like Milton's Eve beside the lake in Paradise.[28] The Madresseh, or theological college, recalled to me a similar building in Fez, but the former has an exotic loveliness, an other-world atmosphere, notably absent from its Moroccan counterpart; and its cloistral garden, drenched with the fragrance of many blossoms and resonant with the song of many birds, is surely a haven of peace in which to linger . . . Often in this wonderful city I was saddened by signs of approaching ruin and decay. A delicately wrought panel stained with rust; a statue missing from a marble fountain; a gaping wound in an exquisitely enamelled wall; a cracked pavement beneath my feet, or a mouldering cornice above my head; broken tiles, scaling paint, shattered porcelain, these are no minor blemishes, but indelible marks of time's jealous touch on the priceless and irreplaceable work of man. The artist destroyed the mould in which he had formed his masterpiece, and the precious fragments have long since crumbled into dust. Ispahan is a place in which to dream on a summer day, or to walk with ghosts on a moonlit night, but all its poetry and romance are overcast by a shade of melancholy, exhaled, as a subtle perfume, by a beautiful flower about to die.

Awakened one morning before dawn by what sounded like an orchestra, I found that the music was produced by the camel bells of

28. John Milton, *Paradise Lost* (1667), book 4, lines 456–59: "I thither went / With unexperienc't thought, and laid me downe / On the green bank, to look into the cleer / Smooth Lake, that to me seemed another Skie."

a huge caravan filing slowly past my window. Appreciating the early call, as I had before me the long journey to Shiraz, I started as soon as possible on a road, once so dangerous that when the governor general of the province passed that way he was protected by a regular army, and a military escort accompanied all travellers, a precaution no longer considered necessary since the recent disarmament of the powerful Bakhtiari tribe. Still following the footsteps of Shah Abbas over the finest of his many bridges, I visited Julfa, an adjacent town built by him for Armenian emigrants who had fled, during his reign, from trouble in their native land, and have been settled here ever since. There is nothing remarkable about the exterior of the cathedral, but the interior is gorgeously decorated, with a beaten silver the reredos behind the altar, the floor covered with wonderful carpets, and the walls literally lined with paintings. An adjoining museum contains illuminated missals, rare specimens of old needlework, historical documents, and many other interesting objects. On leaving here we passed through fertile country with many trees, abundance of wildflowers, and acres of purple and white poppies, cultivated for the manufacture of opium, one of the chief exports of Persia. Prominent features of the landscape are many domed, arcaded caravanserai enclosed by high walls with only one opening, and villages designed to withstand a siege. One of the latter, called Izad Khast, meaning "God willed it," is perched on the summit of a precipitous rock, rising, like the prow of a ship, from the depths of a ravine. It has no visible entrance, and I wondered if the inhabitants ascended and descended in nets or baskets, like the monks of the similarly situated Meteora monasteries in Greece. All these obvious precautions against intrusion proved that this was no place in which to linger unnecessarily, and, as if in sympathy with my feelings of discomfort, Mohammed announced that we were now in the district where, a short time ago, our arrival would have been greeted by a hail of bullets! Not at all reassured by the casual, carefree tone in which he spoke, considering it was possible that a remnant of the bandit tribe might have eluded the disarmament, I knew my companion well enough by then to believe that an atom bomb could hardly plumb the depths of his placidity. For miles we drove through

200 Unaccompanied Traveler

arid country over an extraordinary road, exactly like a switchback, with such regular hills and hollows, that we bobbed constantly up and down like a "Jack in the Box," and it was with a feeling of mental and physical relief I arrived at Naghsheh Rajab. In this sequestered spot, almost concealed by a recess, are three Sasanian carvings, dating from the third century AD, and in this neighbourhood is the site of the important city of Istakhr, of which nothing now remains but a pile of stones awaiting an archaeologist to endow them with speech. About three miles across the valley is Naghsheh Rustam, where, high on a cliff, facing the immense plain, are four tombs, of which only that of Darius I can be identified with certainty, as it alone bears an inscription, but the others are believed to be those of his immediate successors. The subject of all the superb sculptures here is the glorification of a king of the Achaemenian dynasty, which ruled Persia until its conquest in 334 BC by Alexander the Great. So overwhelmingly impressive, in their classic simplicity, are these royal burial places that the Ming tombs of China and the imperial mausoleums of Annam, both of which I visited subsequently, seemed to me to be marred by a touch of flamboyance and ostentation. At almost ground level, and dating from many centuries later, are several bas-reliefs of enormous size, the most notable of which commemorates the victory of Shapur I[29] over Valerian,[30] the triumphant figure of the Persian monarch mounted on his battle charger, with the humiliated Roman emperor kneeling at his feet. Another panel represents Bahram,[31] the "great hunter"[32] of Omar; and a third depicts Auramazda, the Zoroastrian

29. Shapur I, also known as Shapur the Great (died 272), was Persian king of the Sasanian dynasty who reigned ca. 240 to 270, consolidating and expanding the empire founded by his father Ardashir I.

30. Valerian, Latin in full Publius Licinius Valerianus, also known as Valerian the Elder (died 260), was Roman emperor from 253 until his death.

31. Bahram V, also known as Bahram Gor (400–438), was the fifteenth king of the Sasanian dynasty, who ruled from 420 to his death.

32. Edward FitzGerald, trans., *Rubáiyát of Omar Khayyám* (1859), XVII: "They say the Lion and the Lizard keep / The Courts where Jamshyd gloried and

god, investing Ardashir,[33] the founder of the Sasanian line, with the emblem of kingship in recognition of the fact that this sovereign reinstated the old religion when he overthrew the Parthian dynasty,[34] and became the first Persian on the throne, after five hundred years of foreign rule. The most interesting of all the monuments in this region are two Zoroastrian altars, considered so sacred that for centuries they have attracted pilgrims from all over the earth. The remoteness of the site, the primeval solitude, the silence more eloquent than any sound, the atmosphere of an unearthly peace that transformed the whole vast area into a sublime place of worship, all combined to fill me with a feeling of awe in the presence of those primitive structures, which had witnessed the march of countless armies, the rise and fall of many dynasties, and yet stood as defiant of time as the precipice from which they were carved. Massive pedestals supported huge stone slabs, in which is hollowed a cavity that once contained the precious flame, which the priests never allowed to be extinguished; and it was in the discharge of this duty that Zoroaster[35] met his death at the hands of assassins. He founded a monotheistic religion, teaching his disciples to venerate fire and the sun as symbols of divinity, but to worship only one supreme being, the god of light; and to this faith probably belonged the three Wise Men who followed the star to pay homage to the Light of the World.

From the main road no track led to this isolated sanctuary, but Mohammed decided that it was possible to save time by going there in the car instead of on foot, as the small river encountered on the way could be crossed on an apparently substantial bridge. All went well on the outward journey over a tract of barren ground where we

---

drank deep: / And Bahram, that great Hunter—the Wild Ass / Stamps o'er his Head, and he lies fast asleep."

33. Ardashir I (180–242) reigned from 224 to 241.

34. The Parthian Empire, also known as the Arsacid Empire, ruled over ancient Iran from 247 BCE to 224 CE.

35. Zoroaster, also known as Zarathustra or Zarathushtra (ca. 628–551 BCE), was the Iranian prophet and religious reformer associated with Zoroastrianism.

seemed to be the only living things, but when we returned to the bank of the stream we were dumbfounded to see that the bridge had vanished, a heap of rubble on the opposite side being the only proof of its former existence. Suddenly, a few hundred yards away, appeared a group of natives who so evidently enjoyed our discomfiture that they supplied a key to the mystery. They had deliberately destroyed the bridge, and now offered to rebuild it for a sum which, considering the circumstances, was not exorbitant, especially if, as I suspected, these men were disarmed bandits. The thought of how much more tragic the whole episode might have been dissolved my exasperation at being forced to remain, during this tedious process, only a few miles from Persepolis, which I was so eager to reach . . . This famous capital of an empire, to which the West owes so much of its civilisation, stands in the shadow of steep, grotesquely shaped hills facing an immense green plain, bounded by a chain of mountains. During their comparatively brief intervals between wars it was the home of the Achaemenid monarchs,[36] at the sound of whose voices so many nations trembled, who boasted of their conquests in cuneiform script on the rocks of Persia, and who, in their pomp and pride, might be said to have "swung the earth a trinket at their wrists."[37] Here, on this imposing site, in the midst of a veritable garden of Eden, unknown artists and architects created a series of buildings which, for sheer beauty and magnificence, have never been surpassed, and which have doubtless been the inspiration for oriental tales of enchanted palaces erected, not by mortal hands, but by the magic power of jinns. All that is visible today is merely the ghost of former splendour, but even these pathetic remains afford ample proof that descriptions by ancient writers of the wonders of Persepolis are merely attempts to "achieve

36. Descended from Achaemenes, the Achaemenid kings included Cyrus the Great, founder of the Achaemenid Empire in ca. 550 BCE, as well as Darius I (ruled 522–486 BCE), Xerxes I (486–465 BCE), and several more generations, running through Darius III (336–330 BCE).

37. Francis Thompson, "The Hound of Heaven" (1893), line 127, "I swung the earth a trinket at my wrist."

the impossible." This unique city rests on a platform with three different levels connected by a number of stone staircases, the largest forming the main entrance, being considered by critics "the noblest in the world." The gradient of its hundred and eleven steps is so gentle that it can be mounted on horseback, the width being sufficient to allow ten men to ride abreast. At the top, guarded by two monstrous human-headed bulls, is the Propylaea or porch, in which is combined the three principal architectures of antiquity, the Egyptian, Assyrian, and Hellenic. Behind this is the Hall of a Hundred Columns, whose dimensions are so great that the only building of the Middle Ages to which it can be compared is Milan Cathedral, and its only rival in the ancient world is the Temple of Karnak. The bases of the full number of pillars are plainly visible, but one alone rises, elegant and intact, and the ground is strewn with fragments of the fallen, all crowned with double-headed bull capitals, the whole edifice appearing as if it had just collapsed at the hands of a Samson. A graceful flight of steps leads to the Hypostyle or Audience Hall of Xerxes,[38] now a mere skeleton of the masterpiece to which has been assigned an eminent place in the history of art, as the last and crowning achievement of the Bronze Age. Standing a little apart are three palaces, one of which was probably the victim of Alexander's torch, and among the many precious objects devoured by the flames was the only complete copy of the Avesta, or Scriptures of Zoroastrianism. When that religion was revived by the Sasanians, the high-priest of Persepolis wrote here the "Book of Arda Viraf," a "Divine Comedy" of ancient Persia, having many points of resemblance to that of Dante. On the rocky hill close behind these palaces is a tomb destined for Darius III[39] but never occupied, his reign having been tragically terminated by the Macedonian triumph. Amid all these melancholy scenes of

38. Xerxes I, byname Xerxes the Great (ca. 519–465 BCE), was the fifth king of the Achaemenid dynasty, ruling from 486 BCE until his assassination some twenty years later.

39. Darius III, originally Artashata (ca. 380–330 BCE), was the final king of the Achaemenid dynasty, ruling from 336 BCE until his death.

destruction and decay one glorious feature of Persepolis has remained undimmed, one striking characteristic has scorned the ruthlessness of time. Walls, terraces, staircases, door jambs, every available space is profusely ornamented with marvellous carvings, all fresh and vivid as though the sculptor's chisel had but recently galvanized them into life. We can hear the clash of arms, the murmuring of a multitude, the processional chant of many voices, the tramping of numberless feet, the creaking of chariot wheels, the clatter of horses' hooves, imagined sounds sharper than those of sense, as realistic scenes of war and peace pass before our eyes with bewildering variety. An immense panel of great ethnographic value depicts twenty-three nations offering their annual tribute, but it is no spectacular example of this amazing art that lingers most persistently in my memory, but rather a comparatively minor work, which, nevertheless, bears the unmistakable signature of a master. On a solitary block of masonry a superb figure of Darius I emerges from the massive doorway of his palace, clothed in imperial robes, and attended by two slaves, one carrying a fly-whisk, the other holding over the king's head a ceremonial umbrella, the emblem of his majesty. This piece of sculpture, flawless and clear-cut against a background of ruin and desolation, symbolized for me, in a most eloquent manner, all the grandeur and glory that was Persepolis.

Descending the royal staircase, we drove for many miles through poppy and wheatfields, passed the jade-green lake of Miris, and headed straight to the foot of a mountain which rises as abruptly as a wall, seeming to bar further progress. Skirting this for a considerable distance we reached a narrow opening, and leaving the plain behind at last, we entered a sterile, boulder-strewn land, whose reputation for being infested by robbers was not exaggerated, judging from its numerous police posts. Gladly bidding goodbye to this rather disquieting district, we plunged into a wilderness of utter solitude where dismal, leaden-hued mountains cast a shadow even on my thoughts, until I was suddenly startled by the unexpected and incongruous sight of a monumental gateway or triumphal arch across the road, only a few hundred yards ahead. Looking down on the valley below, flooded with the molten gold of tile setting sun, I stopped for an eternal moment to enjoy, what must be "a purple patch" in the itinerary of all travellers in Persia, the first view of the turquoise domes and glittering minarets of Shiraz. That night I dined under the stars in a garden of roses, and, lulled by the plaintive sound of Persian music plucked from the sweetest of strings, I drank a cup of the celebrated local wine, and thought of Omar Khayyam. In such circumstances it was impossible to forget him, and, despite the fact that many of his admirers have honoured him as a mystical poet, it was difficult to believe that his "Heavenly Vintage"[40] was anything more than the literal juice of the grape.

A silence even more profound than that of the desert settled, like a pall, over Shiraz when twilight suddenly deepened into darkness, and a nocturnal walk through its labyrinth of narrow streets might well convince a stranger, abnormally conscious of his own footsteps, that he was trespassing on a place sacred to the dead. But at dawn the call to prayer was an imperative and irresistible command to arise from sleep, and from that moment the noise of human activity, though never strident as in our western cities, was incessant as the buzzing of a swarm of bees. The muezzin's melancholy chant had scarcely died away before a caravan made its harmonious entrance, the many differently toned bells producing a melody always to me most welcome. A stroll through the bazaar was accompanied by a still greater variety of sounds, ranging from the beat of the coppersmith's hammer to the muffled drone of the potter's wheel; from the dulcet cajoling of the carpet seller, seated in the midst of his magical wares, to the raucous whine of the beggar squatted in the dust. This building occupies a large area, and some of the arcades, with their pointed arches and groined ceilings, look like Gothic naves, a resemblance accentuated by the dim light provided by occasional openings in the roof. Throughout those tortuous passages sounds were scarcely more varied than scents, the perfume of the queen of flowers predominating over all others, masses of the lovely

40. Edward FitzGerald, trans., *Rubáiyát of Omar Khayyám* (1859), XLIII: "As then the Tulip for her wonted sup / Of Heavenly Vintage lifts her chalice up, / Do you, twin offspring of the soil, till Heav'n / To Earth invert you like an empty Cup."

blossoms glowing in all the dark corners, and even in the carafe of the narghile smoker floated the petals of a red rose. Such a setting for merchandise of every conceivable shade of colour could hardly fail to be picturesque, but its harmony was marred by the false note struck by the men's European clothes with which the shah had replaced their national costumes. It is always incomprehensible and depressing to me to find people such as the Persians, or other ancient oriental races, the origin of whose civilisation is shrouded by the mists of time, sacrificing their individuality by imitating those whose culture is comparatively modern. Even by day Shiraz was enveloped in an atmosphere of mystery. Veiled women no longer glided like phantoms through its streets, as in other Moslem towns, but the gardens for which it is famous, and the homes of its inhabitants, were as impenetrable as fortified strongholds. In the residential quarter tall trees overlooked high walls, pierced at intervals by a grille or lavishly decorated doorway, designed to repel the boldest intruder; and the whole neighbourhood was pervaded by an air of secrecy so overpowering that, even at noon, I trod those solitary ways with bated breath, my imagination so stimulated that every dwelling was set in the midst of an Eden, and transformed into an enchanted palace. In Shiraz, as in Ispahan, I was acutely conscious of the hardship of being denied access to the mosques, their exteriors being so tantalisingly beautiful that I longed to penetrate to their inner sanctums. Coming here from the treeless waste and wilderness of stone I found these astounding structures, dazzling as jewels in the sun, as unreal as a vision. Blue, in every imaginable shade, was their dominant colour, but in tiles, enamels, and mosaics, it was exquisitely blended with many other hues, in intricate patterns, fine as old embroidery, implying an artistry so far above the skill of any modern craftsman that one realised sadly their inevitable decay.

Many lovely things in Persia show unmistakable signs of mortality, but time has been powerless to bring forgetfulness to the poets. Jalal,[41] a

41. Rumi, in full Jalal al-Din Rumi, also known by the honorific Mawlana ([Persian] "Our Master") (ca. 1207–73), is regarded as the greatest Sufi mystic and

contemporary of Saint Francis[42] and resembling him in many respects, is considered supreme among that astonishing group of mystical writers who have won high rank in the history of literature; but Hafiz[43] and Saadi,[44] both natives of Shiraz, are also stars of the first magnitude in Persian poetry, being read with enthusiasm by all classes, in the study of the scholar and by the camel driver's campfire. Hafiz has been called one of the world's greatest lyricists, and, even in the necessarily anaemic form of translation, such an estimate hardly seems exaggerated. Born of humble parentage in the fourteenth century, he began his working life as a baker's assistant in what was literally a cage, for, like Heine,[45] he sang instinctively and naturally as a bird. Rapidly winning fame, he became the friend of princes and grand viziers, charming even the fearsome Tamburlaine himself. His grave is a sacred spot outside the city, set in the midst of flowers and fountains, cypresses and orange trees, and dotted with blue-domed kiosks for prayer and meditation. These gems of architecture have wonderfully decorated walls and ceilings, floors covered with priceless old rugs, and vases of freshly culled roses constantly renewed. First reserved for the poet alone, many admirers, in the course of centuries, have been granted the coveted privilege of resting beside him, where the spring breezes scatter showers of pink blossoms on their white tombs. A few miles away, Saadi is buried in a severely plain little building, like a chapel, and I came here gladly to pay my respects to a kindred spirit. Because I believe firmly that beauty is as essential for the nourishment of the

poet in the Persian language owing to his lyrics and his epic *Mas navi-yi Ma'navi* ("Spiritual Couplets").

42. Saint Francis of Assisi (ca. 1181–1226).

43. Hafiz, also spelled Hafez, in full Mohammad Shams al-Din Hafez (ca. 1325–89).

44. Saadi, also spelled Sa'di and also known as Saadi of Shiraz (ca. 1213–91), was one of the greatest medieval Persian writers.

45. Heinrich Heine, in full Christian Johann Heinrich Heine (1797–1856), German writer best known for his lyric poetry, especially the *Buch der Lieder* (*The Book of Songs*) (1827).

mind of man as food is for his body, this twelfth-century poet long ago endeared himself to me by a single couplet, in which he advises his reader, whose only worldly goods are two loaves of bread, to sell one and, with the proceeds, to buy hyacinths "to feed his soul."[46] A green turban rests on his tomb, proclaiming the fact that he had made the pilgrimage to Mecca, but his travels brought him much farther afield. He visited Abyssinia, Egypt, Palestine, Asia Minor, Armenia, and India, an almost incredible feat for those times; and, after wandering for thirty years, returned in his old age to his native town, and only then began to write poetry. A contemporary of the troubadours, his memory has never faded from the hearts of his compatriots, the humblest of whom are still his ardent admirers. His last resting place is much simpler and less imposing than that of Hafiz. It is built in the midst of no elegant pavilions or flower-filled parterres; no agate slab bears an indelible record of his virtues; there are no companions to banish the everlasting solitude; but he lies at the end of a pathway which, in May, is strewn with the petals of eglantine; the surrounding thickets are fragrant with the breath of countless roses; and the trees that keep constant vigil beside him are tremulous with the requiem chanted by a choir of nightingales.

I had now reached the farthest point of my journey to the south, and had to retrace my steps back to Ispahan before turning northwards to the capital. The sun was sinking as we entered the plain of Persepolis, and I had a memorable last view of the ruins, all scarlet and gold, as if the ghost of Alexander had set the crumbling walls aflame; while a shepherd, resplendent as an ancient god, was leading his flock to the safety of home, because, as he murmured fearfully, we drew near to "the hour of the panther."[47] A waning moon accompanied us for the rest of the way, shedding an eerie atmosphere around villages and caravan-series and transforming them into abodes of adventure

---

46. Saadi, "Hyacinths to Feed Thy Soul": "If . . . from thy slender store two loaves alone to thee are left, Sell one, and . . . Buy hyacinths to feed thy soul."

47. *The Book of Sajaha, Nineteen Writings of the Babylonian Seer*, Sajaha 10.

and romance. We arrived late in Ispahan, and next morning I bade farewell, from the balcony of the palace in the great square, to the wonderful turquoise city in its emerald setting, encircled by copper-coloured hills and snow-capped mountains, where poetry seems to be distilled in the very air, and where even the beggar, in return for an alms, presents his benefactor with a full-blown rose.

We left in the early afternoon, and, in sympathy with my mood, heavy rain fell for the first time for many weeks, but it ceased long before we stopped in darkness at a tea-shop, so picturesque that it made me forget their usual squalor. The open front revealing the whole interior, the dramatic expressions on the faces of the customers, the colourful clothes, the graceful grouping of the figures, were all fused in a perfect harmony of light and shade by the red embers of a cooking stove and the orange flare of a huge lamp, the whole forming a scene worthy of the brush of an old Dutch or Flemish master. We were now on the borders of a district which, early in the present century, was virtually ruled by a robber chief who built for himself a fortified castle near Kashan, and whom the government, having failed to capture, invited to assume responsibility for the safety of those roads where every caravan had been his victim. Unfortunately we passed through Kum by night, but the golden dome of the famous mosque, the lighthouse for the ships of the desert, shone through the gloom. Beneath its radiance is the tomb of the saintly Fatemeh, which for centuries has been a place of pilgrimage, and many kings and princes are buried here, including Shah Abbas. One of the most sacred cities of Persia, Kum was destroyed by Tamburlaine on his march to Baghdad, but was afterwards rebuilt. Soon after leaving here we entered the Valley of the Angel of Death, a wild desolate region of which, in bygone days, many grim tales were told, and my companion's recital of some of these enlivened the dreary hours, until, at midnight, we reached Teheran.

This city, which was formerly an insignificant village, becoming the capital of Persia only in the eighteenth century, contains no antique monument, and looked blatantly modern when I first saw it bedecked with flags and bunting in celebration of the present shah's homecoming from Europe, where he had been educated. Coming straight here from Shiraz and Ispahan, my first reaction was a feeling of bewilderment at the effect of Reza Khan's[48] mania for westernisation. All the different schools of European architecture seemed to have been rifled to produce a mongrel, if not indeed a monstrous style, some buildings being composed of such incongruous parts that they resemble the grotesque animals of mythology. European dress, almost universal for both men and women, robs the bazaar of all eastern glamour, and despite its precious and colourful contents, transforms it into a common marketplace. I was fortunate to see the last of the beautiful old tiled gates, which were being gradually pulled down, and one day I hired a droshky[49] and drove a considerable distance to see an exceptionally lovely specimen, only to be told by the driver, when we reached the spot, that it had recently been demolished. He evidently thought I had a morbid curiosity to visit the scene of the crime. Of the few purely oriental edifices that remain, the mosques, with their green and gold domes, are a picturesque sight nestling amid the numerous tree-bordered avenues, and the whole city is overshadowed by a rampart of snow-crowned mountains, at the foot of which, in some fascinating villages, are the summer homes of wealthy natives and foreign legations. An aroma of old-world charm, of the ageless traditions of the past, lingered in the quaint little shops, where descendants of ancient artists and artisans still flourished, where mosaic workers still assembled particles of copper, ivory, and gold into elaborate designs, and where miniature painters still portrayed haughty shahs with flowing beards, and dainty princesses, with lustrous eyes and finely penciled brows, holding between their fingers a never-fading rose. During my meanderings on foot I found, in an obscure lane, a small church, served by French priests, where I attended a Chaldean Mass at which an acolyte sustained a wailing chant during most of the

---

48. Reza Shah Pahlavi, original name Reza Khan (1878–1944), was an Iranian army officer who became shah of Iran (1925–41) and founded the Pahlavi dynasty.

49. A droshky or drosky is an open horse-drawn carriage.

service. Concealed from the public by high walls are many delightful private gardens, of which I got an occasional glimpse through a half-open gate, as when a sudden breeze blows aside for a moment the veil of a beautiful Moslem woman. When, on one of these walks, I first saw Mount Demavend, the glory of Teheran, I gazed at it for some minutes, believing it to be a mirage. Like a gigantic opal; so ethereal, so visionary is its loveliness that I could scarcely believe in its reality. Surely even the renowned Fujiyama, which unfortunately was enveloped in mist while I was in Japan, cannot be a worthy rival of this colossal white pyramid which, perhaps because it stands alone in the sky, quite detached from all other peaks, gave me the impression of being much higher, although only 18,000 feet, than any mountain I had ever seen, appearing to dwarf even Aconcagua, the queen of the Andes. One of the most interesting places in the outskirts of Teheran is the site of Rey or Rhages, once the capital of the country, and one of the oldest towns in Asia. Alexander the Great made a short sojourn here during his campaign against Darius, but it was destroyed by the Mongols in the thirteenth century. Several buildings have been excavated, in one of which is a Sasanian bas-relief of a horseman slaying a lion with his spear, like a well-known Assyrian hunting scene in the British Museum[50] . . . The celebrated Peacock Throne had always been so associated in my mind with Persia that my determination to see it was my chief reason for visiting Teheran. Not anticipating any difficulty, I was keenly disappointed when told that it was quite impossible to obtain admittance to the palace where the treasured object is preserved; and, in desperation, I called on the British Minister to ask his assistance. On presenting my card at the Legation I was immediately ushered in before a picturesque queue of tribesmen awaiting an audience, and, to my surprise, was received by a compatriot, who betrayed a decided touch of homesickness by his warm welcome, eager questions, and wistful reminiscences of his native land. At the end of

50. "The Lion Hunt of King Ashurbanipal" is part of the Assyrian palace reliefs on display in Assyria Room (10a) of the British Museum.

a long conversation which I found most stimulating after so many weeks of silence, I told him I intended to start on a trip to the north the following day, but expected to return in about a week, and he promised to do his best, during my absence, to procure for me the necessary permit.

Early next morning when Mohammed called at my hotel I was astonished to see a soldier, armed with a rifle, installed in the back seat of the car, and he remained with me the whole journey, but always disappeared each time I arrived at my destination. This fact helped me to tolerate his presence, as I realised how much worse the situation might have been, remembering my experience in Belgrade, where I was constantly shadowed by a detective from whom I found it impossible to escape. On leaving Teheran we traversed the fringe of the great central desert, where the dreaded Simoon blows destruction to men and animals; and then, after many miles of flat, arid country, with a mountainous background, we reached Kasvin, a former capital, founded by Shapur I. Completely destroyed when the Mongols devastated the Middle East in the thirteenth century, none of its fine buildings remain, except a beautiful gateway and the royal palace, now used for government offices. This town was often plundered by the notorious twelfth-century band of assassins, whose chieftain was known to the crusaders as the "Old Man of the Mountains,"[51] and, only thirty miles away, the ruins of his impregnable fortress still tower above the Rock of Alamut. Soon after leaving Kasvin a transformation scene took place in the landscape. Densely wooded hills and mountains appeared, trees overshadowed the roadside, and the whole country became suffused with that intensely vivid green generated only by an abundant rainfall. The mud-walled, square-topped hovels, to which I had become accustomed, were changed, as if by a fairy wand, into charming little houses, with conical, steep overhanging roofs, thatched

---

51. "Old Man of the Mountains" or "Chief of the Assassins," bynames of Hassan-i Sabbah or Hassan as-Sabbah (ca. 1050–1124), was the founder of the Nazari militia known as the Order of the Assassins.

with straw, and forming verandahs supported by slim pillars. The sight of so much verdure proved a powerful tonic for eyes dimmed by the drabness of the desert, and, in spite of the journey of almost four hundred miles, I arrived without a trace of fatigue in the town of Resht, near the shores of the Caspian. Here I found bazaars which were not covered in the usual fashion, but were situated in very narrow cobbled streets of quaint houses with open fronts. In the neighbourhood are extensive rice fields in which the ox, the ploughman, and the plough were all partly submerged in mud, a familiar sight in all eastern lands. A group of girls, knee-deep in the cold water, were busily transplanting the delicate seedlings, and sang a merry song as they performed their unpleasant task. In a small boat I crossed a lagoon to Pahlavi, formerly Enzeli, the port of departure for Russia, where most of the buildings are in Russian style. Here the shah has a rather flamboyant villa, and myriads of flowers of every variety and colour flourished in public gardens beside the sea.

Retracing the route as far as Resht, we continued through tea plantations where brilliantly dressed women worked; passed a string of camels, the first I had seen in the north; and, accompanied by peals of thunder followed by a deluge, arrived at Ramsar, in the province of Mazanderan. This charming spot, situated on the slopes of the Alborz Mountains, is a health resort, with hot springs for the cure of rheumatism and other ailments. The new hotel, not yet opened, looked imposing, with its long flight of steps and many statues, and the sanatorium was about to be replaced by a larger and more modern establishment. A chain of hills, wooded to the very summit, formed a background, at the foot of which lies an immense carpet of flowerbeds and grass plots, formally arranged in geometrical patterns, the whole facing a verdant plain bounded by the blue Caspian. In the evening, after the storm, I wandered into a grove of orange trees: each standing in a pool of fallen petals, and was so exhilarated by the perfume that ever since I have imagined a paradise for the sense of smell, fragrant with orange blossoms after rain.

My next stopping-place was Chalus, which had a dishevelled appearance owing to a large building scheme in progress, and here I was suddenly elevated, from the depths of primitive accommodation, to the apex of luxury in a hotel owned by the shah. My usual washing facilities had consisted of an ingenious arrangement of petrol tins, one filled with water placed in a cupboard above the basin, and an empty one on the ground below, and this contraption worked quite satisfactorily; but in my Teheran hotel, the absence of the essential plug rendered the water literally "running," and I never succeeded in capturing it before its final departure. Another memorable feature of this abode was the fact that the doors of even the most private apartments had no such superfluous gadgets as locks or bolts, but privacy was secured by the simple, if strenuous, method of rolling a rock against all intruders. After these, and similar experiences, it was hardly surprising that I felt as bewildered as Alice in the Looking Glass[52] when I awoke in my luxurious suite, or dined in a glittering salon with precious carpets beneath my feet and crystal chandeliers reflected a hundredfold in an endless array of mirrors. The atmosphere of fairyland was intensified by the consciousness that all this baroque magnificence, and the undivided attention of a well-trained staff, were exclusively mine, because I happened to be His Imperial Majesty's only guest!

Mazanderan is the home of many of the earliest Persian myths and legends, the battleground of the superhuman warfare described in the epic of Firdusi,[53] the scene where the national hero, Rustam, slew the White Demon, as illustrated in a miniature in the Bodleian Library. My happiest memories of that delightful province are centred in my evening walks, during which I used to meet crowds of gaily clad women returning from work in the rice and tea plantations. Some wore the pastel shades of an old rug, while others were resplendent as a Dutch tulip-field in full bloom. Wide, swaying skirts of scarlet, saffron, or emerald green; narrow black trousers under long, flaming tunics;

52. Lewis Carroll, *Through the Looking-Glass, and What Alice Found There* (1871), the sequel to his *Alice in Wonderland* (1865).

53. Firdusi or Ferdowsi, byname of Abul-Qasem Ferdowsi Tusi (ca. 940–1020), was a renowned Persian poet and author of the *Shah-nameh* ("Book of Kings"), the national epic of Persia.

head-scarves gleaming like strands of a rainbow; rose-tinted veils soft as a cloud at dawn; the whole blending into a mosaic of colour that surely formed one of the most picturesque sights in Persia. Another pleasant scene was the cooking of the family supper, which took place in the open air outside the pretty thatched houses, where steaming pots over blazing fires were stirred with large ladles by the housewife, who carried out the entire routine in circumstances far better than in a hot kitchen on those lovely May evenings. I had noticed in many villages a strange low building which aroused my curiosity so much that one day I decided to discover its purpose. I descended a short flight of steps and found myself beside a perfect miniature of a Roman bath, hollowed out in the middle of the little room, with raised stone seats on each side. A door led into another apartment of a series, and I realised it was a public bathing establishment, primitive according to modern standards, but equipped with all necessary amenities.

Leaving Chalus, and remaining still close to the sea, we drove through Mashhadsar and Noshahr, both of which have become important ports, and for a considerable distance the road was flanked by dense jungle, the haunt of many wild animals, including bears, leopards, and Shakespeare's "Hyrcan tiger."[54] Passing the large town of Babol, with its two beautiful ancient buildings and a modern royal villa, we turned inland and were soon in the midst of wooded mountains and magnificent scenery. My military aide had availed himself of the opportunities for shopping provided by Mazanderan and now monopolised the whole back of the car to accommodate his purchases. Placid as an image of Buddha, and with the same indestructible smile, he sat amid a collection of parcels of various shapes and sizes, including a bag of coal and a large basket of fish. I became aware of the former when a gentle breeze wafted a shower of smuts around my head; the latter betrayed its presence by turning the orange groves of Ramsar into a poignant memory. Gradually the woods disappeared, and the peaks became stern and rugged as we mounted to an altitude that

54. Shakespeare, *Macbeth* (1606), act III, scene 4.

blocks this route with snow for most of the year. From these heights I looked down on the first section of the railway destined to run from the Caspian to the Persian Gulf, but I had no regret for its unfinished condition. My dust coat of Irish linen, noted for its hardwearing quality, was worn threadbare by the friction caused by abnormally bad roads, but I realised that I could never see or know so much of this interesting country, had I been merely a passenger in a train. Descending slowly through a gorge, where the steep sides seemed hewn from a block of amethyst, and the earth and stony ground glowed with the same lovely colour, every nook and cranny filled with pods of purple blossoms, we came to Firouzkuh, a most picturesque village. It consisted of a high hill excavated into a perfect honeycomb of diminutive dwellings, and a narrow, twisted street with single-storey shops, the doors and shutters painted a vivid green bordered with gentian blue; and, rising sheer at the very end, a stupendous rock reminiscent of Gibraltar. The contrast between the latter and the dainty little hamlet, which looked like a toy, was startling and altogether unique. Now the mountains became wilder and more barren, and soon appeared the snowy peaks flushed by the vermilion of the setting sun, which lighted our descent into an enormous plain, where hundreds of goats, sheep, and camels, grazing under the watchful eyes of their shepherds, formed a pastoral scene of Biblical simplicity.

Next morning in Teheran I received a letter from the British Legation announcing that the Iranian authorities had granted me permission to visit the Golestan Palace. The old rulers of Persia always endeavoured to give their homes the semblance of enchanted caves, a custom still followed and exemplified in this royal residence. Surrounded by tree-shaded gardens where swans and flowers were reflected in deep lakes, it is entered by a massive marble staircase, partly covered with exquisite rugs. A series of rooms, some entirely lined with crystal, scintillating with mirrors, chandeliers, and glass stalactites, contain works of art from many nations. Here are treasures of ancient Persia, Chinese vases of the rarest periods, Sèvres porcelain with borders like lace, and one apartment hung with Gobelin tapestries. The most spectacular items of the whole collection are the crown jewels, which surpass even those of the sultans of Turkey; and I now realised that the description of a ruby "as large as a pigeon's egg"[55] was no ridiculous exaggeration, but the literal truth. The most cherished gem of all is the Peacock Throne, once the property of the Great Moguls, brought as a war trophy from Delhi in the eighteenth century. Its base is of solid gold, with eight spiral feet; its sides embossed with sheaves of flowers, the foliage of emeralds, the petals of rubies and pearls. Resting on this is a gold, ruby-studded seat, shaped in oriental fashion; and, on the back, a "sun" encircled by rays of enormous diamonds. Another throne, encrusted with precious stones, is scarcely less magnificent, and in a hall with gilded red decorations, is the Marble Throne, carved from a single block, and supported by figures of goddesses and strange monsters, an outstanding example of Hindu art.

Having now finished my whole programme, I decided to leave Teheran next day, but, to my bitter disappointment, I was stopped suddenly by something absolutely unforeseen. When I applied to the police for an exit visa, they discovered that I had broken the law by bringing into the country a sum of money which I had failed to declare at the frontier, and, owing to my ignorance of the language, I was quite unconscious of having committed this crime. The British Minister, to whom I fled, hoping for some consolation, took such a serious view of the matter, that for two miserable days I feared my trip to Persia would end in jail. I was summoned to the Finance Ministry, and, having hired an interpreter, I was subjected to an ordeal so nerve-racking that it was comparable to a Chinese torture. When I arrived early in the morning I was kept waiting for hours, then questioned and cross-examined, and told to return later, when the whole process was resumed with renewed vigour. I spent the following day, with long intervals of waiting, going backwards and forwards from one

55. Edward Gibbon, *The History of the Decline and Fall of the Roman Empire*, vol. 7 (London: Abraham Small, 1816), 271.

official to another, each twisting the screw tighter, until I was quite exhausted, mentally and physically. At last my inquisitors mercifully condemned me to a mere complicated transaction, involving the sale of my currency to the bank and its purchase by me again, so that the amount could be entered in my passport. This was a tedious business next morning, but, luckily, I had already the four photographs required for the visa, and consequently was not long delayed by the police; and when at last I was free to leave Persia, I felt exactly as if I had been released from prison.

Before my journey back to Baghdad I had to bid a most reluctant goodbye to Mohammed, who had served me so faithfully, little realising, at the moment, how sadly I should miss the babbling brook that ever flowed from his lips. My new driver, the sole candidate for the position, spoke only his native tongue, and, as I never knew his name, I called him "Anonymous" in my imaginary conversations. As we drove away towards Kasvin I looked back, and there, unveiled against the azure sky, as if bidding me farewell, Mount Demavend accompanied me for many miles, and I continued looking back, fearful of losing a moment of that companionship. Finally some lesser peaks intervened and shut out forever the wonderful vision, and then, because of that beauty I forgot all the hardships of my journey, and forgave even the Finance Minister and his satellites. Soon after leaving Kasvin, we entered a plain where, in the intense heat, vivid mirages were of such frequent occurrence that I could hardly distinguish them from reality; but they ceased as the evening grew cooler, and it was a refreshing sight, which I badly needed, when, twinkling beneath snow-topped mountains, I saw the welcome lights of Hamadan. I had arranged to spend the night here, but, to my amazement, "Anonymous" drove straight through the town, and my most frantic and eloquent gestures failed to stop him. At that time, so soon after the disarmament of the tribes, people were unwilling to travel by night in this area, fearing it might still shelter some isolated bandits: and, that other dangers awaited us was soon proved by the fact that my timely scream barely saved us from going over a precipice. I was relieved when the car stopped about 2 a.m. as we approached Bisotun, and

"Anonymous" went in search of one of those ubiquitous tea-shops which evidently are always open to customers. Left alone in profound solitude and silence, unbroken even by the chirp of a cicada, I lived through some precious moments which left a cherished memory of that unusual hour when I stood beneath the famous Rock, with its dark, rugged mass rising into a sky glittering with myriads of stars of abnormal brilliance. Fearing that "Anonymous" intended to drive all night, I got a pleasant surprise on arriving in Kermanshah, when he stopped outside a house, and made such a prolonged and vigorous use of a massive knocker that he must have awakened all the inhabitants. Eventually a hastily dressed woman appeared, and conducted me along a stone-flagged passage to a scantily furnished room, where my weary body was confronted by an absolutely nude bedstead. Leaving me for a considerable time sitting on this depressing skeleton, she returned with all the essential material, and made a bed, of which my extreme fatigue prevented me from being critical. After a short rest I rose early, remembering the distance I still was from my destination; and the sunshine on the tree-shadowed road, the fields of purple and white poppies, and the pink mountains in the background, were a real tonic after the long, dreary journey in darkness. My high spirits, however, were of short duration, as I became increasingly aware of the utter recklessness of my driver. He followed such a serpentine course that the negligible amount of traffic alone saved us from disaster; and though he succeeded in colliding with the only lorry we met, luckily it happened to be stationary, and he had slackened his pace to secure accuracy of aim. Wedged between this vehicle and a wall, it was impossible to open the door, but, fortunately, mine was an open car, and I made a rapid exit over the back, as the piled-up load, balanced precariously by the impact, seemed about to crash down and overwhelm me. The incident occurred near a police station and "Anonymous" was promptly arrested, my dumbness disqualifying me from acting as a witness. During his detention I had leisure to cultivate a nodding acquaintance with a group of Kurdish women who had gathered round us sympathetically. One of them brought a basin of milk, large enough for a camel, to strengthen the prisoner for his ordeal, and when he had proved his appreciation of the gift, the donor, seized by a paroxysm of economy, offered it to me to finish. These Kurds wore high, swathed black turbans, with long veils behind, graceful flowing robes, strings of brightly coloured beads, bracelets, rings, and other forms of jewellery. Each carried a distaff, and never ceased spinning, even while she walked, a custom familiar to me in the Balkans, but this was the first time I saw it in Persia.

I now hoped that "Anonymous" would profit from his experience, and emerge from captivity a reformed man, but we had advanced only a few miles when I realised that, on the contrary, our accident had the same effect on him as the first taste of blood on a tiger. In an almost uninhabited region we overtook a tribesman walking on the opposite side of the road, and, to my horror, my companion swooped on top of him, but, happily, the innocent victim of this murderous attack saved himself by leaping into the air with the agility of a ballet dancer. The rest of the way to the frontier was a nightmare, during which I often wondered whether it would be less dangerous to jump out than to remain inside, having by that time come to the conclusion that my driver was either an opium-eater or a madman. Customs and passport examinations were long and drastic, and, on the Persian side, took place in a shed where travellers had the greatest difficulty in dodging a numerous colony of pigeons that inhabited the rafters. When yards of red tape had eventually been disentangled, I started once more, "in face a lion, but in heart a deer," and was strongly tempted to choose the only alternative, and remain behind; but, had I done so, I should probably be there still, unless I was prepared to spend a couple of weeks on the back of a camel. Night fell soon after entering Iraq, and we had covered only a short distance when suddenly we came to a full stop, and the headlights failed, leaving us in utter darkness in the middle of the desert, more than a hundred miles from Baghdad. For some minutes I was too stunned to realise the full significance of this tragedy, and I could only think of the many dreary hours await-ing the dawn, forgetting that even then we had no certainty of relief. The feeling of isolation had a paralysing effect, and the silence was no mere absence of sound, but something positively tangible that seemed to shut me into a dungeon, where I lost all consciousness of space. Not only with my lips, but with every faculty of my soul, I prayed as I had never done before; and, after an age of crawling seconds, I could hardly believe my eyes when, far, far away I saw a dim light in the sky. Slowly, very slowly it grew brighter as it drew nearer, and at last a car stopped beside us, and I could hardly believe my ears, when a man expressed sympathy for our misfortune in fluent English. My knight-errant was a Turk who had crossed the frontier at the eleventh hour, just before it was closed, and he now offered me a seat which I accepted with overwhelming joy and gratitude. Quite unaware of the roughness of the track, quite oblivious of the length of the route, the pangs of hunger no longer poignant, I revelled in my new sense of security, intensified by meeting a member of the Desert Patrol, which had often befriended me during my wanderings in Iraq.

When at last a luminous chain, extending about two miles along the horizon, heralded the approaching end of my journey, I felt as if those illuminations had been lighted to welcome me, I was overcome by the emotion of an exile returning home, and Baghdad, radiant as a newly crowned queen, was indeed for me, at that moment, the enchanted city of the *Arabian Nights*.

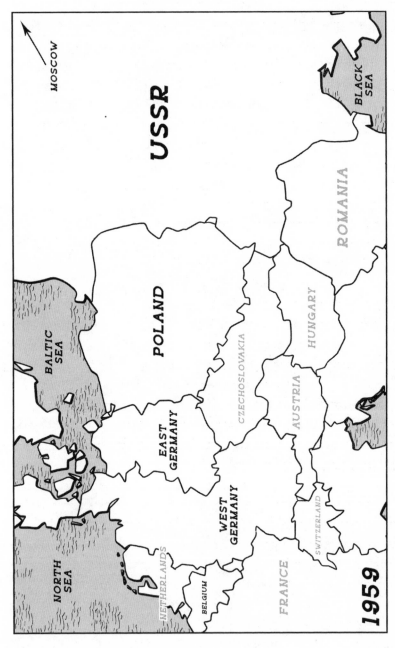

11. Map for A Glimpse behind the Iron Curtain, Brian Bixby, 2020.

10

A Glimpse behind the Iron Curtain

In these days when science has annihilated space, and the ends of the earth can be reached, without apparent motion, in a few hours, it has become a mere commonplace experience to seek information regarding the movements of aeroplanes bound for China or Peru. But when I landed on the quay at Ostend, one afternoon in June, 1959, and asked to be directed to the bus for Moscow, it was for me a distinctively thrilling moment.

The passengers were a heterogeneous collection from the United States, England, Canada, British Honduras, South Africa, and Australia, all speaking English with such bewilderingly different accents that we became a sore trial to our unfortunate guides. I had expected several Communists among my companions, and was surprised to find them all devout Christians of various sects, including two Seventh-Day

Published in *The Capuchin Annual* for 1961, this travelogue recounts a journey undertaken by Murphy just a few years earlier. Although, having reached her eightieth year, she now travels with a tour group, Murphy makes it clear that this is not a pleasure trip: eschewing the ease of modern air travel, she undertakes an epic bus journey, departing from Ostend in Belgium and making her way as far as Moscow. Along the way (more than 1,500 miles or 2,500 kilometers over land), she encounters a Europe in various states of disrepair after the devastation of the Second World War: the specter of the conflict is everywhere present, especially in her visit to Auschwitz. But now, at the height of the Cold War, Murphy makes her way through East Germany and into the USSR, witnessing a world beyond the view of most of her compatriots and others in the West. Her resulting discoveries, along with both her many historical insights *and* her amusing cultural misunderstandings, make for a vivid exposé. Reproduced with permission from *The Capuchin Annual*.

Adventists. An American woman who had already spent many months travelling all over Europe, and who was suffering badly from acute geographical indigestion, assured me so earnestly that Russia was one country she would never visit, that nothing whatever could induce her to go near "those dreadful Bolsheviks," that I often wondered where on earth she believed herself to be while she was in the Soviet Union.

I found the first part of the journey through Belgium a well-worn route, but, despite its familiarity, it provided "a purple patch," during a welcome stop at Ghent, when, after two previous disappointments, I succeeded at last in seeing the famous picture of the *Adoration of the Lamb*, Van Eyck's great masterpiece.[1] Soon after leaving Brussels next morning we crossed the frontier and drove through a lovely landscape, marred by frequent evidence of the ravages of war. To anyone acquainted with the beautiful old towns of prewar Germany, it is a painful shock to see those that have risen from their ashes with no semblance whatsoever of their former selves. Hanover, our destination for the night, is now almost completely modern, and obviously in a flourishing condition, but a small fragment of its ancient self remains, containing a church with a curious carved door, fine bas-reliefs, and a mediaeval town hall, in the museum of which are models of the vanished buildings, whose beauty accentuates the ugliness of the present utilitarian structures. A long journey through wooded country, or immense cultivated fields, brought us to the Russian Zone, and the tedious ordeal of passport formalities before entering West Berlin, a city which was almost entirely destroyed, and has been rebuilt in a very modern, rather haphazard style. There are still large tracts of ruins, and extensive spaces which seemed open country, until I realised that the shrubs, trees, and wildflowers surrounding me were merely the result of nature's kindly attempt, by clothing the naked rubble, to induce forgetfulness of the tragic past. Crossing through

---

1. *Adoration of the Mystic Lamb* (Dutch: *Het Lam Gods*), also known as the *Ghent Altarpiece* (1432), attributed to the brothers Hubert and Jan van Eyck, is a large polyptych altarpiece in St. Bavo's Cathedral.

the park known as the Tiergarten, which was totally devastated but subsequently replanted, we reached the Reichstag, or House of Parliament, for the burning of which in 1933 an innocent man was hanged; and, not far away, is the startlingly original new congress hall, built in the shape of an oyster, and loudly proclaiming the nationality of its architect. Other examples of the latest fashions in architecture are a Protestant and a Catholic church, the former consisting of a plain oblong, like a garage, surmounted by a miniature Eiffel Tower, the latter a huge Nissen hut[2] in the shadow of a wedge-shaped belfry leaning at a most precarious angle; both buildings displaying a cross in a prominent position, as the sole evidence of their religious function. Within the western boundary is an important memorial to the Soviet army's triumphant entry into the captured city, the two tanks that were the first to enter, mounted on blocks of masonry. Ruined residential areas are now covered by up-to-date flats, and at night the principal thoroughfares, such as the Kurfurstendamm, are brilliantly lighted, while crowds of well-dressed people strolling along the pavement, or seated in laughing groups outside the cafes, form scenes as gay, and apparently as prosperous, as those of Paris.

Next morning, under a blue sky and dazzling sunshine, I had the unforgettable experience of a waking nightmare when I passed through the well-known landmark of the Brandenburg Gate, and entered East Berlin. I found myself at once in Unter den Linden, and was confronted by a scene of desolation and decay that seared the memory of what was once one of the finest streets in the world. Crumbling walls, prostrate columns, twisted girders, yawning chasms, the renowned Adlon Hotel reduced to a heap of stones, the empty shell of the Imperial Palace, churches, theatres, mansions, on the verge of collapse, all set in an unearthly silence broken only by my own footsteps, and repeated with monotonous horror as I wandered through acres of what is now merely the ghastly skeleton of a great city. Passing the

---

2. A corrugated steel structure for military use, designed during the First World War by Canadian-American engineer Major Peter Norman Nissen (1871–1930).

remnants of the house in which Goering[3] stored his loot, I looked long at the flat expanse of rubble that now marks the site of the Chancellery, where the gaunt, crooked entrance to Hitler's bunker stands like the last jagged molar in a toothless jaw. Pausing at a spot round which the battle of Berlin once raged, I visited the Garden of Remembrance, where thousands of Russian troops are buried in a common grave. An enormous statue of Mother Russia dominates the main avenue, which is adorned, at regular intervals, with great blocks of stone ornamented with excellent carvings. This leads to a lofty pillar crowned by the figure of a soldier grasping a sword in his right hand, and with his left foot on a swastika, the whole flanked by two colossal flags of red granite. Underneath is a small circular building, like a chapel, with a central pedestal supporting a book containing the names of the fallen, and the walls are covered with mosaics representing the component parts of the Union of Soviet Socialist Republics. From this green oasis I emerged once more on a scene so depressing even by day, that when dimly lighted at night, it must resemble a circle in Dante's *Inferno*, and must be, at all times, a sinister, nerve-shattering dwelling place for its wretched inhabitants. Overcome by gloomy thoughts, I suddenly blinked my eyes in wonder as I entered Stalinallee, an extremely long boulevard built by Russian architects, who aimed at an imposing effect by a meticulous attention to symmetry and proportion. Here, at last, were subdued sounds of traffic, a limited number of pedestrians, shops, restaurants, definite signs of the activities of ordinary human life. And yet this fine street seemed something alien and exotic that aggravated, rather than tempered, the harshness of its surroundings, reminding me of that painting by an old master of a beautiful Magdalene gazing at a grinning skull.[4]

Ever since I first heard of the constant streams of refugees that flowed from East to West Berlin, I had often wondered how they

---

3. Hermann Goering (1893–1946) was one of the primary architects of the Nazi state.

4. A scene painted by a number of Dutch and Italian masters during the sixteenth and seventeenth centuries.

managed to elude the vigilance of the frontier guards. I have now solved the mystery by actually visiting the scene. They succeed in escaping by the simple, but drastic, method of leaving all their worldly goods behind, and, under the pretext of calling on friends or doing some shopping, they come out with only the clothes they wear, and never return. As West Berlin is an island in the middle of the Russian Zone, these fugitives must stay there to avoid arrest, thus creating a situation with which it becomes increasingly difficult for their compatriots to cope. The fact that Protestants or Catholics seeking employment in any industry must possess a notary's letter to prove that they have left their Church probably accounts for a large number of these unfortunate people.

One highlight powerful enough to gild the gloom that enveloped my visit to Berlin was provided by the Dahlem museum, which contains a comprehensive collection of paintings from the thirteenth to the nineteenth centuries. Among these is a *Nativity* by Filippo Lippi[5] representing God the Father sending down a dove to rest over the manger, a symbol of the Trinity, similar to the London Gallery's picture by Pettoni,[6] which had always been labelled *The Flight into Egypt* until a recent cleaning caused excitement among critics by revealing the scene as Bethlehem. While meandering through the numerous rooms, hung with many of the richest treasures of all the great schools, I came to a small alcove, a secluded shrine dedicated to one object alone, a rare gem in the world of art, the three thousand-years-old masterpiece of the sculptor Thothmes,[7] the bust of Nefertiti, wife of the Pharaoh

5. Fra Filippo Lippi, *Adoration in the Woods* (ca. 1459), rescued from Berlin and taken to the United States after the war, was returned to the city in 1949 and displayed in a series of temporary homes over the next five decades.

6. Giambattista Pettoni, *The Nativity with God the Father and the Holy Ghost* (1740), National Gallery, London.

7. Thutmes (also spelled Thutmose), also known as "The King's Favourite and Master of Works," was an ancient Egyptian artist who flourished in the mid-fourteenth century BCE and is believed to have been the official court sculptor of Akhenaten.

who, by establishing monotheism in his kingdom, earned for himself the title of the "Heretic King."[8]

Stimulated by the memory of all these beautiful things, I left Berlin on a grey morning, the rain falling softly on the dismal ruins, and a kindly mist shrouding the stark ugliness of the new city. For a few hours at least, I could forget all horrors and revel in the heavenly peace of the Polish countryside, from which the industry of its inhabitants has obliterated all traces of the devastating footsteps left by its German and Russian invaders. Arriving at Poznan, the ancient capital, I was agreeably surprised to find that a considerable part of the old town still survives, the most outstanding relic of which is the town hall, built at the end of the thirteenth century, a period exemplified by its early Gothic cellars. This edifice was reconstructed three centuries later by the Italian architect Quadro, whose services were then in great demand throughout Europe, and whose chief work here is the Renaissance hall, with its wonderful stucco ceiling. A significant reminder of the severe damage sustained by Poznan is the fact that the cathedral no longer occupies a central position, but now stands isolated on the fringe of an uninhabited area. In this country, no less than in Germany, it is impossible to evade the haunting spectre of war. That the ruins in Warsaw are much less conspicuous than those in other bombed sites seems at first a relief, until it is realised that the city was razed to the ground by the Germans in 1944, and, for the most part, has been rebuilt, a marvellous feat considering that the government was forbidden by Moscow to accept any aid from the Marshal Plan. Dominating the capital is the Palace of Culture, a gift from the Soviet Union, in the form of a gigantic skyscraper containing museums, exhibition galleries, recreational establishments, a swimming pool, theatres, cinemas, restaurants, and a congress hall with three thousand seats. In the shadow of this colossus are many examples of

8. Akhenaten, also spelled Akhenaton, Akhnaton, or Ikhnaton (1353–36 BCE), established a cult dedicated to the sun god Aton (hence his assumed name, meaning "beneficial to Aton").

remarkable reconstruction, including the church where the heart of Chopin[9] is enshrined, the statue of the poet Adam Mickiewicz,[10] the birthplace of Madam Curie,[11] a section of the fourteenth-century ramparts, and a group of dwellings painted to reveal the various occupations of their owners, exact copies of the homes they replace. Many buildings are still undergoing repairs, and the fifteenth-century royal castle, now little more than a heap of rubble, is shortly to be restored according to its original design. The crowning achievement of all this labour is the market square, which, even in the most minute details of the faded frescoes on its walls, has arisen from the debris a perfect replica, at least externally, of its former self. Similar treatment has created in its surroundings such a truly mediaeval atmosphere that a stroll through this apparently ancient quarter is sheer delight for lovers of beauty, although an experience that renders the tragedy of Warsaw more poignant by emphasising the glaring contrast between old and new, and generating an overwhelming regret for the lost loveliness of bygone days. In the extensive Lazienki Park is the elegant eighteenth-century summer palace which, probably due to its remoteness, escaped destruction, and here, too, is the blatantly modern monument to Chopin, which embodies an aesthetically disastrous attempt to make a bronze willow weep. Still erect is the outer frame of the Gestapo headquarters situated in the ghetto, a district now entirely occupied by blocks of flats, whose present inhabitants must have iron nerves to live in a locality where the very air is impregnated with the misery endured by their predecessors. My guide told such appalling tales of the atrocities committed here that I fully endorsed his concluding sentence, "the Hitler Youth were trained to be beasts."

9. Frédéric François Chopin (1810–49) was a renowned Polish-French composer and pianist of the Romantic period.

10. Adam Bernard Mickiewicz (1798–1855) was a Polish poet, dramatist, literature professor, and political activist who is considered to be the national poet of Poland.

11. Marie Skłodowska Curie, née Maria Salomea Skłodowska (1867–1934), was a Polish French physicist, who twice won the Nobel Prize.

Leaving Warsaw early on a Sunday, we drove through a delightful pastoral landscape which furnished abundant evidence of the firm stand made by the peasants against the attempt to turn Poland into a collection of communal farms. The large estates alone have become government property, the small holdings have remained in the possession of their lawful owners. Charming little homes are set in the midst of fields stocked with flourishing crops or dappled with grazing cattle; and on the road we met many long, low four-wheeled carts, drawn by two horses, in which were seated smiling, gaily clad men and women on their way to Mass. The whole formed a most pleasing and picturesque sight, and reminded me of similar scenes, on a Sabbath morning, in the faraway Balearic island of Ibiza. After some hours we stopped at a customs office on the bank of the Bug River, opposite Brest-Litovsk, where two Soviet guides took possession of the bus, and where we were soon involved in the labyrinth of passport formalities. Passing from one country to another is usually accompanied by no particular change of scenery, and, were it not for the artificial barriers erected by nations against each other, the traveller would remain unconscious of any striking difference in his environment; but to step across the frontier of Russia is to enter another world. Gone were the cheerful homesteads, the flocks and herds, the long strings of snow-white geese, the colourful clothes, the friendly workers, and all the pleasant homely things so characteristic of Poland, and in their place was a vast region where nature seemed to have lost her kindliness, her close companionship with man, and to have become aloof and disdainful of all human contact. At first we overtook a few trucks laden with sullen-faced men and women employed on government farms; or passed a solitary woman whose strength was so absorbed by the hard labour of road construction that she lacked sufficient vitality to acknowledge our presence even by a fleeting glance. A patch of bog dotted with ricks of turf, a sight conducive to homesickness, was followed by an enormous expanse of flat green country, thickly wooded in parts, the dense trees often coming close to the highway, along which, stakes were piled in readiness to form fences against the snow, which covers this land for many months of the year. A strange absence of life lay like a shadow on a scene where the small number of cattle and of cultivated areas seemed entirely out of proportion to the extent of the innumerable acres stretching on all sides to the dim horizon. Across the fields, at a considerable distance, isolated clusters of black log cabins, having none of the picturesqueness of tropical shacks, were always too far away to see their occupants, or to realise that their interiors were much more comfortable than their dismal appearance would suggest. All these houses are built round a huge oven with a massive fireplace at one side, while the thick inner walls of stone and clay absorb and radiate the heat. Separated by a partition, but near enough to share the warmth, are sheds for domestic animals, and, at the back, a little windowless building equipped for the typically Russian steam baths, which resemble a canonical penance by terminating in a frenzied flagellation with birch twigs. Strangely out-of-place on this lonely road are gleaming white statues of heroic size, glorifying peace and war with equal enthusiasm. A hefty female figure, bearing on her shoulders a colossal sheaf of corn, is followed, a few kilometres further on, by a grim-visaged warrior clutching an outsized gun. For hundreds of miles, between the frontier and the capital, we met an occasional lorry but no private cars, never passed a village, nor even a house by the roadside, a fact possibly due to the "scorched earth" policy of both Hitler and Stalin, but whatever the cause, we might have been travelling in the Sahara for all the evidence we saw of human activity. The immensity and desolation of the desert have a sublime quality that uplifts and stimulates the mind, and generates the deep thought that leads to infinity; but the Russian landscape weighed on my spirit, paralysed my mental functions, and transformed me into something almost as lifeless as itself.

Our next resting place for the night was Minsk, capital of Bielo or White Russia. Founded at the beginning of the eleventh century and destroyed during the German invasion, it was restored in an almost incredibly short time, and is now a fine city which has become a leading industrial and cultural centre. An academy of sciences, a university, a conservatory of music, research institutes, museums, theatres, libraries, and an important tractor factory are among its buildings, but I saw no church, Orthodox or Catholic, though its population includes 25,000 of the latter faith. The rooms in the hotel were most comfortable, but a deafening jazz band in full blast close beside me at dinner, combined with sweltering heat, became such an almost intolerable torture that hunger alone kept me chained to the table during the two hours required to serve an inadequate meal. At breakfast I was given a pot of hot water when I asked for tea, and so it was that, deprived of my customary stimulant, I started feebly on one of the longest laps of our journey. The route was bordered by tracts of forest and rolling prairies occasionally dotted with collective farms, those lasting memorials of the government's triumph over its unhappy subjects, who fought to retain their holdings with such tragic desperation, slaughtering their cattle, and refusing to harvest their crops, until five million peasants died of starvation. After many hours under a hot sun we made a detour to visit ancient Smolensk, so well known to Napoleon, and mentioned so often during the last war that it was no surprise to find it in the throes of reconstruction. The Cathedral of the Assumption was partially concealed by scaffolding, but its richly gilt interior, gorgeous icons and frescoes, though merely a remnant, are ample proof of its former magnificence. Darkness crept round us before we arrived at the tram-stop, about ten miles from the capital, which was the farthest point reached by the German army, and it was under a starless sky, blurred by heavily falling rain, I first saw the lights of Moscow. If ever I dreamt that I dwelt in marble halls, my dream was realised that night. The hotel, in which the notorious Guy Burgess[12] occupied a suite, was a skyscraper, quite unlike its American counterpart, built in the ornate, wedding-cake style, characteristic of Russian architecture. Dazed as I stepped from the outer gloom into a sudden glare, I found myself in a spacious, marble-lined apartment, flanked by elaborate staircases of the same material, with a lofty, arched doorway

12. Guy Francis de Moncy Burgess (1911–63) was a British diplomat and member of the Cambridge Five spy ring who doubled as a Soviet agent from 1936 until he defected in 1951.

of beaten brass, luxurious furniture, carpets, and upholstery, all surmounted by a ceiling reminiscent of a Venetian palace. Overwhelmed
by such unexpected luxury, I was soon to learn that nowhere on earth
is the truth of the proverb, "all is not gold that glitters," driven home
with such force as in Moscow; and, surely, nowhere else does a passion
for ostentation, carried to a cloying degree, exist side by side with a
depressing monotony and drabness. Everything that dazzled me on
my arrival proved to be merely the work of clever artisans, gifted with
a perfect genius for imitation. My bedroom and private bathroom
were equipped with every possible amenity, but, much to my incon-
venience and exasperation, both bath tub and wash basin lacked the
necessary plugs. Situated, as I was, on the nineteenth storey, early next
morning I opened my window, eager for a new, and, what I expected,
most pleasurable experience. With the vivid memory of so many of
the world's cities seen from similar "coigns of vantage,"[13] I stared at
the spectacle before me, and was pierced by a pang of disappointment,
keen as a physical impact. At my feet, in brilliant sunshine, lay the
metropolis of a vast and mighty empire, but it seemed lifeless as the
face of a corpse. Completely devoid of distinction, something essential
to a capital was missing, and there was a dreary sameness and flatness
in the sprawling multitude of buildings that a few widely spaced skyscrapers emphasised rather than relieved. For some minutes I stood
there, wondering what was wrong, my mind groping for something
it was unable to locate. And then suddenly, in a flash of inspiration,
I found the key. Had I been looking down on a city of the Far East,
my eyes would be gladdened by the picturesque temples and pagodas
that gave character and individuality to the scene; had I before me
a panorama of a Middle Eastern city, my aesthetic sense would be
thrilled by the majestic domes and graceful minarets of its numerous
mosques; and were I gazing at the capital of a Christian land, my spirit
would be uplifted by the soaring spires and belfries that contributed so

13. William Shakespeare, *Macbeth* (1606), act I, scene 6, meaning an advanta-
geous position for observation or action.

generously to its beauty. But in my view of Moscow not a single house of prayer was visible, there was nothing whatsoever to raise the intellect of man above the material world, nothing to fire human imagination except the smouldering embers of the moon. During long drives through the streets, I looked wistfully for a fragment of the Moscow which Napoleon described as "a city of Asiatic appearance with innumerable churches,"[14] but saw only two, of which one was in dire need of repair, and the other was pointed out by the guide as "one of the few that still function." I made inquiries about the only Catholic place of worship, where Requiem Mass was celebrated for the late Pope, and was told it was too far to visit in our limited time. In 1938, at the end of the "great purge,"[15] an event unparalleled in history for the appalling number of its victims, a reaction, probably produced by a surfeit of bloodshed, generated a grudging toleration of religion; and the government, when faced by war in 1939, in a desperate attempt to utilise every source of resistance against the enemy, and realising that fervid patriotism often springs from religious roots, concluded an informal concordat with the Orthodox Church. This, however, has no application to other denominations, and Catholics, Protestants, Mohammedans, and Jews still suffer, in some form, for their faith. The Soviet attitude to religion was well expressed when a foreigner recently commented on the advanced age of the congregation emerging from divine service, and his young Russian companion callously retorted, "Religion is only for old people who will soon be out of our way," and the Communists, true to their principles, have adopted an infallible method of securing this, by making the teaching of atheism compulsory in the schools.

14. Leo Tolstoy, *War and Peace* (1869), chapter 7: "From Vyazma Napoleon gave instructions for an advance straight upon Moscow: 'Moscow, the Asiatic capital of this great empire, the holy city of the peoples of Alexander, Moscow, with its innumerable churches in the form of Chinese pagodas!'"

15. "The Great Purge," also known as "The Great Terror," was a remorseless effort led by Soviet dictator Joseph Stalin to eliminate his political adversaries. Most experts believe at least 750,000 people were executed.

The elder of our two guides, who had been decidedly domineer-
ing, vanished when we reached Moscow, and during our sojourn there,
and until we arrived back at the border, we were completely in charge
of an insipid young man, exuding amiability, incapable of arousing
fear in a mouse, and with no more knowledge of the outer world than
a hermit in the desert. Russia has good grounds for being proud of her
scientific achievements, but it is childish of the government to foster
in its subjects an abysmal ignorance of other lands and to claim that
almost everything worth doing in the world is the work of a compatriot. Exemplifying this policy is the fact that Marconi's[16] place in
science has been usurped by a Russian; penicillin, aeroplanes, and tele-
vision have all been traced to a Soviet source; Dickens[17] is eagerly read
because social conditions in England are believed to be unchanged
since his time; and it is possible that a university student might be
capable of writing a brilliant biography of a jellyfish and know nothing
whatever about the lives of his fellow men outside the Soviet Union.
The naïveté of our guide was amusing and almost incredible. While
driving along the streets, he pointed out all the bookshops en route
and proudly showed us the most ordinary things, obviously expecting us to respond with enthusiasm, as if we had spent our previous
existence in caves. To all my questions he invariably answered "Yes,"
and, as my curiosity was insatiable, I eventually doubted the accuracy
of his information, judging that the large number of my queries ought
to have received, at least, an occasional "No." Looking down at the
commonplace view of Moscow from what readers of Tolstoi know as
the Swallow Hills,[18] I was amazed at his rapturous admiration, and
concluded that, were he standing on a similar eminence above the

16. Guglielmo Marconi (1874–1937) was an Italian physicist who invented a
wireless telegraph and developed shortwave wireless communications. He received
the Nobel Prize for Physics in 1909.

17. Charles John Huffam Dickens (1812–70).

18. [sic] Murphy is referring to Vorobyovy Gory or "Sparrow Hills," one of the
highest points in Moscow, which Leo Tolstoy mentions several times in *War and
Peace* (1869).

wonderful panorama of Florence, he would abandon one of the fundamental tenets of communism and believe in a future life.

Situated on the summit of these hills, now renamed after Lenin,[19] is the university, with its 1,500 rooms, 1,900 laboratories, and 110 kilometres of corridors. Rising to the height of 787 feet, it is the highest building in Europe next to the Eiffel Tower, and fittingly bears the name of Lomonosov,[20] the great scientist, as the main emphasis of its curriculum rests on that subject, and the majority of its students, including a large proportion of women, are trained to achieve Russia's latest ambition to conquer the world by scientific supremacy. Entrance to this institution is abnormally difficult, but once it has been accomplished, the student is free from all financial problems, during his entire course, by receiving a regular salary from the state. Even in the secondary schools every boy and girl is obliged to study chemistry, physics, and biology for several years, and it has been truly said that the Soviet rule has bestowed on these branches of learning all the authority of which it has deprived religion, utterly failing to realise that the deeper the knowledge gained, the more mysterious the universe becomes, and the narrower the limitations of science.

A few miles from the centre of Moscow is the permanent Agricultural and Industrial Exhibition, housed in many picturesque pavilions and occupying about five hundred acres. Here I was overwhelmed by an avalanche of statistics about the multitudinous products, animal, vegetable, and mineral, of the fifteen republics that constitute the Soviet Union, and received a detailed explanation of the full-scale model of the first Sputnik, which I had already seen in Brussels. The most interesting exhibit is a deep pool of distilled water, surrounded

19. Between 1935 and 1999, the hills were rechristened for Vladimir Lenin (1870–1924), the iconic Russian political theorist, revolutionary, and politician who founded the Russian Communist Party (Bolsheviks) and served as head of the Soviet state from 1917 until his death.

20. Mikhail Lomonosov (1711–65) was a Russian polymath who made significant contributions to the natural sciences, literature, linguistics, and other fields, and established the university in Moscow that bears his name.

by a railing, on which the visitor leans and looks down into the blue depths, where energy is created by the fission of uranium, the whole forming the thrilling sight of an active atomic pile, which brought almost too close for comfort the awful force for good or evil liberated by man. Another demonstration, most fascinating to watch, was given by a professor standing inside a glass screen, at a considerable distance from a pair of metallic "hands," which he manipulated by remote control. They picked up minute objects, drew corks from test tubes and poured the contents into miniature vessels, unscrewed the lids of little tin boxes, and, finally, one gave the other a cigarette, which it promptly lighted by striking a match with all the ease and dexterity of real fingers. These amazing mechanisms were destined for use in laboratories where radioactivity would be fatal to human beings.

Having spent the morning among the products of agriculture and industry, I decided to visit the Tretyakov Art Gallery that afternoon, having taken the precaution of eluding the guide by ignoring his appointment, and hiring a taxi myself. My primary object was to see the works of Rublev,[21] born about 1370, many of which were familiar to me from reproductions; but I also expected to enjoy a collection of old masters of different nationalities, as is customary to find in European galleries. Great was my surprise and disappointment, as I wandered from room to room, seeing only an immense display of Russian paintings, and feeling as though I were a guest at a party where I had expected to meet many friends and was chilled at being surrounded by strangers. There are, undoubtedly, some fine pictures here, a few outstanding portraits, some canvases that betray the influence of David[22] and the French classical school, and several others that rise above the morass of post-Revolutionary art, which obviously conforms to the rigid rules of state control. I looked at all with coldly critical eyes until

21. Andrey Rublev (ca. 1370–ca. 1430) is considered one of the preeminent medieval Russian painters, whose masterpiece, *The Old Testament Trinity*, is on display in the Tretyakov Gallery.

22. Jacques-Louis David (1748–1825) is regarded as the greatest French painter in the neoclassical style, leading the reaction against the rococo style.

I reached the section reserved for the icons, where, at last, criticism was consumed by a flame of enthusiasm. Magnificent is the only word to apply to this colourful, glittering array of the best work of religious painters, the majority of whom were unknown monks, whose inspiration was the glory of God rather than their own, and who seldom signed their pictures. No signature is necessary to identify Rublev, the greatest of these, and, not only did I see many of his masterpieces, and memorable examples of the School of Novgorod in the fourteenth and fifteenth centuries, but I found the famous twelfth-century Byzantine *Virgin of Vladimir* and gazed into those wonderful eyes, with their haunting sadness, that seem to look towards a distant horizon darkened by the shadow of a Cross.

I had been so eager to see the ballet in its native setting that I was very disappointed to find the Bolshoi Theatre closed, as was also the celebrated puppet show; but I went to the circus, expecting nothing better than its Parisian rival, and was pleasantly surprised when, both from a spectacular and an aesthetic point of view, this entertainment was altogether unique in my experience. An equestrian performance on two jet-black and two milk-white horses was literally the very poetry of motion; and a ballet danced by an exquisitely graceful girl, in the centre of a fountain on a small island in the flooded arena, contrasted dramatically with another girl's amazing display of mastery over four tigers, swimming in the deep water, and behaving with all the playfulness of kittens. Ignorance of the language prevented me from judging the ability of the clown, but I was convinced that his performance was as perfect as the rest of the programme, believing that anyone who succeeded in wringing even moderate laughter from a Muscovite crowd must be a comedian of the first magnitude. I went one night to an open-air concert in a park, and, though some of the items were excellent, they included nothing distinctively Russian, except the fact that the slim, youthful figure of the announcer was resplendent in a filmy white frock, spangled with silver, while the piano was moved into position, and the score arranged, by a fat matron who looked like a well-known Irish actress playing the part of a charwoman on the Abbey stage.

Moscow is a city of contrasts and contradictions, in which Karl Marx,[23] if he awakened there from his long sleep, would feel as bewildered as Rip van Winkle.[24] Many of the social evils he condemned are still rampant, the dictatorship of the proletariat is a term as ironical to apply to the Soviet government as it would have been to that of the Roman Empire, and absolute power is concentrated in the hands of one man as truly as it was in those of Tiberius[25] or Caligula.[26] In this "workers' paradise" human beings are stripped of all rights except those conferred by the state, and government monopoly, the only real form of ownership, results in an accumulation of colossal wealth, which is spent in sending rockets to the moon, building underground stations resembling Aladdin's Cave, and palatial hotels for the comfort of foreigners, while the natives are obliged, for lack of breathing space, to pass their leisure hours in the streets. A room of one's own is a rare luxury where a whole family is confined to a single apartment, with "partitions" made of cupboards, wardrobes, and other articles of furniture; and even this seems luxurious compared to living within four walls where the beds alone occupy the whole area of the floor. Notwithstanding the sumptuous equipment of our hotel, the unappetising two-course meals, served by dowdy waitresses, never varied, and the meat was so tough that the guests, seated at long tables, looked like apprentices in a carpenter's shop.

The exclusive presidium, the innermost core of the Communist Party, includes one female member. The majority of medical doctors,

23. Karl Marx (1818–83) was a German political theorist whose ideas profoundly influenced Russian communist leaders Vladimir Lenin and Joseph Stalin.

24. Rip Van Winkle is the protagonist of a short story by American writer Washington Irving, first published in 1819. Van Winkle, a Dutch-American villager, falls asleep on an autumn day in the Catskill mountains and does not awake until twenty years later.

25. Tiberius (Latin: Tiberius Caesar Divi Augusti filius Augustus) (42 BCE–37 CE) succeeded Augustus to become Roman emperor in 14 CE and reigned until his death.

26. Caligula (Latin: Gaius Julius Caesar Augustus Germanicus) (12–41 CE) succeeded Tiberius to become Roman emperor in 37 CE and reigned until his death.

and a large percentage of the staff of the Academy of Sciences are women; but their less intelligent sisters sweep the streets even in their old age, repair the roads and railway tracks, build houses, and do all kinds of manual labour, from laying bricks to breaking stones. When I commented to the guide on the bad impression made on visitors by the sight of women employed at work, which in the West is assigned only to men, he answered complacently: "During the war it was necessary, and now they have become so expert," he paused significantly and shrugged his shoulders, plainly implying that it would be cruel to deprive them of the pleasure of exercising their skill.

The last university town I had visited was Coimbra in Portugal, where elegantly dressed students, in their unusual gowns, lend to its streets a delightfully picturesque and cultured atmosphere. The Muscovite professors and their pupils, as, indeed, the whole intelligentsia, evidently dwell in such cloistral seclusion that Moscow gives the inevitable impression, always and everywhere, of demonstrating the success of Marxism in creating a classless society, of being unique among the capitals of the world as a city inhabited only by manual labourers. Nothing ever relieved the monotony of the constant stream of apparently toil-worn women and stern-faced, shabbily clad men plodding along in such an unnatural silence that they might be mistaken for deaf mutes. They recalled to me the eerie tales I had heard in Haiti of recently buried corpses dug from their graves, and transformed by the diabolical power of witchcraft into creatures called zombies to work as slaves in the sugar plantations. The noise of the traffic scarcely suppressed the heavy tread of innumerable marching feet, and was never varied by the cajoling of street vendors, the cries of newsboys and flower-sellers, or the human sound of laughter; and the only smile I saw was the muscular effort of our guide, which looked as if it had been rehearsed at a mirror for weeks before our arrival. The crowded pavements were never enlivened by such signs of vitality as exclamations of greeting or salutation, or cheerful couples enjoying a gossip, or the familiar sight of little ones accompanying their mothers, and, except infants in arms, the only children I saw were abnormally prim and obviously well-drilled, in charge of their teachers. I noticed occasional pairs of young lovers, sprinkled among the crowd, but they conformed strictly to the pattern of life around them, and the listless youth, with a vacant expression, stared into space without uttering a word, exactly as if he were alone in the midst of a boundless steppe, with his arm around a telegraph pole. In the lounge of my hotel I often watched a group of men apparently having a friendly chat, but there was a striking difference between this and a similar scene in the West. They all spoke in hushed tones, as if fearful of being overheard, used no gestures whatever, and, far from punctuating their conversation with peals of laughter, their stolid faces were never for a moment lighted by the flicker of a smile, and, judging from their behaviour, they might have been in a house of death. Often in Moscow I thought of the ragged tramp we once picked up on an Italian road, and who, in a few minutes, filled the bus with the radiance of his personality; I thought of my driver in Capri who sang so buoyantly, as he drove along, that I felt myself on the back of Pegasus rather than in a common, earthbound car; I thought of the young Spaniard who served coffee in a wayside tavern, where I became a regular customer for the sheer pleasure of seeing him effervesce with the joy of life, his whole philosophy crystallized in his question, "The sunshine, the flowers, and the good God—what more do we want?"

In Russia today it is difficult to believe that only about eighty years ago men like Demetrius Lisogub[27] and women like Sophia Perovskaya,[28] sacrificing wealth and rank, died on the scaffold in a vain attempt to win for the common people the liberty they have never known. The fact that they have never been free, as we understand the word, is essential to remember when judging contemporary Russians. Ivan IV,[29] in

27. Demetrius Lisogub, also transliterated as Dmitri Lizogub (ca. 1850–79), was a wealthy noble landowner who gave away his fortune to support the populist "Land and Liberty" cause before being condemned to death as a rebel.

28. Sophia Lvovna Perovskaya (1853–81) was a Russian revolutionary who helped to plan the assassination of Alexander II. She was executed for the crime.

29. Ivan IV, also known as Ivan the Terrible (1530–84) was the first tsar of Russia, ruling in that capacity from 1547 until his death.

the sixteenth century, founded the secret police, who have remained a sinister feature of the government ever since; Peter the Great[30] cast his shadow on the domestic affairs of his subjects, denying them the right to choose even the coffins of their families; the emancipation of the serfs by Alexander II[31] was more nominal than real; and the last Czar, Nicholas II,[32] obsessed, like James I of England, by "the divine right of kings," clung so tenaciously to that doctrine that, despite his weak character, he became the greatest autocrat of them all. Moscow today presents the sad spectacle of a people suffering from psychological anaemia, resigned to their lot with oriental fatalism, and so broken in spirit by centuries of oppression that their dominant emotion is fear; and they seem as incapable of rebelling against tyranny as an assembly of puppets against the manipulators of their strings. The revolution of 1917 resulted merely in the exchange of one form of despotism for another still more terrible, which robbed them of the religion that, for most of them, shed the only ray of sunshine on their dreary lives.

Plunged into the depths of depression by the joyless atmosphere, I suddenly found myself, for the first time, on the edge of the Red Square, opposite the Kremlin, and immediately all my melancholy thoughts and feelings vanished, as if at the touch of a wizard's wand. Magical is indeed the most appropriate word with which to describe this strange citadel rising so unexpectedly from the midst of common-place surroundings, something so unique and exotic in its loveliness that this memorable experience amply rewarded me for my strenuous journey across Europe. Flanked by a single row of pine trees, a mellow dark red wall enclosing a large area, is surmounted by clusters of

---

30. Peter the Great, byname of Peter I (Russian: Pyotr Alekseyevich) (1672–1725), was tsar of Russia from 1682 until his death, though in 1721 he was also proclaimed emperor.

31. Alexander II (1818–81) was emperor of Russia from 1855 until his death. His most significant reform was to emancipate Russian serfs in 1861.

32. Nicholas II (1868–1918) ruled from 1894 until he was forced to abdicate in 1917. He was executed by the Bolsheviks shortly after the October Revolution.

primrose-tinted palaces, lofty towers and pinnacles, and a group of churches whose golden domes glittered under an azure sky. A broad avenue inside the closely guarded gateway leads to a square, at the end of which is situated the Church of the Assumption where the czars were crowned, and which was built by an Italian architect in the fifteenth century. Some years later another Italian designed the nearby Archangel Cathedral, where Ivan the Terrible and his murdered son are buried; and, beside this, is a lovely gilt-topped belfry dating from the sixteenth century and facing the Church of the Annunciation, which is the work of a Russian. The interiors of all these buildings, which are no longer places of worship, are ablaze with lights that enhance the colouring and gilding of numerous frescoes and icons, producing an effect of dazzling magnificence. This byzantine splendour is also the keynote of the wonderful museum installed in the Armoury where, rather incongruously, myriads of priceless jewels scintillate among a formidable collection of antique weapons. Preserved here are many imperial crowns, of which the most outstanding contains 3,800 diamonds; the ivory throne of Ivan IV; the coronation robes of Catherine the Great,[33] woven of silver thread; an Easter egg studded with emeralds; and luxurious coaches and sledges used by royalty before the advent of railways. Far more impressive than all these, in my opinion, are the various items of ecclesiastical interest, the immense gem-encrusted bibles and missals, the gleaming church plate, the jewelled mitres, the marvellously wrought vestments, chasubles and copes, one of the latter of which I remember particularly, in a soft shade of apricot silk, intricately embroidered with countless pearls. Our guide to this treasure-house was a pretty girl with an air of dignity and distinction that seemed to belong to another age, and which was completely at variance with her proletarian environment. Probably a relic of the old

---

33. Catherine the Great, also called Catherine II (Russian: Yekaterina Velikaya) (1729–96), was the German-born empress of Russia from 1762 until her death, making her the country's longest tenured female ruler.

regime, she would be in no way remarkable in a western city, but so obviously was she fashioned from finer clay than her compatriots, that here she seemed a rare jewel in a pinchbeck setting.

Some years previously when I visited Pekin, I often wished I had been there when the emperor himself offered sacrifice at the Altar of Heaven, and opened the agricultural season by ploughing the land with a plough of pure gold. I sighed for the glamorous past until I realised that, instead of having free access to the Forbidden City, as I then had, the most I should have been allowed, in Imperial days, would be a passing glance at its sacred walls. Now, too, I appreciated my good fortune in visiting Moscow after the death of Stalin, who, during his lifetime, had banished all curious eyes even from the precincts of his sanctum. A decided relaxation in the tension of Soviet life undoubtedly followed his passing, but that this affected only comparatively minor matters is proved by the fact that foreign residents, when entertaining guests, still take the precaution against hidden wiring, of turning on the radio; that among the apparently harmless housewives who cook in the communal kitchens of the flats, an agent of the secret police is often concealed; and there is no evidence of any break in the chain of forced-labour and prison camps that stretches across the north of Russia as far as eastern Siberia.

The Red Square derives the name, by which it is known for centuries, from a Russian word signifying superlative beauty. Standing quite detached at its southern end is the curious, multicoloured Church of Saint Basil, which looks like a colossal masterpiece of the confectioner's art rather than a structure of solid stone. Built to commemorate a victory of Ivan the Terrible, it is now a museum, and close by is the Place of Execution, where unspeakable atrocities were committed during the reign of that sadistic monarch, who sought to expiate his crimes by spending his last years in a monastery. Farther on, at a short distance, is the enormous government shop known as GUM, where the various departments are arranged along wide arcaded passages running its entire length, and their contents are guaranteed to free western women from all temptation to purchase anything superfluous. On leaving here, after wading my way through a throng of customers,

I failed to find a taxi to return to my hotel, and, as the word is fortunately the same in all languages, I appealed for help to a policeman,
who not only procured one by means of a peculiar whistle, but held
up the traffic until I was comfortably seated. Opposite Saint Basil's is
the historical museum, the entrance to which afforded me a welcome
shelter, one afternoon, from a sudden and most unexpected storm.
Forked lightning, in a paroxysm of fury, set the Kremlin aflame, and
tore the black clouds into countless shreds; peals of thunder ripped the
silence with terrifying ferocity, and torrential rain swept a purifying
deluge across the blood-soaked pavement. The whole formed a vision
of apocalyptic grandeur, far more congenial to the history of the place
than the sunshine and blue skies under which I first saw that spot, so
indissolubly associated with human misery. On the west side of the
square is the mausoleum, in which the bodies of Stalin and Lenin lie
in state. Built of porphyry, and impressive in its stark simplicity, this
building is visited every day by an apparently endless procession of
people from all parts of the country. What powerful motive impels
these thousands of weary workers to travel long distances, enduring discomfort and hardship, and wait for hours, with inexhaustible
patience, under the burning sun of summer and winter's falling snow?
Is it devotion to communism, a perverted religious instinct, a fanatical
form of hero-worship, mass hysteria, morbid curiosity, or fear? Whatever it may be, whether personal or political, is a secret well hidden
behind the expressionless masks of their faces. Foreigners in Russia
enjoy privileges unknown in other lands, so I was not surprised at
being placed near the top of the mile-long queue, where the reverent
silence of my companions was never broken for a moment, during
the course of what proved to be a most gruesome experience. Confronted at the entrance by two statuesque guards, we descended a
flight of steps, and crawled along a dark corridor until we reached a
recess, where a muted orange glow suffused the ghastly features of the
two occupants, lying side by side. To turn back was now impossible,
and, scarcely conscious of any movement, I found myself at the feet
of Lenin, and realised, with a pang of horror, that his eyes were half-
open, and were staring straight into mine. With almost superhuman

self-control, I suppressed a scream, and maintained the conventional pace until I emerged into the upper air, and awoke from what I now regard as the most awful nightmare of my life. In a city of contradictions, surely the greatest of all is the fact that a man, whom the ruler of the nation, in agreement with the rest of the world, has publicly branded as a monster, lies in death beside the supreme idol of every true communist.

Next morning I mounted the bus, and, with the events of history vivid in my imagination, I began my retreat from Moscow. Separated though they are for more than a century, there are many points of resemblance between the Napoleonic and the German disasters. The combatants on both sides were conquered by cold, hunger, and disease; both suffered an overwhelming defeat on the bank of the Beresina River, and, worn out from similar sufferings, only the mere remnants of the two great armies finally returned across the frontier. The monotony of travelling on this historic route was varied by stops at regular intervals, ostensibly for the purpose of resting the driver, but much appreciated by at least one of his passengers. A frugal lunch of bread and cheese and a hard-boiled egg, so appropriate in the circumstances, was eaten with unusual relish under the welcome shade of a tree; and it was a joy to stroll through the silent, peaceful woods, far from the ceaseless din of crowded streets, and the constant sight of ruin and reconstruction, and all the grim reminders of war. In the course of my travels, different flowers have become inseparably associated in my mind with certain places. Scarlet geraniums shed such a glory on the grey walls of Oxford during a memorable month I once lived in Oriel College, that, ever since, these old-world blooms recall to me that "city of the dreaming spires";[34] the red poppies that blazed amid the ruins, when I first saw Mycenae, seemed to me to symbolise the blood-stained pages of its history; and the frequent masses of purple loosestrife, that lined many miles of the long

---

34. Matthew Arnold, "Thyrsis: A Monody, to Commemorate the Author's Friend, Arthur Hugh Clough" (1866), line 19.

road from the frontier to Moscow, will never fade from my memory of Russia.

After spending another hot night in Minsk, we arrived back in Warsaw that evening, and made an early start next day for Kraków, fortified by an excellent breakfast of sizzling bacon and eggs, which a bevy of waiters served from frying pans only large enough to contain each person's portion. The constant variety in the scenery on this drive, and particularly the sight of mountains on the horizon, were a striking contrast to the flatness and immensity of the Russian steppes; and a most welcome change from our usual experience awaited us at journey's end, when we found, at last, an old city entirely free from the hideous scars of war. So ancient is this former capital of Poland that archaeologists, rather than historians, are best qualified to calculate its real age. It is mentioned in a tenth-century Arabian chronicle as an important trading centre, and all along its streets are stones that speak eloquently of its prosperous and glorious past. Since the days of Copernicus,[35] its famous graduate, the university, founded in 1364, has been noted for the eminent scholars among its professors; and the discoveries made within its walls that led to the liquefaction of air, have won for it a worldwide celebrity. The site of the greater part of the old fortifications is now occupied by a narrow park, planted with trees and flowers, a green belt that encircles the mediaeval city, guarding it, most delightfully, from any intrusion by the modern buildings. Still contributing to the charm of the town are fragments of the old ramparts, among which are a massive gate, the Carpenters', Joiners', and Haberdashers' Towers, named after the guilds responsible for their defence, all of the thirteenth century; and a fortress, known as the Barbican, built two centuries later, one of the few of its kind that have survived. A most interesting relic of the Middle Ages is the spacious market square, with its picturesque cloth hall, imposing watchtower, and beautiful Gothic Church of Saint Mary, containing exquisite

35. Nicolaus Copernicus (Polish: Mikołaj Kopernik) (1473–1543) was a Polish astronomer who famously proposed that the planets orbit around the Sun.

stained glass, and the famous polychrome triptych of the Assumption, the masterpiece of Veit Stoss,[36] the great fifteenth-century German wood-carver. From the loftiest of its twin spires floats an hourly trumpet-call, cut off abruptly, to commemorate the death of the sentry who sounded an alarm seven hundred years ago, during a Tartar invasion. The most prominent feature of the city is its birthplace, the precipitous Wavel Hill, rising beside the river Vistula, and crowned by an architectural group of rare beauty, in which steeply pitched copper roofs and gilded domes strike an exotic note. The most important of these buildings is the cathedral, originally Romanesque, but, owing to numerous reconstructions, gradually evolving into its present Gothic style. Even after the capital was changed to Warsaw in 1596, this edifice remained the coronation and burial place of the Polish kings, and their tombs are among the most superb of its many artistic treasures. The poet, Mickiewicz, and the patriot, Kosciuszko,[37] are buried in the crypt, and, in a central position, is the splendid mausoleum of Saint Stanislaus,[38] the eleventh-century martyred bishop of Kraków and patron of Poland. The most impressive of the secular buildings and the chief historical monument on this site is the castle, which was for centuries the royal residence. In the course of time, under various dynasties, it developed into a palace, predominantly Renaissance, but with obvious traces internally of its Gothic origin, and with baroque exuberance in many of its apartments. Parliament Hall, one of the largest of these, is noted for a most remarkable wooden ceiling, on which are carved forty human heads, the work of a master, who endowed them with such vitality and variety of expression that there can be no doubt that they are genuine portraits.

36. Veit Stoss (ca. 1447–1533).

37. Andrew Thaddeus Bonaventure Kosciuszko (1746–1817) was a Polish military leader and statesman revered for his role in the American Revolution and in a national insurrection against the occupying Russian army of Catherine II.

38. Saint Stanislaus of Kraków, also known as Saint Stanislaus of Szczepanów (ca. 1030–79), became the first Polish saint when he was canonized in 1253.

A short distance from Kraków are the famous salt mines, which have existed for a thousand years, and have been visited by distinguished people of many nationalities, from Copernicus to Einstein.[39] A wonderland of winding tunnels, arcaded passages, caverns, lakes, and chapels, encloses a gallery of sculpture, which for hundreds of years, has been chiselled by the miners from rock salt having the exact appearance of stone. Many shrines with life-sized statues, an altar surmounted by a fine *Crucifixion*, stately pillars with intricately worked capitals, gracefully curved arches, elaborately decorated walls and ceilings, the whole culminates in the spacious cathedral where "a dim religious light"[40] throws into relief many works of art, among which a charming *Flight into Egypt* lingers in my memory. Surely no more worthy setting could be imagined for the midnight Mass celebrated here every Christmas Eve, the members of the congregation finding their way, with lanterns, across the snow, and assembling in this sacred place, far from the haunts of men, to worship like the shepherds of old in the cave of Bethlehem.

Thrilled by all the beauty I had seen in Kraków, I descended into a veritable inferno when I visited, about thirty miles away, the notorious Nazi concentration camp of Auschwitz, where millions of men, women, and children were murdered in circumstances of unspeakable cruelty. No change whatever has been made in this accursed spot. The gas chambers, crematoria, suffocation cells, even the hair and clothes of the victims, have all been preserved in one of the most ghastly memorials in the world today of man's inhumanity to man.

Next morning, driving through a delightful country, we reached the border at Cieszyn, and, after a long delay there, we entered Czechoslovakia, where we were immediately appropriated by a masterful woman, who announced that her name was Elfrida. Soon we stopped

39. In addition to Nicolaus Copernicus and Albert Einstein, notable visitors to the Wieliczka Salt Mine include Johan Wolfgang von Goethe, Frédéric Chopin, and later Pope John Paul II.

40. John Milton, *Il Penseroso* (1632), line 160.

at the lovely old town of Olomouc, which demonstrates its claim that Julius Caesar was its founder by his equestrian statue, prominently displayed on a fountain in front of the town hall. The glimpse I got of the many fine buildings, lay and ecclesiastical, of this former capital of Moravia, left a lasting regret that the time allowed here was only sufficient for a hasty lunch. On returning to the bus, I unfortunately found myself close to Elfrida, whose powerful voice, proclaiming the attractiveness of life in this communist utopia, seemed to resound interminably in my ears, shattering the peace and poetry of the countryside. But "even the weariest river winds somewhere safe to sea,"[41] and eventually, the sixteen hours of our journey trickled to a welcome end, and we arrived in Prague.

Noted for its parks and gardens, this city is a lovely sight in spring, when decked with a brilliant array of flowering trees and shrubs, and an indelible picture remains in my memory from a previous visit, when the fragile white petals of the acacia, with its lace-like foliage, flung round the ancient buildings an atmosphere ethereal as a bridal veil. At all seasons its silhouette is most picturesque, owing to the number of historical and ecclesiastical monuments of various styles, some dating from the thirteenth and fourteenth centuries. Among these is the church in which Tycho Brahe[42] is buried, and the town hall containing a clock, with a colourful apostolic procession, which has heralded the passing hours since long before Jan Huss[43] preached in the adjoining Bethlehem chapel. Spared by the Nazis are two most interesting relics of the vanished ghetto, the Jewish cemetery, where a

41. Algernon Charles Swinburne, "The Garden of Proserpine" (1866), lines 87–88.

42. Tycho Brahe (1546–1601) was a Danish nobleman and astronomer renowned for making the most accurate astronomical and planetary observations possible before the invention of the telescope. He is entombed at the Church of Our Lady before Týn in Old Town Square, not far from the Prague Astronomical Clock.

43. Jan Hus, also referred to as Johannes Huss (ca. 1369–1415), was a Bohemian theologian and philosopher, who became one of the most important church reformers of his time.

tombstone is dated 1439, and the old synagogue whose origin in the thirteenth century is proved by internal architectural features. Like Kraków, the capital of Czechoslovakia is dominated by a steep hill, on which are perched a splendid palace and a great cathedral, the latter dedicated to Saint Vitus,[44] and the former, known as Hradcany Castle, is reached by the royal route across the famous fourteenth-century Charles bridge. Situated also on this eminence is the art gallery, where I spent an afternoon renewing acquaintance with a superb collection of primitives; and, not far off, is the Premonstratensian[45] monastery, with its baroque library, the ceiling of which is decorated with an eighteenth-century fresco depicting philosophers from Plato to Voltaire. The monks have been banished from this long-cherished scene of their labours, which is now state property.

Elfrida was an ardent Communist and her enthusiasm for the *status quo* was sincere, but our local guide in Prague, a woman obviously of higher class, although she pointed out such things as the memorial to the Soviet army, "which liberated our country," she repeated her lessons like a parrot, and her attempts to eulogise the present regime were feeble and lukewarm. She declared that she owned a large four-storey house, where she lived on the top floor and let the remainder to several tenants. When asked who received the rent, she became very embarrassed, and the truth leaked out that she was thankful to be let live in the attic, while the government made money on the rest of her property. When I asked how she reconciled her statement that the church is free with the fact that the archbishop has been in prison for the last ten years, while his flock have no clue whatever to his whereabouts, she looked at me most appealingly, and begged me not to ask

44. Saint Vitus (died 303) was a legendary Christian martyr, who is reputed to have died during the Christian persecutions carried by the Roman Emperor Diocletian.

45. Premonstratensians, byname White Canons (in Britain and Ireland) or Norbertines, members of Order of the Canons Regular of Prémontré, is a Roman Catholic religious order founded in 1120 by Saint Norbert of Xanten at a monastery in Prémontré, France.

her questions impossible for her to answer. It was a great pleasure to me to find Prague, unlike so many other cities, preserved from the ravages of war, but to anyone who had known this stronghold of the faith in former days, it was unutterably sad to see the empty throne in the cathedral, the statue of Stalin in a place of honour, and the hammer and sickle brazenly flaunted beside the cross of Christ.

We were now approaching the last lap of our journey, and a few hours' drive, during which we passed some typical Bohemian castles, brought us for lunch to Pilsen, surmounted by the lofty tower of its ancient Gothic cathedral, and containing many objects of interest besides its well-known beer. After this interval we soon reached the West German frontier, where, without any conventional reference to the possibility of a future revoir,[46] we bade a fervent goodbye to Elfrida. The customs formalities were abnormally brief, and the moment the Iron Curtain dropped behind us, a spontaneous cheer resounded through the bus, and "the cold chain of silence that hung o'er us long"[47] suddenly snapped, and we fully enjoyed, what we had never really appreciated until then, the priceless gift of free speech.

For the next few days we followed the path of destruction left by the war, a route with which I was once familiar, but in its brand-new cities now I felt in strange and uncongenial surroundings. Nuremberg was quite unrecognisable, and I was so bewildered by its garish shops and neon lights that I felt as if the delightful old town of the Meistersingers,[48] which I had known and loved, was only a dream. In bomb-damaged Aachen, where so much had disappeared, it was a relief to find the tomb of Charlemagne, and the Byzantine

46. [French] "to meet again."

47. Thomas Moore, "Dear Harp of My Country," *A Selection of Irish Melodies* 6 (1815), line 2.

48. *Meistersingers* were members of German guilds for musicians and poets from the fourteenth to sixteenth centuries. Nuremberg was home to a particularly famous Meistersinger school led by Hans Sachs in the sixteenth century.

octagon, that important monument of Carlovingian architecture;[49] but Cologne's glorious cathedral, in its present ultramodern setting, looked like a lily in a wilderness of weeds. Spending the last night in Brussels, and strolling round the flood-lighted Grande Place, with its beautiful mediaeval buildings, I felt I had arrived in another world; and my thoughts flew back in pity to that land without laughter, where man is fed on bread alone, and where the golden calf of materialism is worshipped with such tragic fervour.

A few mornings later I watched the rose-tinted disk of the sun rising majestically over Dublin Bay, and when my boat glided along the Liffey, reverently as through the nave of a great basilica, the Angelus bell, ringing out from the spire of a quayside church, called the sleeping city to prayer and seemed to render articulate the passionate *Te Deum* that welled from my grateful heart.

49. Carlovingian, usually known as Carolingian, architecture is the style of northern European design belonging to the period of the Carolingian dynasty, founded by Charlemagne's father, Pepin III, in 750 and continuing until 987.

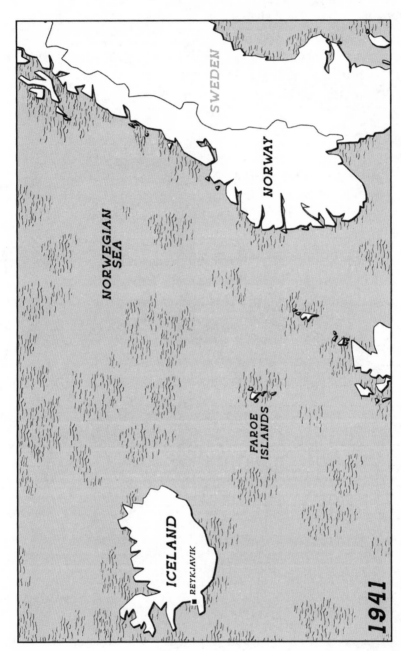

SWEDEN

NORWAY

NORWEGIAN
SEA

FAROE
ISLANDS

ICELAND

REYKJAVIK

1941

12. Map for Northward Ho!, Brian Bixby, 2020.

11

Northward Ho!

When reading accounts of modern Polar exploration, with its comparative luxury, my thoughts drift back inevitably to those early explorers who, with scanty and primitive equipment, abandoned their ice-locked ships and, trusting with sublime courage to their sledges and faithful dogs, faced all the terrors of the unknown in the bleakest and most desolate regions of the globe. A treasured school prize in the form of a "Life of Nansen"[1] proved the spark that set aflame an ineradicable hero-worship of these intrepid men, and this enthusiasm finally evolved into an intense desire to follow, even the merest fraction of

Published in the 1961 issue of *The Capuchin Annual*, "Northward Ho!" recounts a trip inspired by Murphy's youthful reading about Polar exploration. Details in the article provide insight into her abiding motives for European travel: not just her attraction to cultural traditions but her ruling passion for the exotic, the remote, the undeveloped, even the dangerous. Sailing north from Scotland, past the Faeroe Isles, along the coast of Iceland, and eventually to Norway, Murphy does not hope for a leisure cruise. Instead, she focuses on her sense of isolation as she heads into the grey seas, frigid winds, and desolate landscapes that provide her travels with a sense of adventure much like those of the explorers who came before her. But the harshness of the environments she encounters is tempered by the charm of Icelandic culture, of local folklore, and of the history of these lands, both modern and medieval, which she describes with her usual flair. Reproduced with permission from *The Capuchin Annual*.

1. W. C. Brögger and Nordaul Rolfsen, *Fridtof Nansen, 1861–1893*, trans. William Archer (London: Longmans, 1896). The book details the Norwegian explorer's early travels to Iceland and Greenland.

the way, their hallowed footsteps. At last an opportunity came to fulfil this long-cherished wish, and I set forth from the port of Leith on one of those peaceful summer days before Hitler had attempted to bestride Europe like a colossus.

Clinging to the jagged eastern coast of Scotland, as if reluctant to lose contact with our fellow men, we ploughed laboriously through a sea that imprisoned me in my cabin until my tortured imagination had transformed the most minute area of stability, even a rock in mid-ocean, into an earthly paradise. Punctuated by the mournful notes of the foghorn, the crawling moments weighed on me with a pressure that became almost tangible; and then, suddenly, through my porthole, I saw splinters of vivid blue in the leaden sky, and a shaft of sunshine, welcome as Noah's dove,[2] penetrated my dungeon and set me free.

Emerging joyously into the upper air, I found myself close to the Faeroe Isles, one of which, rising sheer from the water's edge, reminded me of Stromboli. This perfect cloud-capped cone, of obvious volcanic origin, stood sentinel at the entrance to an archipelago, where we glided past towering cliffs, yawning caverns, massive granite formations, stately as cathedrals, and stupendous boulders worthy to be the seat of a Polyphemus. And surely this sullen land, sombre, austere, inhospitable, were fitter to be the abode of such monsters rather than the home of man. The largest island is less elevated than the rest, and, scattered haphazardly like mushrooms in the shelter of a small bay, are clusters of little dwellings designed with stark simplicity. No inhabitants were visible, except a stalwart bearded figure, clad in sealskin, who stood erect in his canoe, and, evidently unaccustomed to the sight of strangers, stared at us as if we had dropped from another planet.

Rapidly leaving this lonely outpost behind, we sailed on an ocean haunted by the ghosts of fierce Vikings in search of worlds to conquer,

2. Genesis 8:8–11.

of gallant Irish monks in their frail craft, and of great explorers lured by the lodestar of the Pole. Somewhere in this waste of waters Pierre Loti[3] set the tragedy of his hero's wedding to the sea; and somewhere here a group of enormous petrified forms, like prehistoric beasts, accentuated the forlorn scene, where a few distant fishing boats were the only sign of life before reaching Iceland, aptly named "the Anchorite of the Atlantic."

This remote island, nearer the New World than the Old, was colonized in the ninth century by Norsemen, who are believed to have discovered America five hundred years before Columbus. At the dawn of the Middle Ages, these people possessed a highly efficient legislative system, an organised parliament, and a literature that culminated in those immortal sagas, the greatest of which contains a description of the battle of Clontarf, and extols Brian Boru as "the noblest of all kings."[4] Many of the original settlers had come into contact with Christians in Ireland, and, about AD 1000, the government, suppressing paganism, adopted Christianity, and by the year 1106 several churches and two episcopal sees had been established, followed later by the foundation of numerous monasteries, which developed into renowned centres of culture. In 1550 the official religion became Lutheran and has remained so ever since. The country lost its independence in the thirteenth century, first becoming subject to Norway and then to Denmark, but by 1904 it had regained its liberty and enjoyed its own laws and its own courts, though the Danish king was still nominal sovereign. The majority of the inhabitants, however, were discontent with this status and eagerly looked forward

3. Pierre Loti, pseudonym of Louis-Marie-Julien Viaud (1850–1923), was a French naval officer and later popular novelist. His *An Iceland Fisherman* (French: *Pêcheur d'Islande*) (1886) closes with a Breton seaman "wedding" the waters of an Icelandic cod fishery, so that he will never return to his wife on land.

4. Brian Boru (Old Irish: Brian Bóruma mac Cennétig) (ca. 941–1014), the High King or "Emperor" of the Gaels, who died in the Battle of Clontarf, is chronicled in the thirteenth-century *Njáls saga* and other Icelandic sources.

to a referendum due in 1943, which they confidently expected to result, as it did, in the proclamation of a republic.[5]

This strange land whose frozen face conceals a heart of flame, has had a chequered and tragic history; rising to a Golden Age of material prosperity and literary achievement, sinking into abysmal depths of penury and despair, even the peace which its aloofness from the outside world ought to have secured, has seldom been its portion. The coasts ravaged by pirates from southern seas, the people massacred or carried into captivity, internal strife and family feuds, have all been comparatively minor misfortunes compared to the havoc wrought by the invincible forces of nature. Violent storms, devastating earthquakes, widespread volcanic eruptions, famine and pestilence recurred so persistently that the whole race was brought so close to extermination that at the beginning of the nineteenth century the country contained only 20,000 inhabitants. At last, after a long series of catastrophes, a prolonged period of tranquility and freedom from disaster relaxed the tension of life, and these indomitable people, with the vitality of a phoenix, literally arose from their ashes.

Awaking early on the fourth day, and feeling myself in a most welcome state of equilibrium, I looked out my porthole, and found the boat anchored beside Reykjavik, capital of Iceland. Huddled at the foot of a hill, surmounted by an imposing church, was a large town whose grey monotony was relieved by a splash of colour from an occasional red roof. On going ashore I looked forward to being keenly conscious of a strangeness in my surroundings, similar to what had usually infused a dreamlike quality into my emotions on first arriving in foreign lands. But, with a pang of disappointment, I saw that the dominant fact here was the absence of all individuality, and my sole reaction was a feeling of being already familiar with all its features.

---

5. [*sic*] In May 1941, Iceland served formal notice to Nazi-occupied Denmark that it desired to overturn their Act of Union. A two-part referendum to abolish the union and adopt a new republican constitution was held in May 1944 and approved by 99.5 percent of voters.

There was nothing primitive about the place, but it had the crude, unfinished appearance I had often seen in the recently built housing schemes of various other countries. Soon, however, I caught something of the exotic note I had expected when I met groups of women dressed in an altogether unknown fashion that transformed the commonplace streets into a picturesque scene. They wore their hair in thick plaits hanging down their backs, crowned by a little skull cap, from which a long tassel dangled over the shoulder. Their graceful robes were enriched by regal mantles of velvet edged with fur, under which gleamed a brass belt embossed with designs from the ancient sagas, the whole costume investing the wearers with a dignity worthy of the daughters of Vikings.

The most important buildings are the fine Catholic cathedral in pure Gothic style; the Lutheran church adorned with a white marble baptismal font by Thorwaldsen;[6] a theatre which maintained such a high standard that no actor appeared on its stage who had not acted previously in Copenhagen; and a museum, which contains an astonishing display of painting and sculpture by Iceland's distinguished son, Einar Jónsson.[7] Far from being the result of a long period of evolution, Icelandic art, like Minerva from the head of Zeus, sprang, fully mature, from the brain of this remarkable man. Born in a land apparently incapable of inspiring the creative imagination, he was daringly original in his symbolism and personification of nature, and, although he was acquainted with the productions of many foreign artists, ancient and modern, he was influenced by none; and, pupil of no school, disciple of no master, he was determined that his work should bear only the impress of his own personality. In a gallery rich with impressive statues, dating from 1894 to 1923, my attention was attracted by a small figure of an Irish monk bearing a crucifix and

6. Bertel Thorvaldsen (1770–1844) was a famed Danish sculptor during the neoclassical period.

7. Einar Jónsson (1874–1954) was an Icelandic sculptor known for his portraits and public moments, as well as his profound spirituality.

labelled "the first settler in Iceland," a fact suggesting that the sculptor probably believed the popular legend, which attributes the discovery of this sequestered spot to no other than that adventurous spirit, Saint Brendan, the Navigator.[8]

In a country without railways, and with roads only in the immediate vicinity of inhabited areas, the chief mode of transport was on horseback. About fifteen miles from Reykjavik is the famous valley of Thingvellir, where the world's oldest parliament was founded more than a thousand years ago. For this journey I was offered one of the sturdy ponies for which the island is noted, but most reluctantly refused the mount in favour of an antique motor car, the time limit determining my choice. Lurching along a rough track through a landscape which was lifeless but for a few black, white, and brown sheep, and colourless except for occasional patches of emerald green, like oases in the desert, we suddenly entered the shadow of a precipitous gorge. Cliffs of reddish granite and fantastically carved violet rocks flanked a labyrinth leading to an immense plain partly covered by deposits of lava, relieved by the silver gleam of a large sheet of water, and bounded by a range of snow-capped mountains. Desolate as it is today, this historic place once resounded with the ringing voices of a multitude, when chieftains, armed with swords and lances and clad in armour, rode from the most inaccessible localities, and encamped here for the assembly of the Althing, as it was called, which was held in the spring of every year, and lasted for two weeks. In the long course of its history, this weird spot may well have been the scene of strange events, but surely of none more so than the dramatic advent of Christianity when, without the eloquence of an inspired preacher, or any preliminary missionary labour, the ancient gods, Thor and Odin, who had long been worshipped in numerous temples, were summarily banished

8. St. Brendan (Gaelic: Naomh Bréanainn or Naomh Breandán) also called Brendan of Clonfert or Brendan the Navigator (ca. 484–578), was one of the so-called Twelve Apostles of Ireland, who is famed for his legendary voyage to the "Isle of the Blessed."

by a parliamentary decree, followed by the baptism of all present on the banks of the nearby lake.[9]

Returning from this exciting excursion I stopped for some time to watch several women, enveloped in steam, busily cooking and washing clothes in the hot springs that well from the depths of this land of ice. Suddenly, in the neighbourhood, a loud rumbling reverberated beneath the earth, and, scared by a warning cry, I fled to a safe distance from a geyser, which resembled a gigantic sheaf of ostrich plumes, whose height and volume dwarfed all the fountains ever made by man. We were now approaching the realm of perpetual day, and though we left Reykjavik long after midnight, the western sky was stained as if by an overflowing wine glass, and the placid ocean shimmered with "patens of bright gold."[10]

For the next twenty-four hours, in an arctic temperature, we remained in sight of a rocky coast, backed by leaden-coloured, snow-flecked mountains that contrasted strikingly with a gentian-blue sea, whose loneliness was dispelled for a moment by the passing of a trawler with scarlet sails.

Next morning, although we had now gone beyond the influence of the Gulf Stream, the intense cold had vanished, and we anchored off Akureyri, which sprawls for about half a mile along the shore of a picturesque fjord. The principal industry here was demonstrated by thousands of codfish drying in the sun and countless barrels of oil; and, judging from the number of flags floating from the homes of consuls, diplomatic relations were in a flourishing condition. Polar bears sometimes travel on enormous ice-floes, driven south by powerful currents, and one winter the normally peaceful atmosphere of this town was overwhelmed by all the horror of a nightmare when a cargo of these starving animals invaded its streets.

9. In about 1000, Thoreir Ljosvetningagodi, a pagan chieftain of the Althing, abruptly decided that Christianity would replace Norse paganism as the "one law and one religion" of Iceland, requiring the conversion of all who lived there.

10. William Shakespeare, *The Merchant of Venice* (1598), act V, scene 1.

A surprise awaited me when I drove into the rural area, over an extremely rugged road, bordered with clumps of purple pansies. In the valleys I found an unexpected amount of cultivation, people working in the fields, large flocks of horned sheep, and many pastoral scenes unknown in the vicinity of Reykjavik. The little farmhouses were built of lava blocks completely covered with roughly cut sods of the soil, the interiors furnished so scantily that the most prominent object, attached round the walls, was a broad bench or shelf which supplied the family with tables and chairs by day and beds by night. I visited a tiny church, externally similar to these curious dwellings, but it was lined with wood, which must have been imported if the total absence of trees I had noted characterised the whole country. That evening there was a shade of wistfulness in my farewell to Iceland, a sense of having broken the last link with humanity, with the simple homely things of ordinary life, a momentary shrinking from the unknown, a chill feeling of isolation that quickly dissolved in the fervour of my enthusiasm at finding myself at last on the direct route to the Pole.

We now sailed during an endless day in a world where the flight of time was no longer marked by the periods of morning, noon and night; and that we were not utterly alone in the immense emptiness was proved by the passing of a whaler, so eager to greet us that it approached until we could see on board the dissection of a huge carcass; and soon afterwards two of the victim's companions became partly visible as they frolicked in the waves, evidently rejoicing at their escape from a similar fate.

The next afternoon we got a glimpse of Jan Mayen Land, which has been almost entirely formed by the eruption of a lofty volcano; and then, instantaneously, as if the earth had yawned and swallowed us, everything disappeared beneath the pall of a dense fog. Our speed gradually lessened until we were almost at a standstill; the pilot stood erect at the prow, motionless as a figure-head; and the awful silence was broken only by the unceasing wails of the syren, like the moans of a wounded beast in pain. In this boundless solitude there was little likelihood of a collision, but a far greater danger threatened as we drew near the very birthplace of the dreaded iceberg. Everybody seemed to speak in hoarse whispers, and visibility became so limited that even the forms of my fellow passengers, as they moved about the deck in an earthly gloom, were blurred almost beyond recognition. In this veritable Hades, the bark of Cerberus[11] or the splash of Charon's oars would be a welcome break in the terrible monotony, in which time and space were no longer even mere mental illusions, as some philosopher has maintained. I tried to check the claustrophobic feelings that oppressed me by walking a few yards and stretching my arms as wide as possible, but my mind was filled with gruesome thoughts, and my imagination hovered between the story of Jonah[12] and the tragic destiny of Verdi's hapless lovers, immured alive within their tomb.[13] All this, however, was comparatively cheerful compared to what I felt when some sadistic demon, determined to plunge me still deeper in the Slough of Despond, seized the gong, hitherto associated with appetising meals, and sounded a peremptory summons to attend a lifesaving drill. Whipped by a searing wind, we were marshalled beside our respective boats, while members of the crew instructed us in the complicated process of donning our belts. My instructor thoughtfully warned me that if I failed to adjust this cumbrous apparatus properly, my neck would inevitably be broken when I jumped overboard; and looking down into the black abyss that awaited me, I concluded that this might well be a merciful fate. At the end of forty-eight hours, when endurance had almost reached breaking point, the fog slowly lifted, revealing an illimitable expanse of grey sea that seemed to have existed before the creation of life. Early next morning I looked out my porthole, warmly welcomed the sun, and, in a mood of tense expectancy, got my first impression of Spitzbergen.

This group of islands was discovered in 1596 by the Dutch explorer, Barentsz,[14] during his attempt to find a northern route to China, but,

---

11. In Greek mythology, Cerberus is the monstrous-headed dog that guards the gates of the underworld.

12. Jonah 2:1–11.

13. Radames and Aida in act IV of Guiseppe Verdi's opera, *Aida* (1871).

14. Willem Barentsz (English: William Barentz) (ca. 1550–97).

having failed in his quest, he died of scurvy on the homeward voyage, and was buried in the sea that now bears his name. This event in its history was but the forerunner of such a long series of tragedies, commemorated by the numerous wooden crosses erected round its shores, that this remote region, with its four months of perpetual darkness, has been called "the Country of the Dead," one of its dismal peaks being known as the "Mount of Tears." Attracted by the wealth hidden in waters teeming with whales, walrus, and seals, so many colonies were established here for about two hundred years after its discovery that eventually these valuable animals were practically exterminated, and the place was deserted until its interior was explored by Sir Martin Conway[15] in the last decade of the nineteenth century.

A land without colour, where nature demonstrates her dexterity as a sculptor rather than her skill as a painter, Spitzbergen, at first sight, is so overpowering to a mere mortal, so majestic in its grandeur, so sublime in its primeval solitude, so undefiled by man, that it leaves one breathless with awe, as though one were present at the very dawn of creation. Steep, deeply scarred mountains, black earth partly covered with dazzling snow, immense glaciers crawling stealthily to the edge of an azure sea, where they form shimmering cliffs of ice, all were sharply defined under the glare, at this season, of a never-setting sun. Clinging to the coast for miles, we encountered many icebergs, entered a harbour populated by seals and penguins, passed mountains resembling chocolate cakes topped with white icing, and finally anchored in Advent Bay. Here the landscape conformed to the pattern to which I had now become accustomed, but soon I was dazed by a transformation scene so unexpected that it seemed to belong to the realm of fantasy rather than to that of real life. Climbing to the fringe of a sunlit valley, I found myself gazing in amazement at a cluster of little wooden houses, painted pink, yellow, blue, mauve, and various

15. William Martin Conway, the First Baron Conway of Allington (1856–1937), was a British explorer, art historian, and politician who conducted expeditions in Europe, South America, and Asia.

other shades, startling in such surroundings as a flamboyant flower garden. These minute dwellings, far from being the abode of gnomes or goblins, were occupied by tall, hefty men engaged in laborious work. Incredible as it seemed, this fantastic village was the residence of a colony of Norwegian miners, and, near the summit of the gaunt peak soaring above, was the coal mine which proved that, on this arid spot, green trees once flourished. Some of these workers were accompanied by their wives, who were apparently content and cheerful, in contrast to the men, who looked as though the melancholy of their environment had seeped into their souls. During their sojourn here the government did everything possible for their health and comfort by providing a well-built little church, a large scrupulously clean refectory, a post office, and a hospital staffed with a doctor, a dentist, and two nurses. Nearly all their food was sent from Norway, and, in such a climate, was preserved indefinitely without the aid of refrigerators. The interiors of their homes, compact as ships' cabins, were almost cosy enough to render even the polar night tolerable, and, though some of these people remained only a few months, the majority faced the long darkness and worked for two seasons. During the winter, transport problems were solved by using sledges drawn by the powerful Eskimo dogs that now wandered about in blissful idleness. I considered myself fortunate to have seen this settlement when I heard that water had begun to ooze through the galleries of the mine, one section being already flooded, so that in a short time this region, now such a hive of industry, was doomed to revert to its original silence and desolation.

Such was the fate we found to have befallen King's Bay, another coal mining centre, when we landed there the following afternoon. The huts were deserted, the machinery left to rust, and the sole surviving inhabitants, the postmaster and his wife, performed their last act of public service by stamping and dispatching our letters, and probably returned to Norway on the last mail boat. Confused by the impossibility of distinguishing night from day, I rarely went to bed before 2 a.m., and even then, so stimulating was the sunshine pouring in my window, that I felt little inclination to sleep. Unusually wakeful at this particularly interesting place, I went ashore soon after midnight, and was enjoying a walk over a carpet of wildflowers, rich and variegated as a Persian rug, when I was fiercely attacked by a battalion of angry birds, evidently resentful of my intrusion on their exclusive territory. Swooping down suddenly, they almost succeeded in driving me back to my cabin, but, protecting my face and head with a large scarf, I eventually escaped from their talons, considerably frightened by such an abnormal experience.

A short distance from the shore stands the huge skeleton of the hangar constructed to accommodate the airship in which Amundsen[16] made his celebrated flight over the Pole in 1926, and which was also used in 1928 to house the "Italia" of Nobile,[17] before starting on a similar journey. When news came of the latter's disastrous crash in the arctic wilds, the former, from this very spot, flew to the rescue; but, while the Italian's life was saved, the famous Norwegian was never seen again. A monument to his memory, erected here by his compatriots, records not only his great achievements as an explorer, but also his outstanding act of self-sacrifice as a man. Not very far away is the scene of another daring exploit in the history of polar exploration, the attempt of Andree[18] in 1897 to reach the Pole by balloon. He and his two companions were never heard of until 1930, when his body, his maps, diaries, and logbook were found on White Island.

Our entry into Cross Bay was a masterly feat of navigation by our pilot, who, with all the grace and agility of a Scottish sword-dancer, manoeuvered us to safety through a swarm of small icebergs, which, in their gleaming whiteness and sculptured forms, reminded me of those great Italian cemeteries renowned for the beauty of their marble

16. Roald Amundsen (1872–1928) was a Norwegian explorer who led the first expedition to reach the South Pole in 1911 and later became the first to cross the Arctic by air.

17. The *Italia* was a semirigid airship piloted by Italian General Umberto Nobile (1885–1978) during his second series of flights around the North Pole in 1928.

18. Salomon August Andrée (1854–97) was a Swedish scientist, aeronaut, and explorer.

tombs. And surely this secluded haven, where no living thing was visible, might well be a resting place for the dead. Nature, in her most austere mood, was clad in mourning garb, and there was something sacred in the silence that even a deep breath seemed to profane. The peace of this sanctuary was shattered only when an immense fragment of a glacier, breaking from the parental mass, crashed into the sea with a sound like a peal of thunder that announced the birth of an iceberg. Even this was a mere ripple on the surface which quickly ebbed away, leaving a stillness so profound that our boat seemed to steal on tiptoe from the scene, conscious of being an intruder.

Our next port of call was Magdalene Bay, with its mountainous black and white background, scintillating glaciers, and perfect curve, lovely in shape as the famous Concha of San Sebastian. Myriads of birds, like snowflakes, fluttered and wheeled above a tranquil blue sea, which was scarcely ruffled by a procession of icebergs, graceful as swans. Some of these, transformed into prisms by the sun's rays, were iridescent as a casket of jewels; and the whole spectacle was so ethereal, so exotic, that my wondering eyes eagerly seized all the details, fearful lest such rare loveliness might vanish like a dream. Reluctantly departing from this enchanted spot, the last land on this side of the globe, we were accompanied by an escort of seals, later reinforced by two walrus, their curiosity probably aroused by the unusual sight of humanity. All these soon disappeared, leaving us on a lonely ocean, warned that our voyage was approaching its end by a strange light on the horizon, the reflection of the ghastly wilderness that lay before us. Timidly we crept forward until we stopped abruptly, confronted by an irresistible force that compelled our retreat. In an indescribable and overwhelming loneliness, I looked at this interminable sea of ice, cruel as a monstrous beast of prey, eager to mangle with its claws any vessel venturing within its reach; and I saluted not only the victor but the vanquished, not only the valiant Peary,[19] but the long line of heroes

19. Robert Edwin Peary (1856–1920) was an American naval officer and arctic explorer, credited with leading the first expedition to reach the geographic North Pole in 1909.

who made his victory possible by an almost superhuman fortitude, and, in many cases, by facing the agony of a lingering death.

Our farewell to the Arctic was unexpectedly premature owing to the dense fog that crept round us soon after we turned south. Plunged into an inferno similar to that of the outward journey, we were spared the ordeal of lifeboat drill by the intense cold; but a full measure was added to our misery when the placidity of the polar seas was replaced by waves that tossed the unfortunate boat to and fro like the ball in a game of rugby. We passed Bear Island which, even when the sun shines elsewhere, is usually invisible in a shroud of mist, and at last a chill breath from the Pole lifted the clammy winding-sheet that enveloped us, disclosing the grim precipice of the North Cape, so close and so directly in our path that we seemed doomed to inevitable destruction. We skirted the coast of Norway, got a distant view of Hammerfest, the most northerly town of Europe, and were dazzled by the glory of the sunset, so long unseen, which ushered in a short evening, though, as yet, there was no night. When the sun sank, it remained so close below the horizon that it radiated an eerie twilight, called by Norwegians the "Tussmorke," during which a lovely green glow suffused the western sky.

Next morning I looked out my porthole and saw a new world, which, to eyes ravenous for colour, seemed a Garden of Eden. Flowers, grass, trees, abundant vegetation, all formed a radiant setting for the little town of Lyngen, nestling in the shadow of lofty peaks that lined the fiord, on which we sailed that afternoon on our way to Tromso. Here, in a small public park, the inscription on a statue of Amundsen proclaims the fact that it was from this place he started on his final ill-fated expedition. After several hours ashore we left by evening light, and I enjoyed an unforgettable view of the picturesque pastel-coloured houses backed by blue, snow-topped mountains; and soon I joyfully welcomed the first star I had seen during the whole voyage, a certain sign that the reign of perpetual day was almost at an end. Later we arrived at what is known as the Lofoten Wall, that string of jagged pinnacles rising precipitously from an unbroken chain of islands, fifty miles long, which terminates in a colossal cliff, close to the maelstrom immortalised by Edgar Allen Poe.[20] We were now in one of the world's most important fishing centres, the scene of an extraordinary event which is a dominant factor in the prosperity of this country. Every year, in February, millions of codfish, in immense shoals, often 150 feet thick, migrate along the Norwegian coast, following the flow of the Gulf Stream. The shortness of the six weeks' season combined with the value of the catch, creates an almost incredible congestion in the adjoining villages, and when, at this period of darkness, thousands of lights are suspended from the masts of trawlers and flash from the fishermen's torches, the sea must be a wonderful sight.

Next day we landed at Trondjem, a large town with a royal palace and a very fine cathedral, in which Bernadotte was crowned king of Norway and Sweden in 1814. Here, at last, life resumed its normal course, time was restored to its rightful place, and, under a full moon and a sky glittering with stars, I gave thanks for the precious gift of sleep, and, with something of the rapture of the poet, I realised more profoundly than ever before, "how beautiful is Night."[21]

In the present age, when the motto *Nil Admirari*[22] is written in letters of flame upon rapidly shrinking skies, when speed is almost worshipped as a god, and life has degenerated into an unending race, how gladly I play the part therein of a humble tortoise rather than of an arrogant hare! I rejoice in my good fortune at having visited Iceland while it was still "the Anchorite of the Atlantic," before becoming a mere stepping-stone on the shortest route to the Far East; and I am thrilled at the thought of having crawled beyond the farthest shores of Spitzbergen, "to stand and stare"[23] at that awe-inspiring mausoleum of many heroes, the vast area of pack-ice that forms the last barrier to the North Pole.

20. Edgar Allen Poe, "A Descent into the Maelström" (1841).
21. Robert Southey, "How Beautiful is Night" (1799).
22. [Latin] "to wonder at nothing."
23. W. H. Davies, "Leisure" (1916), line 2.

13. Map for Balkan Byways, Brian Bixby, 2020.

12

Balkan Byways

The hardships and misadventures inseparable from travel in remote areas of the world may be likened, in my opinion, to the nucleus needed by the oyster for the formation of a precious gem. The remembrance of these unpleasant experiences would inevitably tarnish some of my most splendid moments were it not that in course of time they became encrusted with a layer of something magical that develops into a thing of beauty completely concealing the ugliness of the inner core. I could almost rival Saint Paul in the various misfortunes that befell me in my wanderings, and yet my vivid memories of those days have become a priceless possession, a sort of spiritual string of pearls. As are precious stones, some of these are undoubtedly more perfectly formed, or more lustrous, than others, and among the most

Murphy's final travelogue, published posthumously in the 1963 issue of *The Capuchin Annual*, tells the story of her last pilgrimage—across the republics that made up Yugoslavia in 1961—to view the churches and abbeys of the region. Now in her early eighties, Murphy again joins a tour group, but this is no luxury outing. To reach the cultural monuments she seeks, Murphy must travel rough roads in brutal temperatures, endure a harrowing carriage ride, and even find herself on the wrong end of a soldier's rifle. But the rewards are well worth these trials: she encounters the stunning art and architecture of the abbeys, along with the many surprises of social and cultural life in the republics. If she tends to exoticize the Islamic elements of the Balkans, Murphy nonetheless lauds the cultural diversity represented there. To be sure, the sheer variety of what she encounters in the region, the stimulating mixture of East and West, serves as a fitting culmination to her many adventures. Reproduced with permission from *The Capuchin Annual*.

memorable for sheer enjoyment was a tour I once made through the Balkans, a name which, in my imagination, had ever been encircled by an aura of romance.

Tourists were so unknown when I first visited Belgrade that whenever I indulged my habit of lingering in historic places to attempt recreate the life of past ages, I aroused the suspicions of the police and was shadowed by a detective; and, when I penetrated into the wilds of Albania, the bandits, who then infested the country, were so chivalrous that the presence of a woman in a car was an absolute guarantee of its immunity from attack. This was in striking contrast to my experience in other lands. Returning from a visit to a moonlit temple in Sicily I narrowly escaped being captured by brigands. My "emotion remembered in tranquility,"[1] created something more practical than a poem; I achieved the thrill of standing on the Great Wall of China by taking the precaution of joining a party escorted there by a bodyguard of soldiers.

In Dalmatia, Bosnia, Herzegovina and Serbia, I travelled in the ordinary local buses, thus establishing an intimate contact with many places in which, at that time, so universally worn were the picturesque and colourful, national costumes, that the weekly markets resembled fancy dress balls. In some districts the majority of the inhabitants were followers of Mohammed, in others the Cross was triumphant over the Crescent; and once, as I approached a distant village, I saw a mosque, a Catholic and an Orthodox church, all three, silhouetted clearly against the horizon. Everywhere one witnessed a fascinating blend of East and West, found nowhere else in Europe; and no traveller could ever complain of monotony where the scenery was as varied and interesting as the people.

An intensely exciting journey of discovery brought me to places like lovely Ragusa, brooding on its former greatness, the haughty

---

1. William Wordsworth, "Preface to *Lyrical Ballads*" (1798): "Poetry is the spontaneous overflow of powerful feelings: it takes its origin from emotion recollected in tranquility."

rival of Venice in the Middle Ages; Spalato, that unique town built within the walls of Diocletian's tremendous palace; Sarajevo, with its dim-lit bazaars, veiled women, and countless minarets; picturesque Jajce where I heard the muezzin's cry resounding through its majestic gorge and at sunset watched groups of gaily clad men performing the ceremony of washing themselves at a fountain before evening prayer. I enjoyed on foot the beautiful neighbourhood of Vilitvice, where an unbroken chain of sixteen jade-green lakes, connected by a series of foam-white cascades seen during a twilight walk, was a scene unforgettable, to which a truly oriental touch was added by a shepherdess singing on a hillside, and a shepherd leading his flock to the sweet notes of a flute. I traversed immense plains that would delight the heart of a Van Gogh[2] when the westering sun set the cornfields aflame. I entered Montenegro over the Lovcen Pass of precipices and hairpin bends scarcely less terrifying than those I afterwards encountered when crossing the Andes.

I explored all the highways of this most fascinating country but its byways appealed to me irresistibly because in this secluded corner of the world numerous treasure-houses of art are concealed from the public by the remoteness and inaccessibility of their situation. In my mind, this fact, added immeasurably to the allurement of the places, endowing them with a poetic atmosphere, an air of mystery, altogether lacking along the beaten track. Before the Turkish conquest, Serbia and Macedonia were sprinkled with Orthodox monasteries, the walls and domes of which were covered with magnificent frescoes though only a fraction of them have survived the ravages of time and war. It was tantalising to find that, unlike Mount Athas, which is barred to women, I could have free access to these extremely interesting buildings if only I could reach them, but at that time they could be approached only by rugged mountain trails or dried-up river beds; only hefty pedestrians or expert horsemen with unlimited leisure could enjoy their beauty.

2. Vincent Willem van Gogh (1853–90).

Many years elapsed and though I had then seen most of the great galleries of Europe, and much of its monastic architecture, including even the Meteora of Greece,[3] the thought of these secluded shrines in the Balkans still haunted my dreams. The excitement I felt can then be well imagined when, in the spring of 1961, I saw, in an English newspaper, an advertisement of a tour to some of these ancient treasure houses, organised specially for connoisseurs by a Yugoslav travel agency "in co-operation with experts of the National Institute for the conservation of Cultural Monuments." Without delay I secured a reservation, and at Ostend, one night in the following July, I boarded the Tauern Express bound for Belgrade.

Breaking the long journey at Zagreb, the Croatian capital, I visited the cathedral, founded in the twelfth century, so closely associated with Cardinal Stepinac, whom I had seen long ago, and whose spiritual face, with its strikingly beautiful eyes, was impossible to forget. He is buried behind the high altar, and despite a communist government, his faithful flock are determined to keep his memory green by daily tributes of fresh flowers from groups of mourners kneeling beside his tomb.

During the day I spent in this ancient city, I lingered in some of my old haunts, and recalled an amusing experience I once had when travelling from there to Bled, the lovely summer resort in the Julian Alps. I entered an overcrowded train and was trying to wade my way through a densely packed corridor, gloomily facing the prospect of having to stand for several hours, when a man suddenly appeared outside a compartment and, seeing my plight, ushered me into a vacant seat. I had a warm welcome from four other men to whose bows and gesticulations I could respond in similar fashion, for having then been practically dumb for weeks, I had become almost as proficient at expressing myself in gesture as an actress in the silent films. I noticed that the blinds on the inner windows were pulled down, and after a

3. Meteora is a group of Eastern Orthodox monasteries perched on the summits of vertical rock formations in Thessaly.

short time I was bewildered by the strange behaviour of my companions. Whenever we were approaching a station they all jumped up abruptly and rushed out on to the platform, where they remained until we were again about to move, and then strolled back with an air of utter relaxation. During their absence the other passengers thronged round the door, and stared at me in a most embarrassing manner. This occurred at all our numerous stopping-places, and, at the end of the journey, my new friends took charge of my luggage, found me one of the few porters and made a most elaborate demonstration of their sorrow at having to say goodbye. Only then, at last, was light thrown on the whole mysterious affair; somebody, who spoke French, informed me that I had been travelling with the royal detectives, and my fellow travellers had mistaken me for a prisoner.

I arrived in Belgrade at night and was dazzled by the brilliantly lighted streets, richly decked shop windows, and imposing public buildings which had transformed the rather shabby, war-worn capital I had known into a modern metropolis, from which all traces of Turkish domination had been obliterated, and no vestige whatever remained of the Austrian bombardment during the First World War, nor of the dreadful havoc wrought by Hitler's Stukas.[4] I was still more amazed, when, with recollections of my former hostelry, I dined on the terrace of a palatial hotel, from a menu worthy of the most fastidious gourmet, to the delightful strains of a first-class string orchestra. Unfortunately next day was the national holiday, and the museums and galleries being closed, I was disappointed in my intention of renewing my acquaintance with that fine Yugoslav sculptor, Meštrović.[5]

I searched in vain for some familiar landmarks in a place that seemed to have lost its identity and found myself, at last, in the grounds of the fortress, which enshrines the history of the country and is the only ancient edifice in a city which its important strategical

---

4. The Stuka or Junkers Ju 87 was a single-engine dive bomber used by the German Luftwaffe from 1937 to 1945.

5. Ivan Meštrović (1883–1962) was a famed Yugoslavian and Croatian sculptor, as well as a leading figure in the artistic life of Zagreb.

position doomed to a tragic fate. In 400 BC the Celts founded here a settlement which they called Singidunum which became, eight hundred years later, an episcopal see. (It was conquered by a succession of invaders, Greeks, Romans, Franks, Bulgars, Venetians, Byzantines and others, including the Slavs in the seventh century who changed its name to Beograd, and called the whole land Serbia, which then comprised all the countries now known as Yugoslavia. When the Hungarians were in possession they transported the entire fort to Zemun, a town on the opposite side of the river, and later, the Byzantines carried back the whole structure and rebuilt it on its old site, overlooking the confluence of the Sava and the Danube. The supremacy of Constantinople continued over the whole Balkan peninsula until the twelfth century when Stefan Nemanya[6] founded a hereditary, independent Slav state and became king.) Along a path, hitherto unknown to me, I descended a short distance and approached a massive gateway at which stood a soldier, who appeared to be shouting instructions to a man busily engaged unloading a cart full of sand. Then suddenly and swiftly as a flash of lightning, the whole scene vanished and, with abnormal clearness of vision, my eyes saw absolutely nothing but a gun pointing straight in my direction and a steady hand about to pull the trigger. Petrified with horror I remained rivetted to the spot, and it seemed ages before I regained sufficient strength to turn back. The shouts I had heard were the cries of a sentry ordering me to halt.

Contrary to Shakespeare's dictum, I find that for me custom never stales the infinite variety of travel,[7] and early next morning when the tour started, the thrill of expectancy, which I always feel on such occasions, was as keen as ever. My first reaction was surprise at the discovery that, in this part of the world, a connoisseur is a *rara avis*,[8] for, when, instead of the forty members of the species I had expected

---

6. Stefan Nemanya or Nemanja (ca. 1113–ca. 1200) was founder of the Serbian state and the Nemanjić dynasty.

7. William Shakespeare, *Antony and Cleopatra* (1606), act II, scene 2: "Age cannot wither her, nor custom stale / Her infinite variety."

8. Latin: "rare bird."

to meet, I found only seven. There were two Englishwomen, one a doctor, who was destined to have ample opportunity of practising her profession on her fellow travellers; a professor and his wife from Brussels and a textile designer from Sweden; and a Belgian woman whose almost perfect silence might be the result of a vow, so unemotional that she might be a robot. Completing our little company was a young Church of England clergyman who, for comfort's sake, had discarded clerical dress, and wore a dust-coloured suit several sizes too large, and a flamboyant scarf draped, in Arabic fashion, round his head, as a precaution against sunstroke. A small, upturned nose, coupled with a pair of dark eyes, in which laughter always lurked, gave him an impish expression that would be an invaluable asset to a comedian, but must have been a decided disadvantage to a preacher. Resembling a pedlar more than a parson, his slim figure was lavishly festooned with gadgets of various kinds. Cameras of many shapes and sizes, a tape recorder, a thermos flask, a leather satchel, guidebooks, maps, and a bulky volume of unbound notes were so precariously attached to his person that, like a windblown tree in autumn, his movements were always punctuated by a flutter of loose leaves.

I arrived last and was allotted a back seat in a mini-coach which behaved like a ball on the appallingly bad roads we encountered and bounced from one "pothole" to another with sickening regularity. Once I was flung with such force against the roof that, dreading concussion, I determined to keep a permanent grip on some solid fixture in front of me to prevent a recurrence of such a painful experience. This involved a chronic state of tension which, accompanied by constant jerks from side to side and jolts backward and forward, transformed the journey in the torrid temperature of the hottest month of the year into something resembling a penitential pilgrimage. Our first stop was at the village of Topola, a few miles from the birthplace of Karageorge,[9] where a monument has been erected to this heroic

9. Karageorge or Karadjordje ("Black George"), byname of George Petrović (1762–1817), was leader of the First Serbian Uprising against the Ottoman Empire (1804–13) and founder of the Karadjordjević dynasty.

opponent of Turkish domination who gave his name to the dynasty whose rule was ended in 1945 by the proclamation of a republic. Nearby is the church of Oplenac built in 1910 by his grandson, Peter I,[10] to enshrine the tombs of his family, which in a most impressive crypt are distinguished by their simplicity. The interior walls are almost completely covered with admirable mosaic copies by German artists of the frescoes in the old monasteries, and as I turned back for a last admiring glance, the beautiful building was suffused with a lovely blueish light that, despite the massive structure, transformed it into something ethereal and visionary.

Pausing for lunch at the large industrial town of Kragujevac we were soon en route to Ljubostinja, a spot so cut off that until recently it could be reached only over the dried bed of a river. Close beside the bank a road now runs and, though the latter seems to be modelled on the former, I felt well repaid for the turbulent journey by the exquisite atmosphere of peace and the sense of remoteness from all worldly cares that enveloped me immediately once I entered the monastic precincts. Surely no more fitting place could be chosen by one desirous of leaving the world behind than this sequestered haven where Militza,[11] widow of the ill-fated Tsar Lazar,[12] founded a monastery in which she lived as a nun for the rest of her life. The richly decorated church is in Moravian style, and the centuries, which have obliterated much of the beauty of the soft stone carvings, have been more merciful to the numerous frescoes that transform these ancient shrines into veritable galleries of art. We followed the steps of the foundress to Krushevatz,

10. Peter I, byname King Peter the Liberator (1844–1921), was king of Serbia from 1903 until 1918, when he became the first king of the Kingdom of Serbs, Croats, and Slovenes.

11. Princess Milica Hrebeljanović, also known as Empress Milica (1335–1405), was a royal consort of Serbia, who founded the Ljubostinja monastery in about 1390 and took vows to become nun Eugenia in about 1393.

12. Prince Lazar Hrebeljanović, also known as Lazar of Serbia (1329–89), was a medieval ruler who presided over Monrovian Serbia from 1373 until he was killed by the Ottoman army in the Battle of Kosovo.

former capital of Serbia, from which she fled after her husband's death. The remarkable church he built there is still in a wonderful state of preservation, due to the fact that it was covered with plaster by the Turks. Nothing else remains from the past except a fragment of the palace wall and a melancholy memorial of the darkest day in Serbian history, the gateway through which Lazar led his troops to disaster on the battlefield of Kosovo.

We spent the night at Kraljevo, a small town with a dominant Turkish atmosphere in its colourful market scenes, and arrived early next day at the monastery of Zica, a prominent feature of the landscape, owing to the fact that its walls are painted dark red, which gives it a deceptively modern appearance. Built about 1208 by Stefan Peter,[13] who was crowned here by his brother Saint Sava,[14] it became the seat of the newly founded archbishopric, of which the latter was the first occupant. Zica was recognised for many generations as the spiritual centre of the Serbian state. Bishops were consecrated and monarchs enthroned in its cathedral, whose architecture is the full flowering of the Raska School.[15] Almost from its foundation, this monument to the former greatness of Serbia has suffered much from the ruthlessness of war; the last conflict left its mark with a bomb that destroyed, among other things, a large area of the precious frescoes. The oldest of these are preserved in the choir. All the others belong to a more recent date, including the works of the Court School of King Milutin,[16] a group of artists who, during

13. Stefan Peter or Stefan Nemanjić, byname Stefan the First-Crowned (1165–1228), was Grand Prince of Serbia and, from 1217 until his death, the first Rascian king, who helped his brother Sava establish the Serbian Church.

14. Saint Sava (1174–1236), also known as the Enlightener, was a Serbian prince and the first archbishop of the autocephalous Serbian.

15. Raska style, also known as the Raska architectural school, is a Serbian ecclesiastical artistic and architectural style that prevailed from about 1170 until the end of the fourteenth century.

16. Stefan Uroš II Milutin (ca. 1253–1321) was a member of the Nemanjić dynasty and King of Serbia from 1282 until his death.

the twenty-five years of their activity, starting at the end of the thirteenth century, produced numerous mural paintings for ecclesiastical buildings throughout Serbia and Macedonia. These masters, growing weary of old static traditions, and tired of depicting conventional figures, were doubtless fired by the eagerness that swept like a flame through all forms of art in thirteenth-century Europe to create living figures. They introduced many innovations both in composition and technique, in the handling of drapery and the representation of space, in the treatment of light and shade and the harmonious blending of colours, all tending to give a dynamic quality to their work and a realism hitherto unknown in Serbian art. A beautiful arched door, leading to the sanctuary, is exceptionally rich in its decoration, and almost the whole interior surface of the church is covered with impressive single figures of kings, warriors, saints, martyrs, hermits, prophets, Old Testament characters, and large scenes of the *Crucifixion*, the *Descent of the Holy Ghost*, the *Annunciation*, the *Last Supper*, and, despite extensive damage—a scar across the centre— the most striking of all, an enormous *Dormition of the Virgin*, that favourite subject of medieval painters. This one is especially notable for its lovely head of Christ, who stands at the bedside looking down tenderly at his dead mother, and receiving her soul in the form of a winged infant.

Our route grew increasingly rugged as we approached mountainous country but the scenery did much to compensate for the discomfort of the journey. A delightful interlude brought rest and refreshment to mind and body when we lunched in the garden of a wayside inn facing a range of thickly wooded hills. In the foreground, in the vivid sunlight on the other side of the valley, was a golden fleece of ripe corn, which a group of gaily clad women were busily reaping. The scene was so biblical that we seemed to see Ruth and Naomi among the little company, and a poetic touch was added when, at intervals, with the regularity of a ritual, the reapers suddenly stopped work, stood side by side, and flung their arms round each other's shoulders, and sang plaintive, melodious songs of "old, unhappy, far-off things, and battles long ago."[17] With this music in my heart I climbed the steep path leading to the monastery of Studenica, my mood attuned to the full enjoyment of its many treasures.

It is recorded that Stefan Nemanya, while hunting in the surrounding forest, conceived the idea of founding in this remote region a monastic building that would serve as a mausoleum for himself and his descendants. Soon after this project had been realised, at the end of the twelfth century, he renounced his throne and became a monk at Mount Athos. When he died there some years later, his body was brought back enclosed in a double coffin of which the outer one of solid silver, elaborately worked, is now a prominent feature in the Our Lady Church, distinguished by the richness of its decoration. Lavish use has been made of white marble, the whole façade being covered with slabs of this material. A frieze of sculptured human and animal heads ornaments part of the exterior, which is notable for the beauty of its doors and windows. But, as with all these old Serb monasteries, however excellent their other features, its frescoes are the great glory of Studenica. According to an inscription in the dome all the mural paintings here were finished in 1209, but some of them were restored in 1569, much of their beauty unfortunately being marred in the process. Dating from the thirteenth century is an immense *Crucifixion* with a remarkable Saint John; many other scenes from the New Testament; and on the lower walls, countless single figures, powerful and majestic. Of special interest is the portrait of the founder and his family, which is the first realistically painted royal group in the Middle Ages. The little church of Saint Nicholas has an impressive thirteenth-century head of John the Baptist, and in the larger church, dedicated to Saints Anne and Joachim, built in 1314 by King Milutin, all the paintings belong to the first half of the fourteenth century, among which are many fine scenes of the life of the Virgin Mary, culminating in a *Presentation in the Temple*, an outstandingly beautiful

17. William Wordsworth, "The Solitary Reaper" (1807), lines 19–20.

composition. For some time Studenica was the seat of Nemanya's son, Archbishop Sava, later recognised as a saint, who wrote there some of his literary and historical works, and under whom it became a renowned centre of culture.

Hidden in the mountains, in a most picturesque situation, is the monastery of Sopocani, built about the year 1260 by King Uroš I,[18] who, like his grandfather, Nemanya, planned his foundation as his last resting place. Although a large part of the building was destroyed by the Turks in the seventeenth century, the importance of the remainder can hardly be exaggerated, for it is here we find the supreme achievement of medieval Serbian painting. Originally an area of seven hundred and sixty square metres was covered with frescoes, of which scarcely more than half have survived, and of these undoubtedly the most precious gem is the *Death of the Virgin Mary*,[19] a monumental work, in the presence of which criticism seems almost irreverent. We have here a scene in which unity of design, a subtle blending of sorrow and serenity, a loveliness of colour and composition, a delicate balance between the peaceful grouping and expressive attitudes of the numerous figures combine to form a harmony so perfect that it produces the effect of music. The atmosphere of mourning and solemnity that pervades the lower part is tempered by the charming upper section where the apostles are flying from distant lands, mounted on clouds and escorted by angels.

Several weeks would scarcely suffice to view all the beauty of this amazing collection, the impact of which is too overwhelming to assimilate in a single visit. Haunting my memory is the young shepherd pointing out the star at Bethlehem to his old companion whose wonder seems blended with fear; the expression of love, awe, and incredulity on the rugged features of the apostles to whom the Master appears after His resurrection; the poignant grief on the face of Saint

18. Stefan Uroš I, byname Uroš the Great (ca. 1223–77), was king of Serbia from 1243 until he was forced to abdicate to his son in 1276.

19. *Death of the Virgin Mary*, also known as *Dormition of the Mother of God*, is a 430 square foot (forty-square meter) fresco completed ca. 1265.

Peter, the unconventional bust of Saint John the Evangelist; the dramatic figure of a Prophet, clad in wonderfully manipulated drapery who seems to personify all the majesty and grandeur of the Old Testament. At least ten painters, whose names are unknown, worked in this church beginning not later than 1265 with the most famous, who is called in the history of art, the Sopocani Master, and ending with a much inferior artist in the fourteenth century.

While one lingers in admiration among these magnificent frescoes, distinguished, above all, for vitality, the names of Giotto and Duccio,[20] of Orcagna[21] and Simone Martini,[22] inevitably come to mind as possible sources of their inspiration, until one remembers that they were painted before the Italians were born, a fact which makes one wonder if some Serbian art experts are not, indeed, justified in claiming that their country is the true birthplace of the Renaissance.

A difficult climb over a lonely pass, once infested by brigands, brought us to what is now a monastery, but which was not intended as such by its builders. Early in the thirteenth century the Turks were becoming such a menace to the first Serbian archbishopric at Zica that Saint Sava's successor[23] transferred his seat to a secluded spot near the Rugovo Gorge and built a church there in the shadow of a sheer precipice. A hundred years later two succeeding archbishops built two other churches, which were subsequently joined to the original to form a single building, now known as the Patriarchate of Peć. Little remains today of its former artistic wealth, its superb handiwork on

20. Duccio, in full Duccio di Buoninsegna (died ca. 1319), was one of the most important Italian painters of the medieval period, who fused the Italo-Byzantine tradition with the Gothic style, and the founder of the Sienese school.

21. Orcagna, in full Andrea di Cione di Arcangelo (ca. 1308–68), was the most important Florentine painter and architect of the late medieval period.

22. Simone Martini (ca. 1284–1344) was an Italian painter, who made important contributions to the International Gothic style and the prominence of Sienese painting.

23. Arsenije Sremac (1219–66) was the second archbishop of the Serbian Orthodox Church.

gold, silver and on parchment, or its carvings in wood and stone, but some of its oldest frescoes still preserved are worthy of being placed at the very apex of Serbian painting. A striking example is the *Birth of the Virgin* by Master Jovan[24] who treated landscape and architecture in his works more realistically than any of his contemporaries, among whom was the unknown painter of the *Saint Nicholas*, which loudly proclaims its authenticity as a real portrait, though the subject looks more like a shrewd old courtier than a benevolent saint. Reluctantly I left this hallowed spot which had aroused in me so many emotions. The chanting of the monks mingled with the call to prayer from some nearby minaret, the rocky pinnacles towering above the monastery shut out the raucous sounds of a material world. The dove of peace could find no more fitting place to build her nest. Yet we were close to the mountains, grim and forbidding even on a summer's day, over which, in the winter of 1915, the Serbian army, accompanied by thousands of civilians made their historic retreat.

We were now passing through Kosmet, where fortresses on the hilltops and hidden monasteries testify to its former military might and its ancient culture. The most dominant feature of every village is a mosque beside a Christian church, a convincing proof that the old hostility has vanished. The national costumes are still worn; the colourful voluminous trousers of the Mohammedan women and the black-embroidered white garments of the Albanians. I noticed many men wearing the distinctive headdress of the Siptars[25] who, unlike their fellow Moslems, claim descent from one of the tribes with whom Rome maintained a state of almost chronic warfare, judging from how frequently their names are sprinkled through the pages of Tacitus.[26]

24. *Birth of the Virgin* (1346), on a lateral wall of the Church of St. Demetrius, Patriarchate of Peć, was painted by Master Jovan, who left only one coded signature to identify himself and remains the subject of debate among art historians.

25. Siptar, also transliterated Shqiptar, is an Albanian language ethnonym naming the Albanian people.

26. Tacitus, in full Publius Cornelius Tacitus (56–ca. 120), was a Roman public official and highly regarded historian.

Softly shaded, evening light harmonized with the sombre grandeur and austere site of the Patriarchate, but brilliant morning sunshine and blue skies formed the perfect setting for my first sight of Decani, considered the loveliest of all the Serbian monasteries. Founded in 1327, it has always been sacred to the Serbs as the burial place of its founder, Stefan Uroš III,[27] known as the "Holy King," because of the sanctity of his life. The church is a masterpiece of mauve and white marble, in the architecture of which the Romanesque and Byzantine styles are happily wedded. The doors and windows are elaborately decorated with symbolic carvings of gargoyles, griffins, flowers, foliage, birds and other animals, and an excellently carved frieze outlines the whole building, contributing much to the rich effect of its exterior. The inner walls are aglow with the colours of innumerable frescoes, many of them belonging to a much later date than those I had already seen. I particularly noted a *Marriage in Cana*, an *Annunciation*, the prophet *Balaam*, an *Expulsion of Adam and Eve from Paradise*, and a family group of King Dušan,[28] whose reign has been called the Golden Age of Serbia and whose ambition of becoming the ruler of a new empire, centered in Constantinople, death prevented him from realising.

Unlike many other monasteries that have undergone extensive restorations Decani has remained practically unchanged for the six hundred years of its existence. Even under Turkish domination and during the great wars no damage was done to an edifice revered both by Christians and Mohammedans. An attempt to capture it was once made by the sultan and his army, and an imam, privileged by his priestly rank, was chosen to be the first to cross the threshold, but when he arrived at the principal entrance, a marble lion fell from its pedestal on the unfortunate man's head, killing him instantly. Terror dispersed the

27. Stefan Uroš III Nemanjić, also known as Stefan Decanski (ca. 1285–1331), was the King of Serbia from 1322 until he was overthrown by his son Stefan Dušan in September 1331.

28. Stefan Uroš IV Dušan, also known as Dušan the Mighty (ca. 1308–55), was the king of Serbia from September 1331 and emperor of the Serbs, Greeks, and Albanians from 1346 after he conquered a large area of southeastern Europe.

invaders and Decani was saved. Another attempt on its integrity was made during the First World War. The Germans wished to remove the leaden roof from the church but the first man who attempted to obey the order had scarcely begun his work when he slipped and fell to his death, and his companions refused to risk a similar fate.

After the battle which ended in disaster for Serbia, the widow of Tzar Lazar visited this monastery and among her various gifts is an immense circular chandelier of finely wrought metal which has been hanging ever since before the sanctuary. Two colossal candles now standing beside the altar were also presented by her, and she expressed the desire, recorded in the archives, that they should not be lighted until Kosovo was avenged and Serbia free. More than five hundred and thirty-three years later the Serbian army, having inflicted a crushing defeat on the Turks, marched to the "Plain of the Blackbirds" to kiss the liberated soil, and the king having bowed in gratitude before the tomb of Uroš, lighted Militiza's candles.

I felt so fortified against the rigours of the road by the stimulating experience of a visit to this famous shrine that I was still absorbed in wondering at its many treasures, and living imaginatively the days of its glory when we had left its hallowed precincts far behind, and were approaching the historic town of Prizren. The royal residence and seat of government for two hundred years, Prizren was once a prosperous city, but its importance and prosperity disappeared and its size diminished when the capital was transferred from here to Krushevatz. It is situated in a natural amphitheatre, climbing tier above tier on the slopes of a mountain, crowned by the hoary walls of a medieval fortress, with numerous minarets rising like lilies in a garden. Its history is forgotten for a moment at the first sight of its beauty. National dress is extensively worn, transforming the steep cobbled streets into scenes irresistible to the heart of an artist. People of varying types, obviously sun-worshipping, sat or strolled in an atmosphere in which speed or strain are unknown.

About 1307, King Milutin built here the remarkable church of Bogorodica Ljeviska. When it was subsequently converted into a mosque, its fourteenth-century frescoes, according to the Turkish custom, were thickly covered with plaster. This has recently been removed, but unfortunately the nave suffered badly from the marks left by the chisel before applying the plaster—a tragic fate suffered by many precious Balkan frescoes.

We were now in what is called "The Land of Blue Shadows" where, at twilight, the country is enveloped by a soft, azure mist that gradually evolves into every imaginable shade of blue from the palest delphinium to the most brilliant gentian, while the sharply defined mountains on the horizon flaunt so intense a hue that here Paul Henry[29] would feel at home and an Irish exile be filled with wistful memories of Connemara.

We spent that night in Pristina, a large town with a good hotel, and as it was Saturday, I asked our guide to find out if there was a Catholic church here, and if so, at what time Mass would be celebrated next day. I was informed that the church was undergoing repairs, but that the service would be held at 8 o'clock in a building about two kilometers distant. I was told there were no taxis in the place but was assured that some form of transport would be procured, and I was thrilled next morning when I found awaiting me a carriage and pair driven by a Siptar. Never in my life had I seen a vehicle so dilapidated and I mounted nervously, fearing that my weight would prove "the last straw," and that the whole thing would fall to pieces. The driver assured my interpreter that he knew my exact destination, and off we started at a brisk trot. At first I was too interested in my surroundings to notice how far we were going, but when we had left even the suburbs behind and were in the open country I began to realise that the distance ought to be little more than a mile, and that already we must have covered at least three or four miles, judging from the pace of the horses. I poked the man with my umbrella and waved backwards with an eloquent gesture, but he pointed onwards with equal eloquence. After another couple of miles we had gone beyond all human

29. Paul Henry (1876–1958) was an Irish painter renowned for his landscapes of Connemara and West of Ireland, rendered in a muted postimpressionist style.

habitations—there was absolutely no traffic, we met no pedestrians and we were driving across the vast, apparently illimitable plain of Kosovo, the scene of the famous battle. I made several attempts to get the driver to turn back but they were always answered by a hand pointing forward, and once he aroused my fury by turning round on his seat and offering me a cigarette, obviously intended to soothe my nerves. Suddenly the monotony was broken by a harsh grating sound, and I was horrified to see one of the decrepit rubber tyres flying off and performing a pirouette in the middle of the road. Jumping down with an angry exclamation, my companion picked up an object that looked like the corpse of a snake killed in a motor accident, and with a leisurely air, and a skill I suspected was the result of long practice, he proceeded to repair the damage. After what seemed an age, the wheel revolved once more, and I was cheered by the certainty that we now must turn back, but, to my horror, I saw the hand still pointing to the dim horizon. Gruesome thoughts filled my mind, and I began to fear I was at the mercy of a maniac determined to drive me on and on until the wretched vehicle disintegrated, or the horses dropped dead from exhaustion. At last he got very excited and with a triumphant expression waved towards a distant spot where a large Orthodox church was visible against the flat background. We then left the main road and drove along a rough track where the carriage behaved like a see-saw and I like a Jack-in-the-box, and when we reached the entrance to the church grounds, we found it blocked by barbed wire. I made a vigorous protest which was completely ignored and realising that I must make a desperate attempt to prove to him that he had gone astray, I boldly faced the risk of leaving part of my clothing on the fence and I followed him to the door of the building which, as I expected, was locked. Now at last we turned back and eventually arrived at the hotel, outside which the guide eagerly greeted me. Soon she and the driver were engaged in a fierce battle about the cost of the trip, and, in an effort to establish peace, I offered quite a substantial sum which he flung back contemptuously and drove off down a side street. Fearing that he was going to fetch the police to arrest me for nonpayment of debt, I fled into the hotel in the presence of an ever-increasing crowd and nearly collided with my clerical friend who was rushing out to find the cause of the uproar. He kindly offered to act as mediator, and before I had finished my belated breakfast he came back to tell me that he had succeeded in pacifying the Siptar, who had returned to the fray and had finally accepted, with every demonstration of friendship, the sum he had at first so indignantly refused.

After this nerve-racking episode I was delighted to hear that we were only a few miles from the monastery of Gracanica, which is considered to be King Milutin's greatest achievement. The monastery church has no marble façade, no intricately carved frieze, none of the wealth of ornamentation that characterises the churches of the Raska school, and yet the architect transmuted the commonplace materials of brick and stone into the acknowledged masterpiece of the Serbo-Byzantine style of architecture. The exterior is classically severe, but the entire interior from floor to ceiling—cupolas, columns, capitals are liberally covered with frescoes, ranging from immense, many-figured compositions to paintings of single persons. Concentrated here is a wonderful exhibition of the art of the Palaeological Renaissance, as it was called in Byzantium, which was adopted in Serbia and which is noted for being full of life, movement, and expression and for an appreciation of the beauty of the human body. These characteristics are well illustrated in numerous frescoes, together with such paintings as: *Expelling the Merchants from the Temple*; *Raising of Lazarus*, in which the crowd seems to push and jostle; *Calming the Tempest*, in which the terror of the apostles is so well expressed; *Abraham's Sacrifice*, with its pathetic little boy so curious about his father's knife; and above all, in the dramatic *Last Judgement*, the creation of a powerful imagination, in which the overwhelmingly realistic hell reminds one of the description of it in Dante's *Inferno*. Many of these mural paintings introduce scenes from contemporary life and literature, and landscapes often replace the traditional gold backgrounds. The long, attenuated figures of some of the saints are reminiscent of El Greco; but the majority are fine specimens of robust manhood such as Elijah in his cave[30] and the gorgeously clad warrior, Mercurius.[31] Outstanding among them all, both for form and colour, dignity of pose and expressiveness of feature, is the magnificent figure of Saint John the Baptist.

Having made a detour to visit Gracanica we had to turn back to join the main road leading to Macedonia, a country remembered best as a district of northern Greece, the birthplace of Alexander the Great. But even after its political unity was lost, the name survived until modern times. Then it became a bone of contention for some of the combatants in the First World War and was incorporated into the new kingdom of Yugoslavia. In 1945 it became an independent republic. We had a long, arduous journey before us, and we were eager to proceed without further delay, but we had gone only a short distance when a fierce storm suddenly bombarded us with almost incessant peals of thunder and flashes of lightning that seemed to set the car on fire. Torrential rain soon brought us to a standstill in the middle of a flood. The deafening noise made speech impossible, but we anxiously watched the swirling waters around us while our little vehicle seemed a cockleshell in the midst of the ocean. After an hour of tense anxiety, swiftly as it had begun, the storm subsided, and the sun burst through the clouds, restoring peace to the earth and dry land beneath our wheels.

Late that evening we arrived in Skopje, once a Roman city, the headquarters of a legion, afterwards the provincial capital of Justinian's empire.[32] In the fourteenth century it became a royal residence where Dušan established a court rivaling in splendour that of Byzantium, but a few years later it sank to the level of a Turkish outpost

---

30. 1 Kings 19:8.

31. [Latin] "Mercury." In Roman mythology, Mercury is the god of shopkeepers, merchants, and travelers, commonly identified with the Greek Hermes, the messenger of the gods.

32. Justinian I, also known as Justinian the Great (Latin: Flavius Petrus Sabbatius Iustinianus Augustus) (ca. 482–565) was the eastern Roman emperor from 527 until his death.

called Uskub and is now the capital of the Federated People's Republic of Macedonia. Here, on the banks of the river Vardar, are two distinct towns, connected by a bridge, the larger built during the last forty years and distinguished only by a palatial station; the other, bearing the burden of centuries, crawls up a steep hillside, and with its narrow winding streets, tiny shops, and numerous minarets, must have changed little since the days of Turkish domination. Situated almost on the summit of the hill is the principal mosque of Mustapha Pasha, designed by Mimar Sinan,[33] the Armenian, a contemporary of Michelangelo. A short distance away, in the middle of a small courtyard, stands the seventeenth-century church of Our Saviour, with its deliberately unimpressive exterior and partly underground construction— the latter in compliance with the Moslem decree that no Christian place of worship should overlook other buildings in its neighbourhood. A flight of steps descends to the entrance and the whole interest of the interior centres in the wonderful iconostasis, as the screen is called, which separates the sanctuary from the nave in all Orthodox churches. Carved in walnut are innumerable figures from the Old and New Testaments: *Jonah and the Whale*; *Salome* in Macedonian national costume; scenes from everyday life; flowers, fruit, animals; even in one corner, the artists themselves, the brothers Filipovski,[34] who were trained in the workshops of Mount Athos, but were natives of a local village. Reminiscent of similar carvings by Veit Stoss, the great German wood-carver, this Balkan work is much more intricate. Despite the perfection of some of its parts, it loses in strength and individuality by this excessive intricacy and becomes comparable in craftsmanship to certain Chinese ivories. In Skopje, as in Granada, a special quarter is reserved for the gypsies, but, unlike their Spanish

---

33. Mimar Sinan (Turkish: "Architect Sinan") or Mimar Koca Sinan (Turkish: "Great Architect Sinan") (ca. 1490–1588) was the most celebrated of all Ottoman architects and civil engineer to several sultans.

34. Petre "Garka" and Marko Filipovski were nineteenth-century Macedonian masters of woodcarving, who worked together in the Church of Our Savior in Skopje from 1824 to 1829.

brethren, who inhabit spacious caves, these unconventional people dwell in houses so diminutive that their occupants are obliged to perform all their domestic duties out-of-doors, a fact which contributes much colour to the picturesque scene. Not far from this district is a large building known as the Kursumli Han, which is the oldest caravansery among the many scattered through Yugoslavia, and is believed to have been built by the Romans. It provided accommodation for the caravans travelling between Constantinople and Dubronik and is now a museum. In another building, once a Turkish bathhouse, is a collection of modern paintings showing fewer "abstracts" than is usual nowadays, and contrasting dramatically with admirable reproductions of the ancient frescoes in the nearby monastery of Nerezi, among which a beautiful Pietà is dominated by a *Mater Dolorosa* of outstanding excellence.

The mountainous region around Skopje is dotted with churches and monasteries all profoundly interesting to artists and architects, but most of them inaccessible except on foot; in fact, judging from information I received, even the goat-footed Pan himself would find the ascent of one of these eyries a formidable undertaking.

A considerable amount of walking but no climbing was necessary to reach our next objective, the Roman Byzantine settlement of Stobi, a large area of which has been recently excavated. An extensive plateau in the shadow of barren mountains is plentifully strewn with ruins dating from the second, fifth and sixth centuries, including a theatre with a well-preserved stage and seats, a luxurious palace with beautiful mosaic floors and stone carvings, public baths, temples, and several churches, the principal of which is dedicated to Saint John the Baptist.

After refreshing ourselves with deep draughts of ice-cold water at one of the wayside fountains which, in the sweltering heat, were a welcome sight on these Balkan roads, we continued our journey to Ohrid, which we expected to reach before sunset. The route lay through lofty mountains riven by the precipitous gorges that form such an impressive feature of this country's scenery. After an exhausting day, we were eagerly looking forward to our arrival, when the car gradually came to a full stop, and the driver announced in a sepulchral tone that the petrol was "finished." Some moments passed before we realised that we must spend the night on the roadside, with no certainty that relief would come even in the morning, but my bones were so tired of being rattled that, with no thought of the morrow at first, I enjoyed the voluntary control of my limbs while I was walking backwards and forwards in the cool evening air. Soon darkness crept along the valley and we began to settle down with all the cheerfulness we could muster, when, suddenly, we were enveloped in a dazzling light, and an angel in the form of a young man appeared beside us and supplied us with sufficient fuel to reach our destination.

Like Skopje, Ohrid consists of two distinct towns, one dating from the eleventh century, the other obviously new. The latter follows the conventional pattern of a fashionable summer resort, with palatial hotels, luxury villas, swimming pools and formal gardens, all facing a treelined promenade along the shore of a beautiful lake; the former climbs a steep promontory surmounted by a ruined castle, and, with its many ancient buildings and maze of cobbled streets, is full of interest and charm.

In the ninth century the brothers, Saint Cyril and Methodius, "the Apostles of the Slavs,"[35] came from Constantinople and established Christianity in this little town, having invented the Cyrillic alphabet and translated the Gospels into Slavonic in preparation for their work. One of their successors, Archbishop Clement, built early in the eleventh century the church of Saint Sophia which contains some of the best mural paintings in the world. In the fifteenth century this building was converted into a mosque and these precious pictures were covered with plaster. But in 1951 a wonderful work of restoration was accomplished by the Yugoslav government in collaboration with a team of experts organised by UNESCO.[36] The walls were badly

35. Saint Cyril (826–69) and Methodius (815–85), known as "the Apostles of the Slavs," were Byzantine Christian theologians and missionaries.

36. Acronym for the United Nations Educational, Scientific, and Cultural Organization, which was founded in 1946 to promote world peace through international cooperation in education, the sciences, and culture.

cracked and leaning at a dangerous angle, and the rediscovered frescoes were actually removed and replaced after the whole precarious
structure had been restored to normal by a most complicated and difficult process. With feelings of deep gratitude to those who made this
pleasure possible for me, I spent some "moments eternal" surrounded
by these marvellous works of art, some of which appealed to me so
irresistibly that they remained etched indelibly on my memory. Among
these are an *Ascension* in which the Blessed Virgin gazes with yearning tenderness at the ascending figure of her Son, while Saint Peter,
standing beside her, is overwhelmed with sadness at parting from his
beloved Master; *Jacob's Dream*, in which an angel, about to mount the
ladder, seems afraid even to breathe lest it should awaken the prostrate
sleeper;[37] Abraham and Sarah, with features expressive of kindliness
and hospitality,[38] entertaining their heavenly guests disguised in the
familiar form of weary wayfarers; the dignified figure and expressive
face of Saint Basil[39] celebrating Mass; and the pictures of many saints
on the lower walls, each distinct with the individuality of a portrait. As
I turned back at the entrance for a last look, it seemed to me a strange
sight to see such an unusual combination of Mohammedanism and
Christianity; a rostrum in which pages of the Koran were often read
and the doctrine of the Prophet was often preached, stood out from a
background on which sacred scenes and personages from the Old and
New Testaments are depicted with consummate skill.

A steep rugged road leads to the important church of Saint Clement built in 1295, now famous for its thirteenth- and fourteenth-
century frescoes which were discovered during the last decade. They
had almost disappeared under many centuries of the smoke, grime
and dust, gradually becoming black under several coats of varnish,
until, in 1889, the surface was whitened to serve as a background for

37. Genesis 28:10–22.
38. Genesis 18:1–15.
39. St. Basil the Great, also called Basil of Caesarea (329–79) was an early
Church Father and influential theologian who served as bishop of Caesarea Mazaca
in modern-day Turkey.

a set of completely new pictures. Finally, in 1950, all these accretions were removed by expert hands, revealing the original works in all their glory, bearing the signatures of Entihije and Mihailo,[40] artists who always worked together and are as revered in Byzantine art history as are their contemporaries Cimabue[41] and Giotto in the west. Externally beautiful, this church is a fitting receptacle for its precious contents, and the brilliant array of paintings form such a perfect whole that it is impossible to emphasise or underline any of its parts, and one stands before these masterpieces, profoundly thrilled at being privileged to see something whose loveliness, for more than six hundred years, was hidden from human eyes.

It is recorded that during the long period of Turkish rule, Ohrid had a large number of Orthodox churches; today, under communism, there are still many, but very few are now used for religious purposes, the vast majority, like Saint Sophia's and Saint Clement's, are museums. I had to search for a custodian to unlock one of those I visited; the others I luckily found open. All the interiors are covered with frescoes, which are so dark that it was difficult to recognise their subjects.

At 7 o'clock on our second morning in Ohrid we boarded a boat for the twenty miles' excursion to the end of the lake, above which, on a lofty promontory, close to the Albanian frontier, stands the monastery founded in the tenth century by Saint Naum,[42] a great Slav scholar. This enchanting spot, now deserted, became a centre of culture, and before the last war was famous as a place of pilgrimage and as a religious sanatorium, where many people sought comfort and healing for spiritual and physical ills. At one time there was a community

---

40. Entihije and Mihailo, also spelled Eftichios (Evtihij) and Chrostiras Michael, were fresco artists active ca. 1312 to 1320.

41. Cimabue, original name Bencivieni di Pepo (1251–1302), Florentine painter and mosaicist, is remembered as the last great Italian artist of the Byzantine style and as the mentor of Giotto.

42. Saint Naum, also known as Naum of Ohrid (ca. 830–910), was a Macedonian writer and theologian, who became one of the seven Apostles of the First Bulgarian Empire.

here so large that religious ceremonies were almost continuous but in 1945 the monks left, probably compelled to do so by the extreme poverty we found in other monasteries, crushed by a heavy burden of taxation. Inside the front door of the church are two baptismal fonts, dating from the tenth and the thirteenth centuries and in a chapel to the right is the marble tomb of the saint, surrounded by frescoes much older than those in the rest of the building, which dates only from the early nineteenth century, but all were irreparably damaged by fire. In the neighbourhood of this lovely lake are many things of great interest to the architect and the historian, the painter and the poet, but one thing here that makes a direct appeal to the scientist is the fact that in these intensely blue waters shellfish are found which are the only living specimens in the world of a species which survives from the Tertiary Age.[43] Found here also and nowhere else is another fish, having no claim to such ancient lineage as the shellfish, but of so delicious a flavour that when we tasted the dish we were not surprised to hear that in Byzantine times it was sent regularly to Constantinople by special messenger, so that it reached the emperor every Friday.

We had now arrived at the farthest point of our journey and next morning we turned back towards Belgrade through some of the most attractive regions of Macedonia. Our first stop was far from any town or village where apparently there was nothing of any importance to be seen, but, completely hidden by trees, towering above us, was the monastery of Saint Jovan Bigorski.

"Excelsior" is the most suitable motto for all travellers in search of ancient Balkan art and here we had to climb a track, probably exhilarating for goats, but obviously untrod by men. On entering a massive gateway, we were rewarded by the sight of a most picturesque building, with outside wooden balconies on each storey of the residential portion, and a church with frescoes painted not only on the internal

43. Tertiary Age, also called the Tertiary Period, is an outmoded geological term for an interval stretching from approximately 66 million to 2.6 million years ago.

but even on the external walls. The resplendent interior has the brilliance of a jewel and contains a magnificent gilded iconostasis carved by the artists responsible for a similar work in the church at Skopje, who were natives of one of the local villages where a tradition of excellent wood-carving has been cherished for hundreds of years.

A short drive brought us to the lovely Treska Gorge where we left the main road and had a delightful walk along a narrow, winding path between towering cliffs until a sharp turn wrung from us a cry of admiration at sight of the monastery of Saint Andrew standing beside a lake and backed by a sheer precipice. According to an inscription over the entrance, the church was built in the tragic year of 1389, by Andrew,[44] younger son of Vukasin,[45] one of the puppet rulers, on whom under Turkish domination the title "despot" was ironically conferred. The architecture of this building is of particular interest as an elegant specimen of the Macedonian style, and its frescoes are no longer painted by anonymous artists but can be definitely identified as the work of John Zograf, the Metropolitan,[46] and the monk, Grigorije,[47] whose ambition aimed at achieving freedom from all Byzantine tradition. Here we find a preoccupation with the problems of perspective and foreshortening, for example in *The Agony in the Garden*, *The Last Supper*, *The Washing of the Apostles' Feet*, and *Descent from the Cross*, while a knowledge of anatomy is displayed in the unusual figures of the Holy Warriors, clad in coats of chain mail, and armed with shields and spears, who here replace the ascetic forms and haloed heads of the traditional saints.

---

44. Andrijaš Vukašinović Mrnjavčević (died 1395) was a Serbian noble who ruled Prilep from 1371 until his death; his brother was Serbian King Marko, who ruled Macedonia during the same period.

45. Vukašin Mrnjavčević (ca. 1320–71) was king of Serbia, as co-ruler with Stefan Uroš V, from 1365 until his death at the hands of the Ottoman army.

46. John or Jovan Zograf, also known as "the Metropolitan," was a Macedonian icon painter active in the late fourteenth century.

47. Grigorije of Gornjak, also known as Grigorije the Younger (fourteenth century), was a Serbian Orthodox monk who was later canonized.

298 Unaccompanied Traveler

That night we spent at Nis, the birthplace of Constantine the Great, a prospering, industrial town with good hotels, attractive public gardens, situated amid beautiful surroundings. Its only object of interest seems to be the "Tower of Skulls," a gruesome reminder of the rebellion of 1809 when, rather than surrender, the Serbs blew up their own powder magazine, destroying both the enemy and themselves. In revenge, the Turks built this mausoleum setting in the mortar nine hundred Serbian skulls, which remained there for many years until all but two were removed when the country finally achieved its liberation.

Manasia, our last monastery, hidden amid the silence of the hills, was founded in an age of constant peril from the Turks, a menace that long hung over the heads of the Balkan people like the sword of Damocles. Remembering this fact lessened the shock of surprise when we first saw here no sign of a peaceful monastic site, but rather the very symbols of war in the massive high walls and gigantic towers of a fortress. Inside this formidable barrier we found, like Brunhild within the circle of fire, a beautiful church with five cupolas rising even higher than the fortifications, and representing the loftiest peak of Moravian architecture. Built in 1407 by Visoki,[48] son of Tzar Lazar, this church was so rich in decoration that its columns were originally inlaid with pure gold, afterwards removed by the Turks. But even at the present day its early thirteenth-century frescoes set the whole interior aflame with a galaxy of glorious colour. Biblical scenes occupy the upper sections of the walls, while the lower portions are filled with life-sized figures, majestic prophets of the Old Testament, a pope beside an Orthodox patriarch, and most striking of all, a powerful portrayal of the Church Militant, an army of holy warriors, in chain armour, bearing all the weapons of their age, eagerly awaiting the word of command to march to battle against the infidel. It was in the monasteries some of the revolts against the Turks were planned; monks and priests

48. Vuk Lazarević (ca. 1380–1410) was the younger son of Tsar Lazar and brother of Stefan Lazarević, who became ruler of Moravian Serbia after the death of their father.

taking part with the people in the struggle for freedom. Manasia was for centuries a centre of learning and contained an extensive library of old manuscripts, together with a huge volume of the Gospels bound in solid silver and gold, a gift of an empress of Russia.

Returning reluctantly to the everyday world after so many delightful hours spent in these sequestered abodes of peace where nature and art are wedded in such perfect harmony, I shrank from the imminent impact of a great city. Beside us, for many miles, hundreds of university students were engaged in the construction of a new road, earning for themselves a fortnight's free holiday by this voluntary labour, and the long line of scantily clad, suntanned youths was like a gallery of bronze statues. Overgrown with grass, close to the roadside were ancient cemeteries, several of which we had already seen during our tour. Some of them were Turkish but the majority belonged to the Bogomils, that strange Manichaean sect, whose hold on the Balkans, especially on Bosnia, was so tenacious that, despite persecution, it continued to flourish for centuries.

Some days before, we saw, on a lovely hillside, the last resting place of a partisan who had fought with Tito.[49] Unlike many pagan tombs, with their strong emphasis on a future life, this monument was an embodiment in stone of a blatant disbelief in immortality. As we drew near our journey's end most members of the party showed obvious signs of strain, and we were alarmed when, about twenty miles from the capital, the driver, a man of powerful physique, became so ill that we feared we would be unable to continue. However, after a long rest, and some attention from the doctor, who was now on the verge of collapse herself, he recovered sufficiently to reach Belgrade, and we were firmly determined never again to undergo such a gruelling experience.

The lights of the city brought me an overwhelming sense of achievement, a realisation of having accomplished something supremely

---

49. Josip Broz Tito (1892–1980) was a Yugoslavian communist leader who commanded the Partisan (Serbo-Croatian: Partizan) guerrilla forces in their fight against the Axis powers during the Second World War and later became president and prime minister of Yugoslavia.

worthwhile, and the pains of the journey were already receding into a background, against which the pleasures were indelibly etched. Feeling "like some watcher of the skies, when a new planet swims into his ken,"[50] I had discovered a chapter of absorbing interest hitherto missing from my history of art, another "magic casement" had been opened on far horizons, and my lengthening string of travel memories was enriched by the addition of another priceless pearl.

50. John Keats, "On First Looking into Chapman's Homer" (1816), lines 9–10.

Timeline —⚬✤⚬— *Index*

Timeline

1879   Kathleen Mary Murphy (KMM) is born on December 15 in Tulla, County Clare.

1882   James Joyce is born. The Irish Land War comes to an end.

1889   Charles Stewart Parnell, leader of the Irish Parliamentary Party, is implicated in the divorce proceedings of Captain William O'Shea and Katharine O'Shea.

1898   KMM enrolls at University College, Dublin of the Royal University.

1901   KMM graduates from university and returns to Tulla.

1904   The Abbey Theatre (National Theatre of Ireland) is founded.

1914   The Third Irish Home Rule bill is passed, but its implementation is suspended due to the outbreak of the First World War.

1916   The Easter Rising takes place in Dublin.

1917   KMM receives "special commendation" for a lyric entered in a prize competition sponsored by *The Bookman*.

1918   German surrender brings an end to armed conflict in the First World War. Thomas "Thady" Murphy passes away. KMM begins publishing a series of four poems in *Studies*.

1919   Sinn Féin, led by Éamon de Valera establishes the first Dáil (Parliament) of the Irish Republic. The Irish War of Independence begins with an Irish Republican Army campaign against British forces.

1920   KMM publishes her sonnet "On Reading the Apocalypse" in *Vision: A Magazine & Review of Mysticism and Spiritual Reconstruction*. The British Parliament passes the Government of

Ireland Act, establishing a parliament for Northern Ireland and another for the rest of the island.

1921   Anglo-Irish Treaty establishes the Irish Free State, an independent dominion of the British Crown separate from Northern Ireland.

1922   The Dáil Éireann ratifies the treaty in opposition to the wishes of de Valera and his allies, leading to the Irish Civil War. James Joyce publishes *Ulysses*.

1923   The Irish Civil War ends. The Irish Free State enters the League of Nations.

1928   Sara Agnes Murphy passes away.

1931   KMM attends the Paris International Colonial Exhibition.

1932   KMM publishes *Poems*, which receives first prize in the *Aonach Táilteann* literary competition and the papal decoration *Pro Ecclesia et Pontifice*.

1933   KMM's *The Fortune of Kings: A Drama of Erinn in Three Acts* is broadcast on Belfast radio.

1935   KMM hosts Spanish nobleman Don Carlos de Goyenche y Silvela at her home, Stada Cona, in Birr.

1936   The Spanish Civil War begins. KMM travels to Jerusalem, Petra, and Haiti, among other destinations.

1937   Voters reelect de Valera and ratify the Constitution of Ireland, which replaces the Irish Free State with Éire (Ireland) as a sovereign state. KMM travels to Indo-China.

1938   Douglas Hyde becomes the first president of Éire.

1939   Germany invades Poland, initiating the Second World War; Ireland declares its neutrality in the conflict. KMM travels to Bolivia and Peru.

1945   The Second World War ends when the Allies accept the unconditional surrender of Nazi Germany.

1948   KMM begins publishing travelogues in *The Capuchin Annual*.

1951   De Valera is reelected Taoiseach and holds office, with a two-year interruption, until 1959.

1955   Ireland is admitted to the United Nations.

1959   KMM travels to Moscow via Ostend, Ghent, Hanover, West Berlin, East Berlin, Warsaw, Minsk, and Smolensk.

1961   KMM travels to the Balkans and visits Sarajevo, Belgrade, Zagreb, Topola, and Kosovo.

1962   KMM passes away on March 22.

1963   KMM posthumously publishes her final travelogue in *The Capuchin Annual*.

Index

Patrick Bixby is associate professor of English at Arizona State University and Resident Director of the University Studies Abroad Consortium Summer School at National University Ireland Galway. He has published widely in the areas of Irish studies, modernist studies, and mobility studies; his next book is a cultural history of the passport.